THE ROUGH GUIDE to

CULT SPORT

ROUGH
GUIDES

www.roughguides.com

Credits

Consultant: Richard Tippett
Layout: Fit4Life Media
Picture research: Lois Wilson
Sub Editor: Lois Wilson
Proofreading: Jason Freeman
Production: Rebecca Short

Rough Guides Reference
Editors: Kate Berens, Tom Cabot, Tracy
Hopkins, Matthew Milton, Joe Staines
Director: Andrew Lockett

Publishing Information

This first edition published September 2011 by
Rough Guides Ltd, 80 Strand, London WC2R ORL
11, Community Centre, Panchsheel Park, New Delhi 110017, India
Email: mail@roughguides.com

Distributed by the Penguin Group:
Penguin Books Ltd, 80 Strand, London WC2R ORL
Penguin Group (USA), 375 Hudson Street, NY 10014, USA
Penguin Group (Australia), 250 Camberwell Road, Camberwell, Victoria 3124, Australia
Penguin Group (New Zealand), 67 Apollo Drive, Mairangi Bay, Auckland 1310, New Zealand

Rough Guides is represented in Canada by Tourmaline Editions Inc.,
662 King Street West, Suite 304, Toronto,
Ontario, M5V 1M7

Printed in Singapore by Toppan Security
Printing Pte. Ltd.

A catalogue record for this book is available from the British Library

ISBN: 978-1-40538-598-5

1   3   5   7   9   8   6   4   2

THE ROUGH GUIDE to

CULT SPORT

by Lloyd Bradley
with Andrew Lockett

With contributions by
Sean Mahoney, James McConnachie,
Matthew Milton, David Parkinson,
Christopher Lewis and Derek Ballard

www.roughguides.com

About the authors

A regular marathon runner, an enthusiastic (and often entertaining) golfer and an avid spectator of curling, soccer and cricket, **Lloyd Bradley** has worked as health and fitness editor of *GQ*, consultant editor at *Men's Health* and *Runner's World* magazines, and is the author of *The Rough Guide to Running* and *The Rough Guide to Men's Health*. He is also one of the world's leading experts on reggae and the author of *Bass Culture: When Reggae Was King*. His forthcoming book, *Sounds Like London*, is about the shaping of the city's soundtrack through the many disparate music genres arriving from different parts of the world.

A keen footballer and dabbler in numerous other sports, **Andrew Lockett** has contributed to *The Rough Guide to Cult Football* and has previously written on film, media and other cultural topics. He is currently Rough Guides' publisher for reference and custom titles, and worked mainly on the "Around the World in 80 Sports" chapter for this publication.

Acknowledgements

The authors would like to thank all sportsmen and women everywhere for inspiring this book and for generally brightening up our lives. They would also like to thank all the abovementioned's families for putting up with these obsessions. Of course, this includes the authors' families too. Lloyd would like to thank Lois, Chris, Richard and Derek – especially Lois – for all their brilliant work, Nina for the photo of her dad and uncles, and Diana, George and Elissa for not doing anything differently; Andrew would like to thank the bagel boys and Dunstan Bentley for quality banter, and Andrea Klein and Jonas Lockett Klein for their love, tolerance and inspiration.

Contents

Dragon boat racing in Hong Kong (see p.30)

What is Cult Sport?

A different kind of fervour

ociologists have unearthed several candidates as alternatives to religion, but none seem to overlap with quite the same degree of intensity as sport. It's not difficult to see why, either. Sports stars are worshipped. Sports fans gather in prescribed venues at regular times of the week, observing and taking part in collective and individual rituals before the main proceedings. Communal singing and chanting is then a vital part of that programme. Congregation members willingly fork out large sums of money just to partake in these ceremonies, then, without objection, stump up even more in order to be able to wear the relevant robes and insignia.

Outhouse racing (see p.60), Lake George, New York.

For little tangible reward, seemingly sound-minded men and women give over waking hours that should be spent with their families, money that should be spent on, well, something useful, have their whole week affected by what goes on at the weekend, and live in a perpetual state of hope beyond all reasonable expectations. If they could be lured into behaving like this by anything other than a sport it would be called a "cult", and a "sinister cult" at that.

Sport has its saviours too, who have brought glory back to a club or a country, to be enshrined in a Hall of Fame, either real of imagined. It also has its prophets, its messiahs, its prodigal sons and daughters, its demons and its saints. Indeed the naming of off-spring after the latter is an equally accepted practice, while images or effigies gain even greater significance should they have been touched by sport's Chosen Ones, a situation requiring a signature as verification. Dressing in homage to Virender Sehwag or Michael Jordan or Peyton Manning is considered entirely appropri-ate behaviour too, even among otherwise responsible adults. Likewise tattoos depicting individual deities as well as team names or logos. Or sometimes worship manifests itself in an entirely inexplicable manner: a line of surfboards stuck nose first into the sand alongside an inland desert highway or a fairly large museum devoted to a type of baseball bat – not baseball bats in general, just the one.

> "Some people think football is a matter of life and death. I assure you, it's much more serious than that."
> **Bill Shankly, manager**
> **Liverpool FC, 1959–1984**

Responsible adults at soccer's 2010 FIFA World Cup (see p.101).

For every rising star that promises a new dawn, many more will be dumped unceremoniously by the wayside, and for more reasons than merely failing to deliver their disciples unto the Promised Land. The pursuit of pieces of silver will usually be tolerated, but set yourself up as Mr Clean, then get caught with a string of cocktail waitresses and high-priced hookers, and the world gets to see just how far an angel can fall. Sports prompt debate, commentary and exegesis as much as the sacred texts generate rival interpretations and different understandings. In each case these "discussions" will never be resolved and frequently end up getting ugly.

Sport, however, has a far more complicated relationship with its followers than religion, simply because there is no such thing as a typical sport, therefore, there is no such thing as a typical sports player or fan. And with cult sport things get even knottier. Why travel a couple of hundred miles in the winter just because there *might* be a wave you could ride that weekend? Why continue to watch a football team whose repeatedly poor performances actually make you feel ill? Why risk a broken neck charging down a very steep hill in pursuit of a piece of cheese? Why, out of office hours, do you dress like a professional basketball player, when in reality you're an overweight, pasty estate agent? Why do you have to lose eleven brand

Philippine eskrima (see p.33) championship in Los Angeles.

new golf balls just to convince yourself you need to lay up to get over that lake? Why get your car resprayed then spend a fortune on a state of the art barbecue, just to enjoy freshly cooked frankfurters in a stadium car park? Is running fifty miles with no shoes on really such a good idea? And exactly how long do you plan on wearing those lucky underpants? These are the sorts of questions that can never be answered – except, clearly, the one about the underwear: until your partner actually puts a match to them – but they are the issues that come closest to defining cult sport. Where things veer off into the strange, the counter-cultural, the anti-orthodox and, most importantly, the free and indepen-dent, it becomes a cult in its own right. Welcome to *The Rough Guide to Cult Sport*, where that leftfield world is given full acknowledgement.

> "Sweet are the uses of adversity."
> **William Shakespeare**

It doesn't matter how big or how small a sport is – and some of the sports in this book have very little following indeed – to be recognized for its cult qualities, all it requires is that it inspires a passion, commitment and love which is bigger than the sport or the players and the fans caught up in it. Therefore, a game as big as cricket can enjoy cult aspects, while tennis, equally as popular, might not. And just because not many people have heard of wakeboarding doesn't mean it won't be cult by virtue of its relative obscurity. Cult sports, and sporting cults – seldom the same thing – are those which bind people together in a common fate. That fate might not always be kind – losing to one's greatest rivals is an experience no one likes though few escape at some point – but even shared misery can be weirdly uplifting. And it's in this notion that cult sport has one huge advantage over reli-gion – whereas the latter thrives on its relentless search for meaning, at the core of the former is an essential and deep-rooted meaninglessness.

The Rough Guide to Cult Sport recognizes not only the importance and reso-nance of such pointlessness, but celebrates it with due reverence. Likewise, the men and women who have become cults in themselves are hailed for their appeal rather than just their achievements. Cult contests are fondly remembered, scandals are relived with no hiding place for the guilty – although perhaps the occasional admiring glance – and a number of major league sports have their cult status evaluated and exhumed. We also celebrate the sport of the margins from across the world, where it seems nearly anyone can dream about being world cham-pion of an ancient village tournament or of an eye-catching hybrid game they have recently invented. This is sport as it should be enjoyed, once again removed from mammon in the form of the corporate cash register, and returned to a world where character, courage and love of the game reign supreme.

> "Grass grows, birds fly, waves pound the sand. I beat people up."
> **Muhammad Ali**

This is Cult Sport.

Lloyd Bradley, May 2011

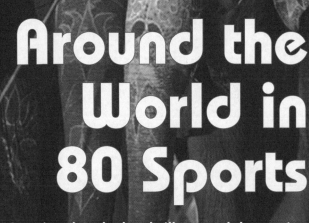

Around the World in 80 Sports

Global, national or the local village: a globetrotting look at some of sport's hidden gems and rising stars

◀◀ Previous pages: a day in the life of our sporting planet – Sri Lankan elephant polo (see p.33) is hardly the sport for adrenaline junkies.

Around the World in 80 Sports

"Life must be lived as play."

Plato (adapted)

For all the sporting world's focus on the big-money events, it's often those quirky local games, mad new sports, or weird ancient traditions that really hold a fan's affections. This chapter pays tribute to that other world of sport: the survivors from days of yore; the close relatives of major-name sports that have lingered on; the quirky hybrids, or simply those competitive activities that somehow define their community. Some of these sports operate at the edge of legality or survive due to the perceived needs of the local tourism industry. Others, such as the martial art eskrima, have an almost spiritual connection to their locality. Then there's those games, such as slamball or underwater rugby, that reflect a very contemporary need for ever more intense adrenalin rushes. Alternatively, older, gentler sports – for example croquet or boules – are being clasped by today's maximum-impact generation in an "ironic" embrace. Eighty sports may seem like a lot but this list could have been much, much longer – there are an awful lot of intriguing and wonderful cult sports out there ripe for discovery.

AMATEUR RADIO DIRECTION FINDING
(EASTERN EUROPE, RUSSIA, INTERNATIONAL)

GaGa Radio?

The eternal divide between jocks and nerds seems to be one of life's givens: except, perhaps, in the techy area of "radiosports" – more specifically, the large and burgeoning scene of amateur radio direction finding. Russia, Scandinavia and Eastern Europe are prominent in this activity, which involves tracking down several concealed low-frequency radio transmitters, situated across a woody terrain. These are sometimes known as "foxes", hence the sport's alternative US name of foxtailing or foxhunting. The ability to construct amateur radio equipment and knowledge of electronic signalling and Morse code need to be complemented with orienteering skills and a reasonable degree of physical fitness, in order to scurry around an area of a few kilometres and to register your discoveries. More sedate radiosports exist, as well as ones that involve motor vehicles. Radiosport contests consist of competitions to contact as many two-way radio stations as possible from within a specified physical locality according to rules too complex to go into here.

In Eastern bloc countries the educative value of understanding radio was vigorously promoted during the Cold War, and even now the likes of Russia, Ukraine, Poland and the Czech Republic occupied the top slots in the mens' team events in the ARDF World Championships of 2010. Even so after 1989 and as word spread, radiosports have grown, becoming a shining example of sport's capacity to bridge international boundaries. Other countries – 146 in total – now stage numerous events and have collaborated on international rule standardization. According to the US's leading radiosports website, homingin.com, you don't need to be a "combination of rocket scientist and marathoner" to enjoy the sport; you should even expect much "head-scratching". That said, you can't help feeling that radio-ham proclivities must help in a sport where the astronaut-dense countries Russia and the US have consistently excelled.

AUNT SALLY (OXFORDSHIRE, ENGLAND)

Six sticks a throw

The phrase "Aunt Sally" means an easy target: a person or idea set up expressly for the purpose of being knocked down (politicians seem to be particularly fond of them). Less well known is the game that gave birth to the expression, now mostly confined to pubs in Oxfordshire and Berkshire, with Abingdon (as well as Oxford) being a particular epicentre. Aunt Sally's heyday was in the late nineteenth century but there's uncertainty over whether it was originally a purely English invention or an American import. Some date it back to the English Civil War, or to a game in which chickens were the unlucky target.

Aunt Sally takes root in Oxford, England, 1938. Radio star Bertha Willmott takes aim.

The game itself consists of the pitching of wooden batons at a wooden doll's head from about ten yards. Two teams of eight players throw six clubs apiece, aiming to knock said "dolly" clean off a "swivel" two and a half feet off the ground. Hits are "dolls"; misses are called "blobs".

Like coconut shies, games of Aunt Sally were popular in fairgrounds, and in its heyday the doll's head was made up as a "black mama", with a clay pipe in her mouth forming the actual target. It settled down into its Oxfordshire heartlands in the 1930s, when pub teams started to compete in leagues and the target was stripped of its dubious racial and misogynistic associations, becoming a single stubby skittle. Many enigmas still surround the game. Is it a relative of West Country skittles? Is Aunt Sally the English cousin of the French game known as jeu de massacre? No mystery, however, about where the future stars of the sport are likely to be found. Over seventy pub and club venues (and even more teams) are listed by the Oxford & District Aunt Sally Association, which must make it one of the most geographically concentrated games in the world.

AUTOBALL (BRAZIL, INITIALLY...)
Football with wheels

In 1970 a daring new hybrid sport was born in Brazil. Teams of between three and six rich Brazilians – who could afford to write off the odd Ford or Renault – would try to score goals with their car bonnets or boots, using a huge ball that might have been more suited for a lead role in *The Prisoner*. What sounds like a lad's mag style jape rather astonishingly became, for the next five years, a professional league, supported by five major football clubs and drawing crowds of up to fifteen thousand. Cars were painted in team colours and there was a referee on the small-ish field of play; automobile injuries were predictably plentiful. What killed the sport was not lack of a following but instead a complete ban on motor sports by a Brazilian government struggling with the effects of an oil crisis.

Fast-forward to the twenty-first century and the *Top Gear* team have indeed reinvented the game, anglicized as "car football", with Toyota Aygos and other diminutive, nippy vehicles. Competition has inevitably come from Germany, another country obsessed with cars and football. German TV personality Stefan Raab's *Autoball EM* has since 2008 presented a more gladiatorial one-car-a-side version of the sport, which lacks some of the spectacle of the original but is none-theless keenly followed: it has trailed both the European soccer championships and the World Cup, with national pride very much at stake. If the sport could develop better eco-credentials and find enough car-friendly arenas on a regular basis, you wouldn't bet against it having a serious professional future.

BANDY (RUSSIA, SWEDEN, NORTHERN EUROPE)
Russian hockey

An example of how fluid the fates of sports were in the nineteenth century is that a future European soccer championship winning team actually began life in 1865 as Nottingham Forest Football and Bandy Club. Bandy was one of several hockey-like sports vying for the Victorian spotlight. Named after the curved stick used by players and played with a ball, the sport subsequently slid onto the ice. It gained major traction in East Anglia, where the legendary Bury Fen club in Cambridgeshire codified the rules in 1882 amidst an undefeated run of games lasting a hundred years. Prince Albert also once turned out in a game as a goalkeeper.

Likewise, fellow royal Peter the Great of Russia played the odd game of something very similar long before his country later adopted English rules from Bury Fen. The sport grew in popularity in northern climes, whereas it was to decline and then disappear from a UK that, climate-wise, was hotting up. Bandy has cult status in Russia where it is sometimes called "Russian hockey" and attendances are claimed by some fans to be higher than for soccer. It is also huge in Sweden (the 2010 world bandy champions) where the opening Boxing Day fixtures in the national league pull in big crowds.

Differences to ice hockey include a larger (football-size) pitch, the use of a ball and rules which are particularly strict on body contact and use of the body to direct the ball. It is a fast game with shots on goal reaching a hundred miles per hour and there is the likely prospect of bandy appearing at an Olympics before long – there are national associations developing in many other countries including Australia and the US. Respect too is due to a sport that serves up blue and white cards for penalties as well as the usual red and yellow.

BEACH FLAGS (AUSTRALIA, INTERNATIONAL)

The quickest sport in the world?

The surfer/lifeguard sport of beach flags seems to have been invented expressly for the purpose of keeping lifesavers alert and in good shape. Contestants race to claim beach flags over a distance of approximately twenty yards, beginning from a prone position. The catch is that there are always fewer flags than contestants. The empty-handed are eliminated round by round until two are left. This sand-sprinting version of "musical chairs" is strangely compelling when viewed on YouTube but with the Australian passion for all matters sporting it is even better watched live, with an overexcited compere whipping up enthusiasm over the loudspeakers.

Rules and regulations devotees will be delighted to know that the International Lifesaving Federation Competition Manual (which, oddly, originates in Leuven, Belgium) legislates over a large range of sand and surf sports and keeps a watchful eye on participants. "Deliberate impedance" spells disqualification and at the start contestants are watched carefully to ensure that "no scooping of the sand or digging or digging in of the feet is permitted." By the time you have read and digested these and other rules, several beach flag races could have taken place. A top-end men's race on Sydney beach could be over in less than five seconds.

BEACH VOLLEYBALL (CALIFORNIA, US, INTERNATIONAL)

Not a glorified bikini contest

Why would the Olympic Committee have voted to include beach volleyball in 1996? This is a sport in which bronzed, muscular men and women dive around in golden sand, hugging and high-fiving every few seconds, while players' behind-the-back hand signals give TV cameras an excuse for lingering shots of tanned buttocks, and regulations ensure that the bikinis and swimsuit bottoms are revealing.

It's easy to mock, but beach volleyball is actually a high-skill, high-pace and extremely high-energy game: the combination of two-player teams (in competitive matches) and a court made of absorbent sand makes it athletically demanding. The game was first played in Hawaii by beach-bums fed up with waiting for the surf to get up, but as a proper sport it's a Californian invention which first sprang up in an organized way in the 1920s in the beach clubs of Santa Monica. Since then, it has grown exponentially, and there's now a professional tour, high-prize championships, and of course a place on the Olympic roster. In the 2004 and 2008 Olympics, the American star duo of Kerri Walsh and the splendidly named Misty May-Treanor convinced plenty of sceptics that this was a real sport, not just a glorified bikini contest. In 2012, the beach volleyball venue will be that most formal and regal of London's public spaces: Horse Guards Parade. The sport has come a long way, in other words, since a few doped-out surfers strung up a volleyball net on a beach.

BEER PONG (US, INTERNATIONAL)

"It's a sport. It just happens to involve alcohol."

Frat-boy favourite beer pong has been working assiduously on acquiring cult status after having truly arrived on the scene with the creation of the Beer Pong World Series. Truly a grassroots phenomenon with intense niche appeal, the sport's origins are still debated. Possibly invented by Dartmouth College students in New Hampshire, it also goes by the alternative name of "Beirut" (no serious connection to the capital of the Lebanon yet confirmed), a circumstance endlessly mulled over in Internet chatrooms. Two players (usually men in their early twenties) must pitch ping-pong balls into a triangle of ten cups laid out by their opponents. The arch throw is favoured by pros though flat hits and one bounce pitches are allowed. A hit, or a strike, and the opposition must drink the beer poured into the cups – for stabilization and other purposes. The winning team must hit the final cup.

Niche documentary *The Last Cup: Road Trip to the World Series of Beer Pong* (2008) proudly celebrates the camaraderie of the sport, though it may not entirely wipe away the bad taste left by the frenetic straight-to-video gross-out comedy *Road Trip: Beer Pong* (2009) that did little to dispel the sport's boozy jock image. More successful in that respect was the *Book of Beer Pong: The Official Guide to the Sport of Champions* (2009), which nicely encapsulated the game's marriage of levity and intensity. At "professional" level, it's comparable in atmosphere and technique to UK darts tournaments, though it's a lot younger and more inclusive. What may elevate beer pong into something not far off unique is the rule that allows opponents to distract the throwers using any tactics short of diverting the ball, be that abusive provocation or distracting costumes (which have ranged from thongs to nappies). Amidst numerous other distracting options, *The Book of Beer Pong* recommends the "Copperfield" – described as "waving your hands over the cups in a magical way". A burgeoning Internet market in accessories from "blinging" gold balls to customized tables suggests players and fans will keep coming back for more.

Who needs the seaside? The Oak Street "Beach" is in downtown Chicago.

The loneliness of the long-distance bog snorkeller.

BOG SNORKELLING (WALES)

A fine mess

With its strikingly mud-drenched contestants, bog snorkelling has become something of a dirty poster boy of cult sports. The annual world championships in August, which started some thirty years ago at Llanwrtyd Wells ("the UK's smallest town"), is always guaranteed column inches and a picture of a smiling be-snorkelled contestant. As a sport it is simple. Participants have to swim two water-drenched sixty-metre stretches of a trench specially cut into a Welsh peat bog. They must use no specialist swimming strokes, only doggy paddle with flippers. There are men's, women's, locals' and junior events, with the winning time for the men usually being around the 1:40 mark. That was until the record was smashed in 2010 by Dan Morgan of Brecon, who managed 1:30.66, winning a princely £50 in prize money. This feat, *The Daily Telegraph* surmised, was in part due to the clearing of the course of "discarded snorkels and flippers from previous events" though, in fairness to Morgan, you can only swim through the mud put in front of you.

Despite such modest incentives bog snorkelling is taking off, with competitions also arranged in Ireland and Australia. Then there are the spin-off sports also hosted at Llanwrtyd Wells: the bog snorkelling triathlon and the world mountain bike bog snorkelling championships. Bikes used in the latter, have a "lead-filled frame" and water-filled tyres for extra grip. The snorkellist/cyclist wears a lead weight to ensure he doesn't float away, in one of a cluster of sports where the going is always heavy.

BOSSABALL (INTERNATIONAL)

"Even the refs will get your hips moving."

It's hard not to like the idea of this recently invented sport, which represents one of the many variants of volleyball, that has added elements of soccer, trampolining, gymnastics and capoeira to the mix. Invented by Belgian Filip Eyckmans in 2003, when bouncy castle technology had been perfected, the game is played by between three and five players on a giant inflatable, in which a small inset trampoline is placed near the net, both to assist spectacular volleyball "spikes" (though any part of the body is allowed) and to offer the bull's-eye of a target for players to aim for. Three points are awarded for a direct hit on the trampoline and one for the rest of the court.

The inspiration for the game came when Eyckmans visited Recife and became enamoured of the Brazilian capoeira craze. Not surprisingly many games have taken place in beach locations, where the playful vibe of bossaball can be best enjoyed. The master of ceremonies is a DJing samba referee, who puts the cherry on the stick of this Brazilian cocktail of fun which is probably as much about the party and the show as gritty win-at-all-costs sportsmanship. Though Belgium and the Netherlands are both big in bossaball circles, the sport is swiftly going global.

BRITISH BULLDOG (UK)

Playground pariah

According to folklorists of playground games, British bulldog has been officially "banned" as long as it has been played – which is, incidentally, for the last hundred-odd years. You can see why schoolteachers would fret. Players – generally children in school playgrounds – have to charge across the playground to get to the other side, while their opponent, the bulldog, has to stop them. Sometimes, a mere tag is enough, but the traditional game required the runner to be brought down by a rugby tackle, or picked up with both feet off the ground long enough to chant "British bulldog 1, 2, 3", or some other such ritual phrase.

The similarity to India's kabbadi (also featured in this section) is striking, but there is one enormous difference. In India, kabbadi evolved to become a national sport. In the UK, British bulldog was generally outlawed by schools, forcing it to remain an underground sport, self-organized by children themselves, its rules and local traditions (which are many and various) passed down in semi-secret.

BOULES (FRANCE)
Tres sérieux

Don't be fooled by the stereotype of the French boules player, with his cloth cap, Saturday stubble and implanted Gauloises cigarette. Don't be fooled, either, by the setting: typically a quiet town square in the warm South, with glasses of potent pastis close at hand. This is a sport in which, at its best, a stunning level of skill can be displayed. The rules, however, are simple. The *cochonnet* (or "piglet"), a little cork jack, is thrown to one end of the sandy gravel *piste*, and the players try to lob their boules as close to it as possible, from a standing position. (The French call the game pétanque, from the Provençal dialect *pés tanqués*, or "stuck feet" – and the game's spiritual home is Provence.)

The balls are satisfyingly heavy, shiny and metal, roughly the size of an orange. The classic throwing technique is a laconic underarm swing, with the palm pointing down to impart a ruthless backspin. That's the grip for placing (*pointer*),

Worth a flutter? Buffalo racing, Negara, Bali.

Finesse is everything for the accomplished *bouliste*.

anyway; for shooting (*tirer*) so as to knock another ball aside, the style is more aggressive. You must bomb the boule of a winning rival, knocking it aside and leaving yours smugly in its place, basking in the honkings of disgust or admiration. Acquiring a good *carreau*, as this move is called, takes a lifetime's dedication.

BUFFALO RACING (THAILAND, INDIA, INDONESIA, ASIA)
Beauty of the beast

Across Asia, buffaloes are indispensable companions, used for ploughing, and for their rich milk and lean meat. In a few corners, however, they have become unlikely racing animals too. At Vihear Sour, a village fifty kilometres northeast of

Phnom Penh in Cambodia, villagers ride exuberantly decorated buffaloes through the streets to mark the end of the fifteen-day Pchum Ben festival, which honours dead ancestors. Admittedly, this is more of a parade than a race.

The same isn't true of Thailand's frantic chon buri races. Around the time of the full moon in early or mid-October, locals and tourists descend for a week-long jamboree of concerts and traditional Thai sports. There's even a tongue-in-cheek buffalo beauty pageant. The focus, however, is the buffalo races, held on the last day. Young men ride the animals over a hundred-yard dusty dash, clinging on to their slim hindquarters with nothing but pressure of knee and either a rope rein or just a hand on the buffalo's loose skin. Urged on by vigorous whipping, the buffaloes – usually placid, lugubrious animals – achieve astonishing speeds. In the crowd, money changes hands just as quickly.

Less well-known, and less international in flavour, are the kambla races, held in the Tulu regions of South India during the winter monsoon period. Here, two pairs of yoked animals storm splashily through an artificial paddy field, filled knee-deep with water, while the whip-brandishing handlers sprint desperately behind. The connection with traditional buffalo ploughing is certainly deeper-rooted than Thailand's races, but the associated gambling is just as furious.

BUN CLIMBING (HONG KONG, CHINA)
Buns of steal

The centre of the bun climbing, or bun snatching, universe is an area outside Pak Tai Temple in Cheung Chao, an island in the Hong Kong region of China. Part of a traditional Taoist festival, bun climbing was one of a series of celebratory activities reputedly designed to bring good luck and ward off attacks by pirates. Others have linked the events to the need to help appease the spirits of the victims of a nineteenth-century plague on the mainland from which the festival had transferred. Individuals climbed sixty-foot bamboo towers, pocketing squidgy buns as they came down. The highest bun achieved was deemed the luckiest. With several of the ingredients of a jolly *Jeux sans frontières* (*It's a Knockout*) jamboree, it was no surprise the local citizens took the event to their hearts. Sadly, 1975 saw the end of the competition after a hundred people were injured when a bun tower came crashing down.

The dream, however, would not die. In 2005 bun climbing returned, albeit in a more health-and-safety conscious form. Now, twelve carefully selected mixed contestants sportily scramble up one steel tower, strapped to mountaineering-quality harnesses. Contestants win more points the higher the bun they reach. The buns too had to change. Disturbed at the thought of steamed buns festering for three days on a bamboo structure, organizers initially wrapped up the buns, before ultimately replacing them with plastic ones. Bun climbing may not yet be the decathlon in terms of organized Olympic zeal, but it's getting there.

BUZKASHI (AFGHANISTAN, CENTRAL ASIA.)

It'll really get your goat

Literally translated as "goat grabbing", buzkashi is a centuries-old sport kept alive by horsemen across the Great Steppe region of central Asia. Linked first with Alexander the Great and the skilled riders of the Macedonian armies, there are perhaps stronger connections to the Golden Horde of Ghengis Khan, who were notably adept at lightning fast attacks on horseback, sweeping into camps and scooping up livestock while barely slowing to a canter. Whether the game evolved alongside, or as a countermeasure to, such attacks is unknown. Although, considering the present rules, such conjecture is purely academic.

The game begins with a few hundred mounted participants divided into two sides, the exact number of riders being determined the night before at a gathering of elders, with the parameters of the field dictated by the number of participants (except in Kabul, where the Afghan Olympic Committee have limited sides to ten players each on a four hundred-metre square pitch). At the same time, the centrepiece of the contest – the goat, or sometimes a calf – is made ready. First slaughtered then beheaded, it is gutted and soaked in water until just before the match, when it's filled with sand and sewn shut.

Now called a *boz*, the heavy carcass is placed in a small depression defined by a circle, with the object being to deposit it in another small circle, called the *hallal* (justice) some distance away. Simple enough, except for the crush of horses, whip-wielding horsemen (*chapandaz*) and general lack of uniforms save for a small coloured saddlecloth. Sport as war indeed.

CABER TOSSING (SCOTLAND)

Highland game

Tossing the caber is one of those traditions weird enough to almost define the nation that practises it. For Scotland it's up there with the wearing of the kilt or the eating of the haggis. Ultimately, there's nothing intrinsically odd about flipping a twenty-foot wooden pole end over end – it's no more or less unusual than throwing an Olympic hammer or doing the triple jump. It's a classic manly feat of strength. (The original legends of clansmen on the warpath throwing tree trunks across rivers in order to ford them are almost certainly spurious; faced with a stream, the average Highlander would just wade across.)

The contender is presented with a vertical caber, typically a larch trunk stripped of its bark – *cabar* means pole in Gaelic. He (rarely she) has to hoick it up so its end settles in his palms, its shaft resting against his shoulder, its far end tottering in the air. He then runs (or staggers – these things weigh up to two hundred pounds) and flings it up and away so it flips end over end. The skill lies in the caber falling so it points straight ahead, without tumbling sideways. The event usually takes place at a Highland Games, a kind of local Olympics-cum-folk music festival dreamed up by the Victorians, in an attempt to restore ancient traditions of Scots clans. At such gatherings, the caber toss is generally regarded as a highlight.

CAGE FIGHTING (MIXED MARTIAL ARTS) (US, INTERNATIONAL)
Full contact combat

Gladiatorial combat or tawdry spectacle? Human dog fighting or the ultimate sporting challenge? No sport in recent years has got the world's adrenalin levels pumping so much as "mixed martial arts" (MMA) – the more respectable moniker of a rapidly burgeoning form of combat. The spirit of cage fighting is well summed up by the name of its Brazilian antecedent, vale tudo, meaning "anything goes", which dates back to the early twentieth century. Older still, and perhaps more illustrious, is the Olympian "total powers" combat sport known as pankration.

But apart from the US, it has been Japanese promoters who have led the way. The cage used in cage fighting is pretty superfluous, a neat way of highlighting the hard outlaw edge of a sport which used to operate at the limits of legality (at least until the twenty first century) and which cannot be shown on TV in many countries including Germany. Blows and grappling are permitted and styles of fighting deployed are legion, with out-and-out wrestlers taking on exponents of Thai boxing and countless other variants of martial arts. Only a few rules exist, including: no eye-gouging, groin blows, hair-pulling or fish-hook elbow blows.

Since 2005, pay per view has driven the sport to ever greater heights with several competitions and individual bouts attracting numbers in excess of a million, despite controversies over both the level and disparities within fighters' pay. The UFC (Ultimate Fighting Competition), based in the US, consolidated its position as lead legislator and promoter in the field when it merged with WEC (World Extreme Cage fighting) at the end of 2010. It has also looked to break into new markets such as the UK, where cage fighter Alex Reid, ex-husband of the top-heavy Essex glamour girl Jordan, has focused further media attention on the sport (not least with his reported penchant for cross-dressing). While Reid has hogged much of the UK cage fighting headlines, it's Cambridge graduate and computer science PhD holder Rosi Sexton that is the UK's most successful cage fighter, being the only Brit to have reached number one in any MMA weight bracket.

Women's MMA competitions are also growing more common worldwide and include "Strikeforce" in the US and "Valkyrie" and "Dreams" in Japan (where the women's scene is larger). In terms of betting and audience enthusiasm there is plenty of evidence to suggest that a cage fighting scene ever more slickly promoted and organized is overtaking a boxing world staggering from internal schisms and self-inflicted blows. Once a pariah in public perception, MMA is now punching above its weight in an increasingly "extreme" mainstream.

CALCIO STORICO FIORENTINO (FLORENCE, ITALY)
Renaissance football

Imagine rugby without rules, or American football without helmets, padding or even shirts. Imagine a game where you can tackle off the ball, throw punches and pin an opponent to the ground for the duration. This is calcio storico, Florence's sumptuously costumed and astonishingly violent sport. The name means "historic football", and the game dates back to 1530, when besieged Florentines took to ball games to keep up their spirits. Ever since then, on 24 June, the feast day of the city's patron saint, John the Baptist, feisty crowds process to the gorgeous expanse of the Piazza Santa Croce (or sometimes, for the two qualifying matches, another square in the city), which is covered over with sand for the occasion. Rivalries between the city's four teams – one for each historic quarter – are fierce, and the opposing finalists enter to the beating of warlike drums. Each team has 27 players dressed in Renaissance costume – though it isn't long before most of the finery is torn off. Horns and guns mark the kick off, at which point the teams charge at each other, wrestling opponents to the ground, or tiring them out with shoves, kicks and punches.

Few rules but a lot of spectacle: calcio storico dates back to 1530.

In the fierce fifty-minute battle, the ball is sometimes all but forgotten, and the more vicious fights have to be broken up by feather-waving referees. But then one plucky firebrand will make a break for it, racing for the four-foot-high wall that runs the width of the opposing end, and posting the ball into a net that runs along the top of it. As he scores his *caccia* – pronounced "hacha" in the guttural Florentine dialect – drums roll, trumpets blare and a flag-bearer races triumphantly across the pitch. The winners celebrate with a roast calf and carousing well into the night.

CAMEL RACING
A game of two humps (or one)

As ships of the desert, pack animals built for long journeys with minimal food and water in demanding heat, camels are not naturally inclined to gallop. Neither do their arched backs make for a comfortable ride at anything brisker than a trot. Yet the sport of camel racing is alive and well within the Arabian peninsula, where promising dromedaries are scouted at local races in Oman, Yemen, Jordan and Qatar, and brought to the United Arab Emirates and the wealthiest camel racing circuit on the planet.

Traditional camel racing at Agadir, Morocco.

Camels who make it to the big show are fed the finest grains and are trained for years to achieve peak fitness. When eventually selected to race, they are lined up alongside fifteen to twenty other beasts (though that number may sometime reach as many as seventy for longer races) and, at the sound of blaring horns, are launched into a dusty oval for a four to ten-kilometre sprint. With some fourteen thousand of the animals ready to race at any time in the UAE, the sport employs a large number of handlers and jockeys, the latter of whom have been cause for scrutiny from human rights watch groups. Robots may have replaced humans at major UAE tracks (see p.67), but at smaller venues and in neighbouring countries boys remain the jockeys. And while camel races draw big crowds in India and Australia, they tend to be one-shot events specific to festivals, and neither country can lay claim to such an organized or monied league as those in the Middle East.

CAPOEIRA (BRAZIL)
Style is all

A mixture of African and Brazilian musical, dance and fighting traditions blend together to form this elegant yet powerful martial art. Considered by many to be

The amazing grace of capoeira in Brazil.

the only indigenous American fighting style, the suspected origins of capoeira can be traced to a mixed community of escaped slaves, natives and poor Portuguese living in and around Palmares in the northeastern part of Brazil. Its evolution from defensive necessity to deceptively dance-like spectacle may have been a matter of hiding its powerful potential from slaveholders. Adding musical accompaniment by way of the *berimbau* (musical bow), *atabaque* (drum), *pandeiro* (tambourine) and *agogo* (bells) and coming close to – but not actually connecting with – opponents, made practising capoeira seem like some simple local celebration rather than the honing of a deadly skill.

There are two main schools of capoeira: Angola and regional. The former is the slower traditional style, its movements performed low to the ground with the combatants very close to one another. The latter is a modern version championed by the revered Mestre Bimba in the 1930s, and is the more stylized, acrobatic version practised the world over. In both, fighters circle each other while employing a rocking movement called the *ginga*, a rhythmic motion that prepares the body to attack or defend. What follows is a flurry of whirling kicks, flips, feints and dodges that bring the fighters perilously close to knocking each other's head off. Fighters aren't actually trying to hit their opponent unless they're competing in mixed martial art tournaments and capoeira-specific tournaments are judged for style over strikes, with the winner being the most graceful practitioner of the art.

CARDBOARD TUBE DUELLING (SEATTLE, US, INTERNATIONAL)
"Spreading cardboard awareness"

One of the happiest long-term by-products of the *Star Wars* franchise may just prove to be the sport of cardboard tube duelling. The invention of Seattle-based Robert Easley ramps up a child-like affection for battling with plastic swords, light sabres and the like into something like a sporting art form. Rules are simple. You fight an opponent with a cardboard tube. When their tube wilts to below a forty-five degree angle – or breaks – you win. There are other limitations on the type of moves permitted, and the tube must be held at the end. The game seems best played in a silly costume and where possible, to the accompaniment of a friendly bagpipe-player. (This last feature – perhaps a homage to the 1980s decapitation fest *Highlander* – is understandably optional.) Cardboard duelling is a clear candidate for elaborate and farcical cosplay (role-playing in a costume) and contestants have dressed up as knights and aliens, but also as sandwiches and sushi.

The Cardboard Tube Fighting League (which provides tubes at battlegrounds) administers the fledgling sport, which kicked off with a first event in 2007 and now promotes battles (with cardboard armour) and tournaments of 48 contestants. Enthusiasts duel together in San Francisco, Boston, Philadelphia and Washington, DC, and Sydney and Bristol have also picked up the cardboard baton. It also reinterprets the US constitution's Fourth Amendment – the right to bear arms – as "referring to elite militias of cardboard-tube wielding ninjas". As good a weapon of choice as any other, we'd say.

CATFISH NOODLING (OKLAHOMA, US)
It was *this* large!

If you're willing to wade about in cold murky waters, feeling with your toes for unseen crevices that might house huge flathead catfish, then you've got half of what it takes to become a catfish noodler. The other part to this drama is catching the slimy monsters, done by twisting your arm into that dark hole, and luring the whiskered fish into biting down on your dangling fingers. Though there's no guarantee that a fifty pound-plus prize-winning fish is lying in wait – it's just as likely to be a snake, alligator, muskrat or snapping turtle that will gladly take a finger or two off your mitt.

Also known as hogging, catfisting or stumping, the sport is illegal in all but eleven US states, while the largest tournament and biggest prizes are found in the traditional heart of noodling country, Oklahoma, at the annual Okie Noodling Tournament. The rules are simple: competitors have 24 hours to land the largest catch they can handle; it must be caught within the state; and it must be alive upon judges' weighing. The mostly self-enforced guidelines have led to some controversy, with critics suggesting that ultra-large catches may have in fact been farm-raised and strategically planted by shady noodlers. No such aspersions have been cast upon the current record, a 68-pound monster dragged from the deep by local boy Jon Bridges. For those of us unable to make the trip to the Pauls Valley, Oklahoma tournament, Bradley Beesley's 2001 *Okie Noodling* documentary provides a thoughtful look into the odd but cherished Midwestern practice.

CHEESE ROLLING (COOPER'S HILL, GLOUCESTER, UK)
"Stay upright, or at least fall a lot better than I did."

While it might sound like a stupid stunt dreamed up for the *Jackass* TV series, the annual cheese rolling competition at Cooper's Hill is an event that was first held over a century ago. There's not a great deal to it – essentially a huge crowd of people run down a very steep Gloucestershire hill in pursuit of a big, round piece of cheese. And it's hard to see quite what's "traditional" about it either, other than that it's been done every year for a long time. But there's no denying the appealing absurdity of a contest in which hordes of near-suicidal contenders race down a near-vertical drop to try to win a battered dairy product. Contestants fall into two camps. There are those who don't want to break any limbs – who either take the slope slowly, determined not to fall, or who opt for a downward slide on their

The dash at Cooper's Hill: the big cheese in this sport's annual calendar.

posteriors. Then there are those who are serious about winning the cheese, for whom the course is a brutal tumble of grass and mud. To judge by the testimonies of entrants, a sprained ankle or a dislocated finger is getting off lightly. The official contest is, in fact, currently in a state of limbo – due to inaccurate reports of large crowds that may have raised insurance fears for the organizers. But the hardy men and women of Cooper's Hill refused to give up, and an unofficial cheese rolling scramble took place in 2010 with former champion and organizer Chris Anderson leading the charge in more ways than one. Such is the profile of Cooper's Hill there is now even an app where you are the cheese!

There's also a gentler cheese rolling competition, of a very different kind, held every year in Gessapolina, Italy. There, cheese rolling is a sport somewhere in between boules and yo-yoing: contestants have wheels of pecorino tied to their wrists with twine, and they see who can roll their cheese the furthest.

CHESS BOXING (NETHERLANDS, GERMANY, THE WORLD)

"Fighting is done in the ring and wars are waged on the board."

New sports are developed all the time but only a tiny minority start life in a comic book. This most schizophrenic of sports first cropped up in cartoonist Enki Bilals's graphic novel *Froid Équateur* (1992), from where the notion of splicing together chess and boxing was first picked up by Dutch performance artist and all-round maverick Iepe Rubingh. He staged the first match of the fledgling sport in 2003 – adapted so that opponents alternated rounds of speed chess and boxing – and thereby became the inaugural world champion.

The World Chess Boxing Organization, now run by Rubingh, is designed to promote "aggression management" (see their slogan, above) and from its start in Berlin has expanded to associations in the UK, Siberia and L.A. Ability in both sports is crucial: players must have an "Elo-rating" in chess (named after the system's Hungarian-born American physics professor, not the 1970s rock group) of 1800 or above. Victory goes to the contender who is the first to win at chess or boxing, though in the event of everything being all square at the end of the eleven alternating rounds the player with the black chess pieces is deemed to be the winner. Quite an advantage you would think. Although so far, with heads reeling from a surprising "Latvian gambit" or a "neo-Grünfeld defence" – or, of course, from heavy blows to the nose or the brain – it is a sport that pretty much always delivers a clear winner. The ultimate dream for chess boxing enthusiasts is to see Lennox Lewis take on Vitali Klitschko, as both are known to like a bit of the old knight-on-bishop action. Mike Tyson, on the other hand, might struggle. The first round in chess boxing is always conducted seated.

DEMOLITION DERBY (US, INTERNATIONAL)

Carpocalypse Now!

If the number of related videogames were the only criterion, then demolition derby would be the king of all games. The 1970s was the peak decade for this subculture with a county fair vibe, before a decline and then a revival propelled by cable channels and pay per view TV. Victory is not, as derby implies, about winning a race but about being the last car standing in a dodgems-style fight your corner smash-up. Large sedans and saloons ruled the roost in the 1970s but with economy vehicles coming to the fore in the 1980s it has become more a case of what you can get your hands on and are prepared to write off. In more recent times the monster truck has become the super-heavyweight face of demolition events as vehicle size has grown again.

Local promotion has been crucial to the sport as well as TV input like *TNN's Motor Madness* and Spike TV's documentary series *Carpocalypse*. With new cars needed all the time and a fluid and highly dispersed racing scene in the US, the sport has lacked consistent momentum and a running narrative to keep it in the mainstream media eye. In the UK and Europe, banger racing fills a similar space with a race to the finish line taking place amidst the carnage. So demolition derby is a cult sport by every conceivable yardstick. But it will forever remain a big fish in a small pond: the ruler of its small-screen universe.

DODGEBALL (US)
Not a true underdog story

A staple of gym classes in primary schools across the US, dodgeball is one of the more obvious ways of separating quickly maturing athletes from the less physically inclined. The game consists of hurling an air-filled rubber ball with as much force as you can muster at one another. If you're hit, you're out. But to keep the game from devolving into total chaos there are some basic rules. The game is most often played on an indoor basketball court, its centre-line splitting the playing area across the middle. Participants are divided evenly and sent to their respective halves, where they must stay while trying to hit opposing players. At the start, players from each team race to a random number of balls set in the middle of the court, where the first close-quarter volleys are exchanged. Those who survive the initial wave must retrieve balls in their own half to launch further attacks, all the while dodging incoming waves from across the court.

The slow, weak and near-sighted are usually the first to go, and once struck must sit out until either the next game starts or a teammate catches a ball thrown by an opponent. In this latter case the thrower is called out, and the catcher can bring a previously ejected teammate back onto the court. Dodgeball was mostly relegated to childhood memory until the movie of the same name came along in 2004, suggesting to adults that they should form a professional league where they wear proper uniforms and take the whole thing too seriously. At the amateur/phys-ed level there are a number of variations on the game, including bombardment (teams must protect a number of pins from being knocked over), jailbreak (struck players must sit in "jail" until a teammate releases them), and trampoline dodgeball, which requires a special facility wherein trampolines are lined up side by side and players launch themselves into the air to avoid being hit.

DRAGON BOAT RACING (CHINA, HONG KONG, INTERNATIONAL)
Bang the drum

The more colourful and inclusive cousin of traditional rowing has a venerable history. Other peoples have buried objects or slaughtered animals to appease the gods or bring on the rains, but some Chinese villagers took the more sensible step of having a bit of fun and holding boat races. So it was that, over two thousand years ago, on the fifth day of the fifth Chinese lunar month, races were held to propitiate the dragon symbol of water and thus encourage the rains needed for prosperity. Today's races feature colourful vessels (with dragon head) of up to forty feet long, with up to twenty paddlers and a drummer beating out the paddlers' rhythm over distances of anywhere between two hundred and two thousand metres.

It's not always been fun and games though. The other legend surrounding dragon boat racing's origins connects it to exiled leader Qu Yuan, who committed watery suicide in AD 278, distraught at the destruction of his Chu homeland by neighbouring armies. Friends and followers frantically paddled out to him in boats to save him – but in vain. The dragon boat festivals that continued thereafter are said to have been held in his honour. Hong Kong created the first international event in 1976, and the Chinese added dragon boat festival days to the roster of national holidays. The sociability of the sport has won it many friends, and it continues to spread internationally with charity events especially popular in many countries.

Dragon boat racing keeps the gods happy, and gets you a day off work.

DWARF THROWING (AUSTRALIA, US, INTERNATIONAL))
Political incorrectness gone mad

The phenomenon of dwarf throwing is probably the most bizarre pub game you're ever likely to hear of. Bar billiards it ain't. Banned by law in many countries and US states, it's generally practised by big men in various degrees of inebriation and involves throwing a dwarf, clad in padded protective clothing, as far as possible in a room cushioned with crash-mats – or at a velcro-treated wall. The longest dwarf-toss ever recorded is said to have been made by Jimmy Leonard, a UK truck driver, who is said to have thrown "Lenny the Giant", who was four feet four inches tall and weighed ninety-eight pounds, a distance of eleven feet five inches. As you'd expect, dwarf throwing is vilified for being exploitative of people with dwarfism. But it has some staunch defenders among its participants. Manuel Wackenheim, a three feet seven inches Frenchman, appealed to the UN human rights committee against his country's ban on dwarf throwing, which had previ-

Washington, DC take on the Sri Lankan police at elephant polo.

ously been his livelihood. Supporters of dwarf throwing claim dwarves can earn several thousand dollars by taking part, and frequently draw analogies with basketball or modelling – lucrative activities that are equally height-dependent. Don't expect dwarf throwing to ever feature in the Olympics: its shady existence is likely to remain the preserve of rednecks, sports jocks and bingeing millionaires.

ELEPHANT POLO (NEPAL, ASIA)
Elite exercise

If polo is an elitist and aristocratic sport – largely because you've got to be loaded to keep a polo pony – then elephant polo ought to be the sport of maharajahs. In fact, it's a recent phenomenon, invented in 1982 at Tiger Tops, an exclusive resort in the jungle flatlands of Chitwan, in Nepal, which keeps its own domesticated elephants for wildlife-watching excursions. The game is still played there each year, on the grassy expanse of the local Meghauli airstrip, and has since spread to Sri Lanka, India and Thailand.

It's basically a tourist attraction, and not exactly thrilling as a sport, given that the elephants lumber about in a confused and peevish sort of way, and the players struggle to find the ball with their nine-foot, bamboo-extended polo mallets. It can be spectacular, however – and was never more so than when, in 2007, a particularly fed-up elephant called Abey ran amok in Sri Lanka, throwing his riders and launching himself, with impressive (and perhaps understandable) vindictiveness, at a team's minibus.

ESKRIMA (PHILIPPINES)
Sticking it to the man

Other martial sports can be traced back to monasteries and courts, but eskrima, which hales from the Filipino island of Cebu, is a street sport, and in more ways than one. Back in the colonial days Spanish troops were alarmed by the fighting proficiency of locals, notably at the Battle of Mactan (1521) when explorer Ferdinand Magellan was killed by the army of native resistance leader Lapu-Lapu in the first Spanish defeat. Eskrima is reckoned to have been much in evidence. The full range of eskrima arts includes the use of knives and empty hand fighting but stick fighting is what eskrima is most famous for. Modern eskrima looks back to the foundation of the Doce Pares society in 1932 when twelve eskrima masters who had previously jealously guarded their secrets got together and pooled their knowledge to form a club which became a nucleus around which the activity spread and developed. There is a baffling plethora of lineages, styles and disciplines in eskrima, but what distinguishes it in a general sense is the fluidity, speed and nimbleness of the way in which sticks are handled, so as to avoid easy blocking.

Going to extremes: six sports in the spotlight

Croquet (see p.37) is far from being the only kid on the extreme block. Here are six of our favourites from an increasingly crowded field.

Extreme ironing

Marketed as a dangerous sport combining excitement with the "satisfaction of a well-pressed shirt", extreme ironing was founded in Leicester, UK, in 1997 by Phil Shaw (aka "Steam"). After a much publicized world championships in Germany in 2002, extreme ironing action has recently gone underwater – with international teams vying to have the largest numbers of divers ironing at once.

Extreme kayaking

Not content with simply running class five white-water rapids in a fragile fibreglass shell, extreme kayakers have taken to throwing themselves over the edges of waterfalls in search of an even bigger adrenaline rush. No festivals or major competitions have been announced as of yet, but with these kayakers posting videos of increasingly tall fall runs (the current world record drop is 187 feet) an international organization with full advertising sponsorship can't be far behind.

Mountain unicycling

Mountain biking's smaller sibling may not be one for mass uptake. Unicycling for those not born into a circus family is hard enough for starters. Then throw into the mix rugged terrains, and some serious core stability is needed to stay upright. Photography of the sport is inspiring and it is impossible not to be impressed by the likes of Canada's star unicylist and tireless promoter Kris Holm whether it is his landhop records, photoshoots or just plain ability to stay on one wheel.

Speed golf/Extreme golf

As if golf wasn't hard enough for most of us, this sport ups the ante by combining it with running. Scoring is based on a combined total of time and strokes. At Chicago's Jackson Park, star speed golfer Chris Smith hit a 65 in 44 minutes and 6 seconds (with an overall score of 109:06). Club selection is limited: wise heads use only four to six. Even so, maybe not one for John Daly for the moment.

Street luge

Created when skateboarders in California tried lying down on their boards to bring about a new rather dangerous activity undertaken at speed. It

joins downhill skateboarding – performed in ski suits and helmets –
as one of the twin peaks of the booming International Gravity Sports
Association.

Wingsuit flying

Jump out of an aircraft in a squirrel-shaped suit equipped with a parachute
and you are wingsuit flying. Incorporating elements of hang gliding and
parachuting, there are flight records up for grabs for achievements such as
greatest height, distance and times. With tweaks such as "proximity flying"
near to mountains and rocket propulsion adding even more spice to the
mix, it is all a very long way from crown green bowls!

Dealing with stubborn creases. Extreme ironing is not quite as easy as it looks.

Old masters now regret the fact that the younger generation of Filipinos do not seem to have the time to devote to the sport – which has been promoted successfully overseas as the form of martial arts nearest to street fighting and a very practical form of self-defence. It has attracted interest from sources as diverse as the Russian army and Hollywood fight choreographers. World championships are held in rotation at Cebu itself every other year, where one of the original masters, Ciriaco Cañete (now in his nineties), is the current president of the Doce Pares club.

ETON FIVES (ENGLAND, UK)
Take Five

The world's more recherché sports usually retain vibrant, historic links to the playground games they grew up from. Take the sport of fives, which is played in a basic form everywhere you can bring together a ball and a wall, under names like "handball" or "patball". (In the US, it's sometimes called the fireman's game, as it's apparently popular in the garages while waiting for call-out.) The official sport of fives is a racquetless version of squash, using one of two kinds of official court, each based on the informal play areas originally found at two English public schools. Rugby Fives, as once played at Rugby School, uses a plain, four-walled squash-style court, and a lethally hard ball – the leather gloves are well-padded. Eton fives, as originally played at Eton, has a softer ball and a pleasingly eccentric court that mimics the hazards of the original Eton chapel wall. There's a lethal six-inch step across the middle of the court, for instance, and a buttress, known as the "pepper", which protrudes awkwardly (and often, painfully) into the left-hand side of the court.

Despite its aristocratic origins, Eton fives has recently been promoted in inner-city areas. In 2001, four courts were even built in the Westway Sports Centre, underneath the Westway Flyover on the rough side of London's Notting Hill.

ETON WALL GAME (ETON, UK)
The goal of the decade competition

A rugby-like ruck forms up against a high, long brick wall, along which it staggers and heaves, crab-like, up and down, scraping the skin off the kicking players as it goes. Every so often the ball pops out, and is promptly hoofed upfield. Goals are only scored about once a decade. You can see, perhaps, why the Eton wall game never caught on. And yet there's something captivating about it. The attraction is partly the splendid eccentricity of playing a sport up against a 110-metre stretch of gorgeous, early eighteenth-century brick (which is topped, on the rare match days, by a mass of watching schoolboys). But the allure is mostly about rarity and antiquity: the game is only really played at Eton, England's most elite private boarding school, and members of the public hardly ever get to see it. It's also hundreds of years old, a relic of the ad-hoc days of eccentric public-school sports before they dreamed up the rules that transformed the old mob scraps into modern games like rugby and football.

These days, the wall game is an unofficial side-show, organized by the boys. The *official* Eton school sport is another antiquated oddity, the field game, which is a bit like football but with rugby-like scrums, and try-like scoring. Other public schools have their own equivalents, from Harrow football, with its ungainly, heavy ball, to "Winkies", or Winchester college football, with its long nets running the length of the pitch.

EXTREME CROQUET (US, SWEDEN)
Where the phrase "safe shot" has no meaning

Many sports in the panoply of out-there pursuits have eschewed competition per se for the dangerous photo opportunity: the unicycle on the precipice or the ironing board on the rapids (see pp. 34-35). Not so extreme croquet, which, rather self-consciously it has to be said, turns a tranquil and genteel pastime into something a little more rugged.

Traditional croquet itself has had an interesting history. No one is quite sure how croquet came about, though a French pastime called "paille maille" – which also gave its name to the famous London road – is often cited as a precursor. The modern croquet bug spread rapidly from Ireland, propelled by an equipment manufacturer called Mr Jacques to the mainland in the 1860s. It then had something of a boom in the US some decades later and still attracts a disturbingly intense following, with enough schisms, versions of the rules and historical ups and downs for a sport with five or six times its following. There are many types currently played across the world including association croquet and golf croquet as well as such closely related spin-off games as rocque (a kind of American octagonal hard surface version with rubber balls, now dying off) through to gateball (a faster and allegedly more social cousin invented in Japan and also thriving in Asia and Australia). Somehow the uniquely deranged croquet gene seems to have settled down most vigorously in the US where, in addition to extreme croquet, you can also find the supersized mallet ball and toequet options (the latter in which you kick the ball through hoops).

The spirit of extreme croquet has certainly been alive in the US for some time. A Boston cleric banned croquet in the 1890s because of the gambling, drinking and fighting it entailed and there are reports that a golf-course-size croquet pitch was created for the American millionaire Herbert Swope in the 1920s, complete with bunkers and rough. Sweden then entered the picture with the creation of the Krocketklubben club in 1975, set up by pioneering Linköping University of

Wrestling: six of the best

Wrestling is one of sport's true universals. Here are six from what could easily be sixty – or six hundred – varieties from around the world.

Cumberland and Westmoreland Wrestling (England)

In Captain Underpants style costume (minus the cape), local fighters attempt to wrestle their opponent to the ground (beginning by standing chest facing chest), at events such as Grasmere's Annual Sports and Show. That particular fair dates from 1852 though C&WW's history extends back much further, with its origins linked both to Norse and more likely Celtic traditions – Scotland has a very similar tradition known as Scottish backhold.

Laamb (Senegalese wrestling)

Laamb (or *lutte traditionelle*, as it is also called), has moved from being folk wrestling into a lucrative professional sport in West Africa, with telecom sponsorship and advertising sustaining a scene rivalling soccer in popularity. Traditional laamb differs from what you'd expect from wrestling in that it allows punching (or *frappe*, as it is known). Matches

Cumberland wrestlers ready themselves for combat at the village of Ambleside.

are for real with prizes that can be as much as $200,000 for stars of the ilk of Yékini or Tyson, the two biggest names in the laamb pantheon.

Pankration (Ancient Greek wrestling)

The "all powers" (including hitting and kicking) wrestling style of Ancient Greece, said to be the grandaddy of mixed martial arts (see p.22), debuted in the original Olympic Games in 643 BC. Gladiator-style, it ended either in death or surrender. In Greek myth, Theseus is thought to have defeated the minotaur using pankration. Pankration has been reinvented as an amateur sport under the auspices of the International Federation of Associated Wrestling Styles.

Shwingen (Swiss wrestling)

This "breeches lifting" form of wrestling is a Swiss national sport. It takes place in an arena lined with sawdust; the two wrestlers wear shorts made of jute and grapple with each other by holding onto the back of the belt straps. The object is to force your opponent to the floor. Victory is accorded when both an opponent's shoulders touch the ground whilst the winner holds the opponent's canvas shorts.

Varzesh-e pahlavani (Persian wrestling)

This activity takes place within the unique Iranian culture of Zurkhenah ("house of strength") fitness clubs, which were housed in covered pits. They would also play host to other practices, such as Indian club swinging. The wrestling, in fact, only occurs at the end of a varzesh-e pahlavani session which, rather like some martial arts in other parts of the East, involves music, wooden clubs, metal shields and iron weights. Zurkhenah practice embodies Sufi concepts and philosophy and has taken root in other Central Asian countries. But despite a first zurkhenah world championships in Baku in 2009, traditional-style wrestling is on the wane in its historic form.

Yağlı gűreş (Turkish oil wrestling)

The Kirkpinar festival near Erdine has a tradition of hosting the chief tournament of this popular national sport, which stretches back six centuries. Contestants wear black calf-skin three-quarter-length trousers called a *kisbet*, and are covered in olive oil, which makes it harder to grab and keep hold of an opponent. The objective of the wrestling match is to put your arm through your opponent's kisbet. Bouts originally lasted as long as it took, and there are matches on record as having lasted one or two days before a clear victory. In 1975, time limits were established and nowadays they won't exceed an hour.

Technology students – currently the oldest extreme croquet club in the world. Members of the club got into the habit of getting into period dress and disallowing female participation (though not social involvement) in games which could last up to six hours, with frequent refreshment breaks.

From here the US once again picked up the mallet, founding numerous clubs such as the regulation-setting Connecticut Extreme Croquet society (CECS) that began in 1984. Dress for extreme croquet clubs is casual and of necessity out-doorsy whereas courses vary from forests to gravel beds with rough, varied and even dangerous locations preferred. Mallets and other specially made equipment are used as normal croquet kit is way too fragile for a more hostile game. There are fears that extreme croquet's tongue-in-cheek appeal might have peaked before the end of the first decade of the twenty-first century. The CECS website, for example, proclaims its pride in its widely adopted rules but sadly contrasts this to its disap-pointingly slow growth in membership.

Still, it is a fool who would try to predict the future for croquet in any of its forms. Perhaps the bizarre incarnation of leftfield croquet was Croquet X Machina, an event that took place in the Black Rock desert in Nevada in 1987, where trucks and specially made battering rams knocked six-foot balls through fifteen-foot-high wickets. This petrol-fuelled extravaganza seems a long way from the English Edwardian country house party image with which the parent game seems so inextricably linked. But as any croquet player, extreme or other-wise, will tell you it is a game as riven with cruelty, mind games and attitude, as any yet invented.

FELL RUNNING (INTERNATIONAL)
Over hill and under dale

Taking its name from the fells in the north of England, fell running could be seen as a spin-off of cross-country running, only with steeper and generally longer courses: fell runs cover rough, rugged and often remote terrain. A fell-running course won't necessarily even be marked, so a fell runner needs to have good navi-gational skills: think "speed orienteering".

The categorization of different fell runs is fairly exhaustive. There are three ascent categories, graded A–C. The toughest (A) must have at least 250 feet of ascent per mile. Then there are distance categories, graded L, M and S (long, medium and short). There are also additional categories, such as mountain mara-thons and mountain trials, which may require over a day to complete, for which competitors must carry all the supplies and equipment they need. Fell races take place every weekend up and down the UK, and the Fell Running Association web-site has all the info you could need if you feel the atavistic urge to torture your feet in some bone-jarring sprints over steep and slippery slopes.

GILLI DANDA (INDIA)
Indian nationalist cricket

In rural areas of India and Pakistan, if you stroll on some wasteground of an evening, you can often see children playing a simple game that, for all that it uses just two sticks, is captivating to the point of obsession. In Hindi, they call it gilli danda, though it has almost as many names as there are languages in India. Most mean the same thing: "bat-and-peg". The *gilli* is a short, conical stick about the size of a finger. The *danda* is like a miniature walking stick. You place the *gilli* in the ground, tap it sharply so it flies upwards, then swat it away with the *danda*, hoping you don't get caught. Even if you don't, the fielders have one chance to get you out by throwing the *gilli* back at your *danda*, which you've meanwhile inserted in the ground like a wicket.

If you think it sounds like cricket, you're not alone. The strange similarity hasn't been lost on Indian nationalists, who like to claim that they, not the English, invented cricket. In truth, similar traditional games have been played from England to Korea. The seventeenth-century writer John Bunyan, author of *The Pilgrim's Progress*, even claimed to have first heard the voice of God commanding him while playing a very similar game, known as tip cat, on his village green: "'Wilt thou leave thy sins and go to heaven?', God asked him; 'Or have thy sins and go to hell whilst playing tip-cat on Elstow Green?'"

GLÍMA (ICELAND)
The art of combating trolls

Whatever happened to glíma, Iceland's unique form of wrestling? Though glíma sounds like the name of a dwarf in J.R.R. Tolkein's *Lord of the Rings* fantasy, it was actually one of a select group of exhibition sports that have appeared at Olympic Games just the once. Standing tall at the Stockholm 1912 games in the company of an obscure pastime called baseball, glíma then promptly took a tumble back into the shadows along with such would-be global titans of the professional sporting world as pigeon racing (1900) and kaatsen (Frisian handball, 1928). Baseball, for the record, was admitted eighty years on from Stockholm before getting dropped in 2012. In Iceland, however, glíma has never been away. According to the International Glíma Association the beginnings of the sport date back to the foundation of the Icelandic commonwealth in 930, with folk tales telling of heroes using glíma as a useful "tool to combat trolls and beasts".

Compared to other types of wrestling sports, glíma is rather dance-like – a form of wrestling with carefully defined rules, ideas of fair play and precisely prescribed holds which legislate against, for example, just pushing your opponent to the floor with force. The classic image of glíma is an arresting one with a man, upended legs pointing to the sky, the other participant an entangled but imposing head and shoulders at ninety degrees to the floor. Women too can fight, with the honour of being crowned Queen of Glíma up for grabs.

HAKA PEI (EASTER ISLAND, CHILE)
Over the hill *and* far away

Easter Island, with its strange gigantic Maori stone faces, does weird on a grand scale. But it's not all granite-faced inscrutability there. There are fun and games too. The annual, fortnight-long festival of Tapati, which encompasses all sorts of indigenous festivities, hosts as a centrepiece the glorious event of haka pei or banana tree stump sliding, a somewhat reckless undertaking which makes your average luge run look like a stroll in the park. Between thirty to forty locals and the odd visitor slide down the vertiginous slopes of Maunga Pu'Il and a stopwatch records the fastest time – generally in the region of ten to twelve seconds.

Minor injuries are frequent in haka pei – and the odd major one. It's not so much the impressive speed of descent, which can top fifty miles per hour, but the not especially aerodynamic banana-stump "carriages" and the bumpy but very steep ground they traverse; eager prospective contenders can size up the terrain on YouTube. Nor are most locals cosseted by the latest thermo-padded outdoor pursuits gear. Traditional dress for competitors is the order of the day.

Originally the event is reputed to have been an integral part of the local culture and somehow connected to the training of warriors. If so it must be one of the more exhilarating options on the soldierly curriculum on Easter Island or anywhere else.

HORNUSSEN (SWITZERLAND)
Creating a buzz

Some sports retain a whiff of medieval warfare about them. Hornussen may just be one of those. After all, propelling a projectile at a speed close to two hundred miles per hour in the direction of a neighbouring village does not sound like the friendliest of gestures, but since the seventeenth century, when the sport is recorded as distracting the folk of Lauperswil from church, it has been popular in Switzerland, particularly in the area of Emmental otherwise famous for its cheese. The original missile was a bone but is now a "nouss". This is whacked up a ramp by a whip, which has something of the feel of a cross between a one wood in golf and a fishing rod whereupon it travels up to 300 yards into a field of players defended by an opposing team of eighteen men armed with paddle boards a bit like wooden pizza spatulas ("*schindel*"). Their aim is to stop the nouss hitting the ground. If they fail they concede points to the opposition. Longer shots yield better scores. As it travels, the nouss makes a whirring noise like a hornet, hence the name of the sport.

Aside from areas of countries bordering Switzerland and rumours of a few South African hornusser, the game remains the preserve of a few specialist clubs in agricultural regions of North Switzerland.

HURLING (IRELAND)

Gaelic fun and games

To outsiders, hurling is said to resemble the bastard child of hockey and lacrosse, though it's a more venerable sport than either, and for a true comparison you might want to add rugby, baseball and maybe netball into the mix too. Scots high-landers would recognize it pretty much as "shinty". In atmosphere, the sport is to hockey what Aussie rules football is to the ordinary kind: it's faster, rougher, harder and definitely much more exciting – and yet hardly known outside the home country. It might just be that if you're not born to the game, you'd have to be insane to choose to learn it.

Players wield a steroidal version of a hockey stick, the hurley, and they're not restricted by the hockey rules that keep sticks below shoulder height and balls mostly on the ground. (You can also catch the ball in mid-air, run with it in the hand for three steps, or dribble with it balanced on the hurley – all of which really keeps things moving. Opponents' hurleys can be blocked or hooked, meanwhile, or you can just shoulder-barge them.) The ball is softball-like in size and hardness, but the pace is so fast and the action so direct that players nowadays wear helmets with face guards.

As one of the two "Gaelic games", alongside Gaelic football, hurling holds a particular place in Irish nationalist hearts. The home of the sport is Croke Park, or "Croker", as Dubliners call it, which has been the third largest stadium in Europe since its refit in 1991, with a capacity of more than 82,000. That fact alone bears vivid testimony to hurling's domestic popularity. Croker's own nationalist associations, of course, were bloodily reinforced in 1920, when Royal Irish Constabulary troops entered the stadium during a Gaelic football match – the stadium hosts both sports – and fired into the crowd killing fourteen people.

IDIOTAROD (NORTH AMERICA)

Best in class for sabotage

Take one shopping cart, five thematically matching costumes, an abundance of offensive projectiles and plenty of strong liquor. You've got yourself an entry for the idiotarod (liquor not required, but encouraged). The idiotarod may be best known for its New York City incarnation, but the original urban iditarod, named after the Alaskan dog race, took place in San Francisco in the mid-1990s.

Participants in fancy dress tethered to a rolling cart dashed through a series of checkpoints in the City by the Bay. The mood was madcap, dog costumes abounded, and the event was more party than competition.

Not so in New York City, where the idiotarod has a more menacing feel – not to mention the fact that it takes place in the dead cold of the mid-Atlantic winter. The race route isn't released until the morning of the event, a tradition that encourages the spread of misinformation between teams, and is a helpful step toward securing one of the most highly sought after prizes: Best Sabotage. Other common modes of disruption are throwing rotting fish, and dropping marbles and banana peels to slow down other teams. That's child's play compared to 2010's Best Sabotage winning team, who hacked the event's online registration system, then sold it back at a profit. Finishing first is, in fact, only the second highest award, following Best in Show.

With teams decked out as mime artists, action figures, traffic cones, Chippendale dancers, pilots from the movie *Top Gun* (including a cart transformed into a fighter jet, complete with smoking exhaust) and one group stuffed into Star Trek uniforms, calling themselves the Mighty Rappin' Shatners, it's always a difficult call.

IDITAROD (ALASKA, US)
Seward's folly

At the turn of the twentieth century, Alaska was little more than a frozen collection of tiny villages separated by hundreds of miles of near-impassable terrain. During the summer thaw, prospectors seeking gold in the hills would travel by way of the Yukon River into the heart of the state, but come winter the waterway was a solid block of ice, and with no train tracks yet laid the route was unnavigable. Except to sled dogs. Native breeds like the malamute and Siberian husky (and even wolves) were prized for their strength and speed, plus they were light enough to move across loose snow without sinking.

Fast-forward to 1973, when Alaskans were looking for a unique way to commemorate the centennial of "Seward's folly" – the seemingly mad purchase of wild Arctic wasteland by Secretary of State William Seward. Could there be any better way to celebrate the pioneer spirit of Alaska than pitting a lone man (and his dogs) against raw nature over 1049 miles in sub-zero temperatures? The race starts in Anchorage and runs northwest to Nome along the Iditarod trail, passing through the namesake ghost town on odd-numbered years while taking a northerly route on even-numbered ones. The drivers, known as mushers, each control a team of approximately 16 dogs and make the journey in roughly 10 days, with the current record held by Swiss-born Martin Buser at 8 days, 22 hours, 47 minutes and 2 seconds. The race is a point of controversy for animal rights activists, who point to dog deaths along the route as evidence of abuse.

IRISH ROAD BOWLING (IRELAND)
Back road bullets

Is there not something stereotypically Irish about a pub-based sport that takes you out on the rural back roads in a great amicable gang, talking and laughing and betting on the outcome? Road bowling has the simple genius of all truly great sports. It's a bit like golf, without ties and clubhouses (although it's certainly chauvinistic), and without clubs or holes or courses. All you need for road bowling is a road, and any tennis-ball-sized cannonball you may have lying around (28 ounces is the standard weight). Plus a few big friends to stop the traffic. Then you sling your "bowl" or "bullet" down the road, skittering it around bends and corners, and picking it up again in the road next to where it lands. Two players compete to see who can travel the distance of the course (usually a mile or so) with the fewest throws.

Experienced players judge lines and angles with astonishing accuracy, and they bowl with amazing power. In 1964, the great Mick Barry legendarily lobbed his bowl right over the roof of Mary Ann McConnell's pub, in Cork, while in 1955 he sent one an astonishing hundred feet up onto the Chetwynd Viaduct, on the Cork to Bandon road. It's a pity that the game hasn't taken off much beyond its homelands of County Armagh (where it's called bullets, or long bullets), and County Cork – though it's getting pretty big in West Virginia, US. Maybe other nations just don't have the same Sunday afternoon spirit. Or the same quiet back roads.

Monument to Balto, the husky who (with colleagues) famously saved the city of Nome from a diptheria epidemic in 1925, when the mushing wasn't recreational, but a matter of life and death.

JIÀNZI/SHUTTLECOCK (CHINA, VIETNAM, SOUTH EAST ASIA, INTERNATIONAL)

"Be inspired by shuttlecock sport."

Southeast Asia is definitely the region of the world to go to for the last word on keepy-uppy-sports. In the Philippines you'll find sipa (played with a ball), in Malaysia there's sepak tekraw (with a shuttlecock), visit Japan and find kemari (ball) or hanetsui (with paddle and shuttlecock). Typically the formal versions feature a badminton net and similar style court; the informal a group of people on the street, park or market square artfully keeping the ball or a shuttlecock off the ground. The rules of the game are not at all dissimilar to volleyball, though use of hands is forbidden.

China, in the fifth century BC, is believed to be the point of origin of the game, where it was designed as part of military training and to improve agility and reflexes, which it certainly does. A first competition took place in China in the 1930s and there have been world championships since 1997. Though the game's heartlands are in China and Vietnam, where the teams do particularly well, Germany and Hungary have taken to the sport. Nowadays the weighty hand (sorry – foot) of the International Shuttlecock Federation (motto reproduced above) is taking the game to the world, where it faces competition with the likes of its South American counterparts peteca and indiaca. Spectacular scissor kicks, coupled with incredible agility and hamstrings stretching to a degree that would make a ballerina wince, should mean the obesity-threatened populations of the UK and US have their work cut out to catch up. Jiànzi goes by many names in the region, notably da cau in Vietnam; in Hanoi it is a popular street sport.

KABBADI (INDIA/BANGLADESH)

Take a deep breath

In the rankings of world sports, kabbadi really is an odd one. You don't need any equipment to play it, not even a ball, and its most distinctive feature is that you spend a lot of time holding your breath. Two teams stand on either side of a badminton-sized court. From one team, a "raider" emerges, dashing across the centre line towards the enemy. As he crosses the line, he has to hold his breath (and start chanting "kabbadi"). He tries to tag an opponent and then get back across his line so he can start breathing again; his opponents have to stop him escaping home, by forming a chain of hands, by tagging him or, in the full-on version, by wrestling him to the ground until he submits or takes a breath.

Kabbadi may date back to ancient warriors' training games, or to wrestling exercises – or it could just be a grown-up children's game. Plenty of people have

Redneck Games (Georgia, US)

The Olympics came to Atlanta in 1996, bringing along all the international fanfare these events tend to attract. Not to be outdone, residents of East Dublin in the very heart of Georgia decided to give the world a true taste of Southern-fried culture: the Redneck Games.

What is a redneck you ask? "Just a good ol' boy, never meaning no harm" – looking up the rest of the lyrics to the *Dukes of Hazzard* theme should fill out the description for you. In the words of the Games' unofficial mascot, the toothless asphalt worker L-Bow, "We work hard, we play hard, and we die broke." The competitions themselves are down-home variants of tamer standards. Instead of apple bobbing, competitors bob for pig's feet (this season's championship strategy: Go for the toes). Horseshoes not challenging enough? Replace the metal crescents with toilet seats. Same idea for the discus (hubcaps are the stand-in), shot put (watermelon seed spitting contest), and long jump (the mud pit belly flop, where outrageously clad men and women are judged for style as they leap beer gut first into a pit of wet slop).

But the height of subtle artistry is best exhibited during the armpit serenade. This year's winner was an eight-year-old boy, whose rendition of "Mary Had a Little Lamb" played on his armpits and the back of his knees brought tears to his mother's eyes.

The mudpit belly flop as it should be performed. Winner Gebby Lehman in 2007.

pointed out the similarity to European playground games such as British bull-dog. In India, its home, the game has popular, peasant roots. In one traditional form, players don't just chant kabbadi; they improvise taunting verses to wind up their opponents. One much-loved traditional taunt can be roughly translated as "Your mother is a cripple/Grabbed your leg, you're in a pickle". The modern sport is played, fervently, from Iran to Bangladesh (where it goes by the name hu-du-du, and is the official national game) and in all the countries of the Indian diaspora. As for the meaning of the word kabbadi, no one is quite sure. The most prosaic explanation is that kabbadi is impossible to say while disguising an in-breath.

KAIJU BIG BATTEL (BOSTON, US)
Wrestling but not as we know it

On the surface, the prospect of art students wrestling each other doesn't sound overly enticing. But what if they were wearing outrageous monster costumes and smacking each other over the heads with chairs? Throw in a back-story about an aggression-releasing battle league for city-crushing behemoths, a few sub-plots involving meta-humans and a dash of disco music, and you've got yourself one hell of an interesting evening. Studio Kaiju would have you believe otherwise, but the origins of this event are entirely human. Confused? That's understandable.

Basically, brothers Rand and David Borden started a wrestling league of their own out of a failed video project, and have since expanded the cast of characters who take part beyond the original four monsters who first locked horns on the Halloween night of 1996 in Boston. More performance art than athletic contest, the wrestling matches may look free form but they are wholly predetermined, and participation in the fights is closely controlled by the Bordens. The mythology they have attached to their fancy-dress bouts is much more interesting. Apparently, giant monsters can't help but want to fight each other, and whatever populated human areas get in their way have "historically" felt the terrible fallout (just think of the casualties, and billions in insurance damages, when Mothra fought Godzilla in *Mothra Vs Godzilla*). Along came a wise group of humans who appointed a commissioner to oversee sanctioned wrestling events, and after moments of reflection, the monsters agreed to abide by the rules of the ring.

Eventually, mutated humans supposedly joined the fray, and now the likes of Kung-Fu Chicken Noodle (a man transformed into a soup can) and Unibouzu (whose powers manifested after he was bitten by an atomic sea urchin), can be seen matched up against the filthy giant rabbit Dusto Bunny and the league's primary villain, former Nazi and current plastic surgeon, Dr Cube.

KENDO (JAPAN)

Light sabres for real

With its black grim-reaper style garb (especially its hood-cum-helmet with metal grille) kendo may just have the coolest sporting outfits – or armour, as it is properly known – this side of *Star Wars*. And then there are the weapons. Combatants use weapons known as *shinai* or *bokuto* made out of bamboo or other wood, in lieu of the Japanese swords which their samurai predecessors would have used. A less dramatic and no less important dimension to kendo is that represented by the detachment and mental discipline of Zen Buddhism, which has left its mark on kendo – a word that translates as "the way of the sword". It was introduced as a new term for the activity as part of a governmental rationalization of martial arts disciplines in Japan which also did away with real swords.

Each strike or blow completed in kendo is accompanied by a shout of "kiai", which adds to the sense of menace. Movements, or "katas" (as in karate), are practised to perfection, as students progress up grades based on attainment and performance in bouts. Such fighting pedigree and imagery does seem to have influenced the *Star Wars* franchise, and Nick Gillard, stunt coordinator, cited it as an influence in the light sabre fighting sequences. The Allies even took kendo so seriously that they banned it in Japan for seven years after the end of World War II as part of a general clampdown on militaristic activities and personnel. Now that kendo, like many other martial arts, has gone international, there is wider understanding of its enlightened spiritual side behind the mask, even if that appearance to the outsider still holds elements of mystery and dread.

"Kiai": junior kendo practitioners.

KORFBALL (NETHERLANDS, INTERNATIONAL)

"The only truly mixed team sport in the world."

Basketball begat women's basketball which begat netball, a game designed for the fairer sex. Netball then begat korfball, which was invented in Holland in 1902 primarily to encourage girls and boys to play together in a happy spirit of gender equality and teamwork. "Korf" is Dutch for the game's basket. Players are split into zones out of which they cannot move and are paired against a player of the opposite sex though players swap zones every two goals. This rather neatly cancels out any height advantages, or similar, that might make the game unfair.

The lazy comparison for korfball is with basketball – "co-ed basketball without dribbling", as one wag put it. But the zonal marking and skill place it much closer to netball, a sport which, despite an estimated twenty million players worldwide, is scandalously still not represented in the Olympics in London 2012. (BMX cycling and beach volleyball have made it past the wire.) Korfball has come close – it appeared as a demonstration (exhibition) sport in Antwerp, Belgium, in 1920 and in Amsterdam in 1928.

Unsurprisingly, the Dutch national team dominates korfball worldwide as emphatically as their Australian cousins dominate the netball world championships, though the sport is spreading. You'd have thought a sport so carefully designed not to let the boys rule the roost ought to have a glorious future in these equality-conscious days.

KILIKITI (TUVALU, SAMOA, NEW ZEALAND)

Pacific cricket

Imagine a mixed-gender twenty-a-side version of cricket with two wicket keepers and a colourfully painted three-sided bat, then you'll have something a bit like kilikiti – or *kirikiti*, as Samoans call their national sport. Nineteenth-century missionaries introduced cricket to the Pacific islands but the game was adapted and took on a more Pacific colour. Out went whites and in came colourful *lavalavas,* – sarong-like garments – and a ball made of hard rubber surrounded by tree fibre. In the past games could take up to three days with rules only really known by the participants and the numbers of players variable. It has even been said that the only form of disqualification that existed for a team was not providing enough food, which gives some idea of the festival-like atmosphere of proceedings that could incorporate singing and dancing. The New Zealand Kilikiti Association has made an effort to tidy up the rules of the game to be both more practical and suitable for television with organized tournaments. Even so most players are said to be all-rounders, which must make the captain's role challenging when it comes to batting order and bowler selection.

KUBB (SWEDEN)

Viking chess

You'd think in the age of computer video games that garden-throwing games might cease to proliferate. Far from it. Though Viking antecedents are claimed for kubb, it only really seems to have got going in the second half of the twentieth century in Gotland in Sweden. It has now spread to the UK, US, Holland, Australia and New Zealand where the Kiwis have added the odd contentious amendment to rules still a little in the making. A brand-new kit costs around £25 – £35 in the UK though with handicraft skills you could easily make your own.

Wooden sticks are thrown underarm at a distance of eight metres at wooden blocks with the aim of eventually proceeding to knock over a larger "King" block set in the middle. If you topple the King too early – a bit like potting the black too early in pool- you lose, which is one aspect of the rules that gives the game some of its patina of strategy. As the game progresses the targets become "field" kubbs or remain "baseline" kubbs.

The UK kubb tournament website notes that one element of the "Tjaereborg Handicapping System" that aims to even out ability differences between players is currently "under severe scrutiny". Likewise the Des Moines Kubb Club in the US offers up its extensive rules online for feedback and comment. All of which suggests a sport still a little in flux, but swiftly developing an obsessional interest in detail, a nerdy necessity for any game with aspirations to wider cult status.

LACROSSE (NORTH AMERICA, INTERNATIONAL)

Warrior spirit

In the summer of 1763, teams of Ojibwa and Sauk Indians from the (now) Michigan area played a lacrosse match in front of a contingent of British troops as part of a celebration for the king's birthday. Midway through the match, the Indians picked up their weapons and slaughtered the spectators. A few hundred years down the road the game is primarily played by affluent whites, who've adopted this story as testament to the warrior spirit of the sport. Thought to have been played in one form or another by Native Americans as far back as the twelfth century, lacrosse was far from simple athletic diversion. Running madly into one another while avoiding a stick to the head was excellent training for battle, and rather than launch straight into armed conflict, hundreds of warriors might face each other on massive lacrosse fields, with the losing side bruised, but alive.

Some rules may have changed over the years, but the goal remains the same: catch the ball with your stick and hurl it past a keeper into a man-sized square net. And while today's game is much more refined than those early American clashes – participants now wear helmets – it remains extremely physical, and in the professional ranks even fistfights are tolerated without ejection. Though considering there are now only six pro teams remaining and the games are aired at odd hours, you'll be hard pressed, even in the US, to witness a full-blooded match outside local collegiate affairs though the Canadian scene is relatively larger.

LAWN MOTOR RACING (US, UK)
Mowing down the opposition

Invented in 1973 by a Jim Gavin and other motor sports fans from the town of Wisborough Green, Sussex, as a cut-price alternative to motor racing, lawn motor racing has a dedicated and passionate following. Helping to kick-start the circus in the UK by winning British grands prix in 1975 and 1976 was motor sport elder statesman Sir Stirling Moss. He was not the only one. Hellraiser actor Oliver Reed and cricketer Phil Tufnell are two other British celebrities who have caught the lawn motoring bug. It has taken off in the US too where the USLMRA presides over an active scene which is sponsored but is not professional. Any mower originally designed for cutting domestic lawns can be used with the blades removed and there are several classes of race for different vehicles including a "run-behind" option.

A tough corner in a Class 3 race, Hamstreet, Kent.

The highlight of the UK lawn motor racing calendar has traditionally been the annual twelve-hour endurance race that has also been won by Moss. Speeds of 35-60mph are routine for racers though a new record for a lawn mower was set at a special speed trial of 86 mph by the grandson of speed legend Sir Malcolm Campbell at the legendary Pendine sands in Wales. Such historical links enforce a feeling that this is a sport for which history counts and as you would expect the USLMRA now boasts a "Hall of Fame and Museum of America" enthusiastically promoted by President Bruce "Mow It All" Kaufman. Cost remains an issue. In 2010 economic problems caused the UK endurance race to be shortened.

LINGERIE FOOTBALL (US)
Passing a pigskin in your underwear

Few sports get the publicity boost of being blackballed by the mayor of Oklahoma City and lambasted as "pernicious objectification" by feminists. But then again not many sports operate costume norms that facilitate "accidental nudity" and brandish team names that sound more like "all services" escort agencies: for example, Chicago Bliss, Dallas Desire or San Diego Seduction. A success at securing pay per

In spite of the Lingerie Football League's best efforts, the sport still has its knockers.

view fans during the Super Bowl's half-time "seven-on-seven", this American football-style franchise has rarely been out of the news (or what passes for it in the Internet age). Media coverage of lingerie football has been ample, typically garnished – it has to be said – with close-up thigh-level shots of crouching players considerately unencumbered with the full body armour of their male counterparts in coordinated bikini-like combos and helmets. New uniforms, new teams and the hardly surprising revelation that models and ex-models are well represented in the ranks of players have all added to column inches and to the pixel count.

Less emphasis seems to have been placed on results or strategy but hey, those that do follow the game have apparently found themselves pleasantly "surprised" with the level of skill and competitiveness displayed, despite the occasional heavily reported "bitch-fight" confrontation where someone, or is that everyone, appears to be taking things too seriously. The sexploitation tag is hard to shift though. Spectators at games will not find male cheerleaders nor will they discover many star players not blessed also by good looks. The counter-argument remains that a women's professional league (there are only semi-professional outfits otherwise) is dependent on eye-candy "front of store" as the only way of ensuring a viable competition should be applauded.

Either way the LFL (Lingerie Football League) looks set to expand from its current ten teams for future seasons with the Cleveland Crush the latest team to join the party. LFL chairman Mitchell Mortaza's parting shot to the disapproving – "I thought our plans were for expansion into Oklahoma City, not North Korea"– nicely sums up one half of a lingerie and liberty debate that will run and run.

LUCHA LIBRE (MEXICO)
Selling moves

Alarmingly-becostumed, pantomime-styled, dubiously combative professional wrestling in Mexico predates its US counterpart as mass-market, televised entertainment by some twenty years – south of the border Lucha Libre, or free fighting, has been second only to soccer since the 1930s. Unlike its high earning North American counterpart, this form rarely bothers with any pretence that the "fighters" are actually wading in to each other, as they talk openly about "selling" opponents' moves, which means to exaggerate the effect when impact was in fact minimal, or "putting an opponent over" the term for making sure the audience believes the hero or villain role assigned to each wrestler for each bout. The masked fighters create characters for themselves, and bouts will be virtually scripted with the "face" (the good guy) and the "heel" (the villain) hamming it up to a predetermined outcome.

The bouts provide such popular entertainment because of the skill and acrobatics of the contestants. Rather than rely on strength or holds, luchadores use speed and agility to perform high-flying moves that would be illegal in wrestling's other disciplines, as fighters use the ropes and the rig posts to launch themselves on to opponents who could be inside or outside the ring. Moves are more likely to be executed in series of lightning fast combination rather than as a grappled war of attrition. Unsurprisingly, given lucha libre's inherent theatrics, its stars all enjoy lucrative secondary careers as they take their characters to films and comic books, where they become superheroes without the super powers. A mainstay of Mexican cinema are the generic, knock-about-violent movies portraying the wrestler almost as a superhero – plots inevitably involve a poor community being terrorized by some sort of evil oppressor, who might sometimes be another wrestler.

MALLAKHAMB (INDIA)

Pole positions

It seems unlikely that a yoga-like practice dating back to twelfth-century India and the erotic gyrations of the stroboscopic world of US strip clubs should have anything in common. The link is pole gymnastics – a rough translation of mallakhamb – which is common to both the ancient Indian art, which is now a competitive judged sport, and pole dancing which after two world championships is attempting to shed its sleazy image. Some hope pole dancing can go further and achieve not only respectability but Olympic status in 2016. Mallakhamb however is strictly not erotic and is mostly practised by children and young men and women and stretches to a variety of gymnastic disciplines involving performances on ropes, bottles and even floating platforms.

However it is mallakhamb on poles which really catches the eye with awe-inducing feats of coordination, strength and suppleness which is assisted by the application of castor oil to the athlete's body not least the initial mount during which a competitor will throw themselves onto a pole head down, clasping it with his or her legs. Hindu theology connects the sport with the soul's progression back to eternal light. Certainly the self-discipline required, involving a healthy dose of meditation, goes far beyond a saucy posture or two. Mallakhamb India locates the ancestral homes of the sport in the peaceful spots of Saptashringi and Kothure, which it says are "'untouched' by the perverse modernization." Today Bombay and Pune are active centres but the modern world is nonetheless reaching out to mallakhamb in the unlikely form of Simon Cowell. *India's Got Talent* has featured the sport and wider exposure might even lead to its own Olympic recognition campaign.

MAN VERSUS HORSE (LLANTWRTYD WELLS, WALES)

"I'm going to catch that horse if I can."

These lyrics (above) from The Byrds' hit "Chestnut Mare" could almost be the motto of this typically inspired event from the Llantwrtyd Wells cult sports production line. (See also bog-snorkelling in this section, and their website

TEN SPORTING OCCASIONS TO RELISH

Arctic Winter Games (Canada)
The ultimate event in winter sports takes place biennially in March. Events unique to the Games include the kneel jump and the Alaskan high kick – in which contestants stand on one leg and kick an overhead target with the other. Dene games – derived from an Aboriginal Canadian group – are kept alive at the AWG and include "finger pull" (a game originally used to strengthen the fingers of Dene fishermen), "stick pull" and "snowsnake" – throwing a spear across snow.

Charreada (Mexico)
This take on rodeo is all about cattle, horses, panache and style. Events such as reining and team roping are judged on quality of execution. The games are complemented by parades, costumes and music. Most exciting of the bunch is El Paso de la Muerte, a manoeuvre in which a rider must launch himself from one mount onto an uncontrolled horse and ride it bareback.

Cotswold Olimpick Games (England)
In 2012, Chipping Camden celebrates four hundred years of a rural sports day invented by Robert Dover "in honour" of Ancient Greek sports. It's most famous for its shin-kicking event, a wrestling-style bout in which players hold each other's shoulders and try to force their adversary – shins protected with straw – to the ground. A judge called a "stickler" has the job of deciding if there was correct contact with shins prior to a throw.

Darwin Beer Can Regatta (Australia)
A long-established annual family charity event, held at Mindil beach at the top of Australia, the Beer Can Regatta centres upon races between boats made from empty beer and fizzy drinks cans. The southern city of Adelaide's riposte, a milk-carton regatta, was halted in the 1980s because of public health concerns.

Elfstedentocht (Netherlands)
Global warming was the nemesis of one fondly recalled Netherlands institution: a two-hundred-kilometre outdoor skating race on frozen canals around the cities of Friesland that was last held in 1997. Annual speculation about whether the event might take place again is not far off mass hysteria, always centring on the big question: will the ice be the necessary fifteen centimetres thick? A party vibe always surrounds the event when it has taken place – only fourteen times since the first Elfstedentocht of 1909.

International Birdman (England)

The oldest birdman rally of all returned to Bognor in 2010 after a health and safety enforced respite. Birdmen (and women) "fly" off the end of Bognor pier in bids to win a prize for the furthest distance flown. But it is the comedy, fancy-dress entries that attract most of the big crowds that flock to proceedings that first took place at nearby Selsey in 1971. The record for longest distance so far is Dave Bradshaw's 89.2 metres in 1992.

Lumberjack World Championships (US)

Since 1960, Hayward, Wisconsin, has hosted the biggest lumberjack sports gathering of them all. As well as the chopping and sawing events you'd expect from the burly Desperate Dans there are competitions demanding ninety-foot climbs up a cedar pole. As far as we know, there are no events involving dressing in women's clothing or hanging around in bars. The Tony Wise All Around prize for best lumberjack has its female counterpart in the All Around Lady Jill award.

Naadam (Mongolia)

This sporting festival features the three major Mongolian pastimes of archery, horse racing and wrestling. It takes place in July with the biggest event in the capital Ulan Bator. Some aspects are distinctly Mongolian. Wrestlers have a colleague called a *zasuul* who recites or sings words of encouragement. The horse racing element is very much long distance – as you'd expect from descendants of horsemen who nearly conquered Vienna – with races of up to thirty kilometres long.

Palio di Siena (Italy)

One of the briskest and oldest horse races in the world at around eighty seconds is held round Siena's main piazza. It happens twice a year in July and August. Ten horsemen compete, bareback, for the honour of their local *contrade* (district) in the midst of a spectacular pageant. Horses (mixed-breed only – no thoroughbreds) are allocated by a lottery system, and sometimes are set to race without riders. Italy being Italy, the race is surrounded by rumours of cheating, intrigue, plot and counterplot (see overleaf).

Shandur Top Polo Festival (Pakistan)

The fabled highest game of polo – originally a Persian game – in the world takes place annually at a height of 3700 metres. Shandur Top, also known as "The Roof of the World" hosts the match each year, with local Pakistani teams, no umpires and precious few rules. There is also music and dancing and camping, making the contest quite an occasion. Advocates of the Shandur Top's unruly style call it polo in its purest form: it's certainly a far cry from anything the Windsors get up to.

The Palio di Siena: a sporting occasion to relish (see previous page).

green-events.co.uk.) Man versus horse originated in a pub discussion over whether a runner could cover a long distance quicker than an equine counterpart. Neuadd Arms landlord Gordon Green decided to find the answer and a contest was organized over approximately 22 miles of local uneven terrain in 1980. A few hundred runners now assemble each year with their rival horses starting one by one up to fifteen minutes later, which sadly for our analogy means it is usually horses catching up with men! At the end times are compared with the staggered starts factored in.

Now an annual event, it has to be said that "horse" is ahead overall by more than a neck with only three individual bipeds ever winning the race, one of whom disowned the victory when it was discovered that the judges had, unannounced, deducted some extra minutes for equine health checks. However Huw Lobb in 2004 was the first "two-legs" to win when he secured a £25,000 prize (that had been growing by £1000 every unsuccessful human year). As if in response sponsors William Hill the bookmakers decided not to go the extra mile again in 2005 and may have been hit by successful high-odds bets against the horses in the previous year.

It says something about the event that Screaming Lord Sutch, the founder of the UK's Monster Raving Looney Party (who have contested UK elections unsuccessfully and not very seriously for decades), supported Man v. Horse in years past and after his death his party still attends the event, trying to recruit members amidst all the general spectator fun.

OSTRICH RACING (SOUTH AFRICA, UKRAINE, INTERNATIONAL)
Win by a very long neck

In theory ostrich racing sounds like a neat idea. It's only when you realize that what is meant involves a human rider that it gets serious or rather silly or, in the opinion of animal rights spokespersons, just plain exploitative. (Of ostriches of course.) Oudtshoorn, South Africa, has good cause to be called the ostrich capital of the world. Ostrich magnates from the 1800s built grand houses off the backs of the world's largest flightless birds, buoyed by a worldwide craze for feather boas, though meat, eggs and leather are more popular nowadays.

Oudtshoorn ostrich farms now offer tourists the opportunity of a ride and for the braver souls a race over a few hundred yards. Reins are used with a small bit for the mouth though it is common at the start of the race to keep the ostrich's beak under a hood before later removing. There is little in the way of a competitive circuit but occasional races can be found across the world in the Middle East, the US (Arizona being a particular favourite) and the Ukraine where local conditions favour the upkeep of the cantankerous birds and the sight of man on ostrich seemed to attract the world's photographers to the hitherto unknown Ukrainian village of Yasnogorodk. The *Prince of Persia* videogame and film franchise (which

South Africa gave the world ostrich racing: it has never looked back.

extends to ostrich racing Lego figures) also boosted the ostrich's profile in 2010, but there's no gainsaying it: it is the ludicrous sight of man astride bird that makes the sport such a compelling spectacle.

OUTHOUSE RACING (US)
Superbowel speed

The likes of Dushore, Pennsylvania, Beckingridge, Colorado, Durand, Illinois, or Trenary, Michigan, may not trip off the tongue quite so readily as Wimbledon or Augusta but these towns are veritable capitals of outhouse racing, a community sport that has captured the imagination of large swathes of the US.

Typically staged on an annual festival day, an outhouse race usually consists of a four-person dash that propels a makeshift or custom-built outdoor toilet (or privy in British English) up a village or town main street. Rules vary but most race rules insist on a toilet seat, toilet roll and strict dimensions. The race in Mackinaw, Michigan, like many others allows for five persons including a "rider", with a few variants even having two pullers, carrying the outhouse more like a sedan chair. Doors and windows may be optional. Wheels are usually permitted but ropes are almost always forbidden. Some insist that the "sitter" must have reading matter upon their person. Nudity, as you would expect in this puritan nation, is off the agenda though themed costumes and decorated outhouses are often obligatory.

Events are usually run according to age and outhouse category with several events taking place on one day against the clock or in heats. Though highly popular with spectators, for reasons unknown this remains a US craze that hasn't spread like wildfire across the globe. Not yet, anyway.

PATO (ARGENTINA, EUROPE)
Of ducks and horses

Think football is Argentina's national sport? Or polo? Think again. The honour belongs to the venerable and formerly raucous pastime of pato, which translates very prosaically as duck. This honour was not really such good news for the feathered creatures that were first subjected to a tug of war (*cinchada*) between men on horses and then thrown into a basket/ring for scoring. Pato managed to get banned from the late eighteenth to the early nineteenth century and only really got properly resurrected *sans* duck with new rules, and a ball with six handles, in the 1930s before consecration as Argentina's national sport in 1953, largely on the grounds it was invented on Argentinian soil.

Players attempting to score must hold the ball standing up on horseback at arm's length to allow opponents to snatch it back. Failure to do so is called *negada* and against the rules. Two teams of four players and horses contest a game that is now infrequently played in Argentina but has a following in Europe via the similar French-invented game of "horseball". The two are now formally linked with Portugal winning the first world championships of pato-horseball in 2006 in Buenos Aires.

PANJAT PINANG (INDONESIA)
Climbing the greasy pole

Panjat Pinang has been described variously as a "new extreme sport", a hangover from colonial times equivalent to *The Jerry Springer Show* and a "sport-like" celebration of Indonesian independence. All in fact may be true. It is also huge fun.

The rules are simple. Various objects and prizes including bikes and televisions are suspended at the top of liberally-greased nut or palm tree trunks. Climbing up is not easy and though you would think at first it was a sport for individuals, it is often groups of children and youths working together that secure the best and earliest goodies. The sport dates back to the cruel practice of Dutch colonialists who would amuse themselves by putting desirable provisions or trinkets out of the reach of desperate villagers and then watch them scramble. When independence came in 1945 panjat pinang was incorporated into celebrations in villages across the country.

Some consider the tradition demeaning because of its history; others suggest it is a textbook example of usurping the culture of the oppressors. Stone jumping on the island of Nias, where youths vault six-foot stone towers, is another unique Indonesian spectacle popular with tourists and locals.

PELOTA AND JAI ALAI (BASQUE REGIONS OF SPAIN & FRANCE, US, PHILIPPINES, SOUTH & CENTRAL AMERICA)
Fastest ball game in the world

Despite its obscure origins in Basque, Pyrenean regions of Spain and France, nerdy school kids have always heard of pelota, or "Basque ball". Famously, it's the sport with the fastest ball speed in the world: 302 kilometres per hour, no less. Okay, so that's only in the xistera or jai alai version of the game, which uses a talon-like curving wicker-basket thing to scoop and re-launch the ball (and, okay, some try-hard golfer eventually managed to beat the record), but, still, there is something glamorous about an insanely fast game played by a little-known European ethnic minority.

In essence, pelota is squash played on a long, high court, or *fronton*. Some frontons have three sides, some two. Some, particularly in France, have just one end wall, while a few have projecting, sloping roofs along one side, rather like real tennis (see p.66) – a fact that betrays pelota's deep origins in the great, pan-European Ur-sport of *jeu de paume*, the "palm-game". There are many styles of play. In one, players use the *xistera* basket glove, but in others they use just their hand, rather like a grand-scale game of Eton fives (see earlier in this section). The ball in this macho version is small and punishingly hard – you can know a *pelotari*, it's said, by his bruised and swollen hands (both hands are used, with stunning dexterity). In Argentina they use wooden bats, while in Mexico they play so-called frontenis, using ordinary tennis rackets.

In the US, jai alai was hugely popular in the 1970s and 80s, as much for its pari-mutuel (pooled-money) betting as for anything else. Florida, with its strong Spanish traditions, was the centre, but it was played up in Connecticut and Rhode Island, too, while some Las Vegas and Reno casino-hotels of the period had their own, in-house frontons. In the Philippines, match-fixing by gamblers became so problematic that, in 1986, the Filipino supreme court banned the game outright; it only returned to the Philippines in 2010. At home in the Basque regions, however, the sport has remained truer to its roots. It has commercialized, sure, with big *empresas* or clubs controlling lucrative TV and gambling revenues. But pelota still plays a central role in the folk traditions that underpin Basque nationalism. Championship-winning techniques are jealously preserved within Basque families. Players such as Tintin III and Panpi LaDouche (whose left-handed, cross-court *gantxo* move was legendary in the 1970s) have the status of folk heroes – they are proudly politicized champions such as you might find in Irish hurling (see earlier in this section), but rarely in global sports like football.

PESÄPALLO (FINLAND)
Finnish baseball

Russian urban myth credits the Slavs with inventing a game (*lapta*) from which baseball supposedly developed. That is not any more likely than ex-general Abner Doubleday's enduring Cooperstown tall tale where he gave himself the credit for baseball's invention, but there is a nice symmetry to the idea of baseball going back east to reemerge as a "national sport" with a few rule changes.

Lauri Pihkala, a man with connections to the far right, is the undisputed inventor of the modern game of pesäpallo, itself actually based on a homegrown

Pig-N-Ford racing (Oregon, US)

In 1908 Henry Ford introduced the Model T to the US. It was the first mass-produced car from Ford's Detroit factory, and was affordable enough that half the families in the country bought one over the next two decades. Being the predominant motorized vehicle of the time, it's hardly surprising that it was in a T model Ford that one farmer once pursued one of his recently escaped pigs. At least, that's the story behind the origin of the Pig-N-Ford race that's been staged for the last 85 years as part of the Tillamook County Fair in western Oregon.

Drivers in the race are limited to stripped-down Model Ts, not much more than a frame, wheels, stock engine and a place to sit with your pig. The competitors begin the race standing on the side of the track, and when the green flag is waved they sprint to a pigpen, grab a Babe-sized piglet and make a beeline for the crankcase on their car. A couple of rotations are required to prime the engine, then they slide behind the wheel to direct the slow-moving antiques around a dirt horse-racing track.

At the end of each circuit the drivers must leap from their cars with pig in hand, and exchange the current swine for a new one from the pen. Then it's back to the car for another lap. The first driver around three times is the winner. Space is extremely limited and drivers wait years for their chance to be one of five drivers on the track at a time. Racing memberships are passed down through families, and rules are strictly enforced – the 2010 winner was disqualified after a suspiciously quick lap time spawned an investigation into engine tampering.

predecessor kingball, but informed by Pihkala's observation of baseball. An idea of the game is best conveyed by comparisons to it. Pitching the ball is vertical and though easier to hit this does allow for spin and height variations. Since the ball can be readily struck, it becomes more important in pesäpallo to place strikes. A hit beyond the edge of the playing area is illegal. Likewise a catch is not an out for a batter, who is said to be "wounded"; all runners just have to return to first base.

Use of combat metaphors like these is not coincidental. Scholars have linked the game's huge emphasis on tactics and control of territory to the Finnish military doctrine of forest warfare "fire and move" tactics familiar to Pihkala. The sport's claim to be the most tactical of games is underpinned by the existence of manager coaches who rehearse diverse "plays" with teams playing offence and defence and signalling tactics with hand movements and a multicoloured fan. Though not the most popular sport in Finland, the Superpesis domestic league still commands attention and pesäpallo seems to have a brighter future than the other Finnish innovation of competitive sauna when in 2010 one of the last two competitors in the world championships died in the event. Some modern sports it seems are best left well alone. Pesäpallo has also spread to a limited degree to neighbouring countries, Estonia, Sweden and Germany, and even Australia, though Russia (historically a foe of Finland) still unambiguously prefers lapta.

GIANT PUMPKIN REGATTA (Canada, US)

Man has accomplished incredible things over the course of his history: the pyramids at Giza, the domestication of the dog, Al Gore's Internet, and now, the engineering of the Giant Atlantic pumpkin variety. Renowned for its impossible size and man-supporting buoyancy, the development of this particular pumpkin has made possible the improbable sport of pumpkin-boat racing, or put politely, pumpkin regatta.

Lake Pesaquid in Windsor, Nova Scotia, is presently the site of the most famous human-in-floating-gourd races, with competitions in Vermont, Oregon and Wisconsin creating some regional interest each autumn. Competitors hollow out a portion of their giant orange crafts, leaving the shape of a seat in the innards, the better to support themselves as they paddle like mad across a three quarters of a mile stretch of frigid lake water. They're not exactly shaped for speed, though horticulturalists at the University of Wisconsin are currently trying to perfect a banana squash/Giant Atlantic hybrid that's sure to part waves with the deftness of a wooden bow. Leo Swinamer is the current grand old man of the sport, having won nine consecutive championships though well into his golden years. His unique method of drying his pumpkins and reinforcing them with lightweight foam insulation may lend him an advantage, though it's more likely his massive forearms that help leave the competition in his wake.

PIGEON RACING (BELGIUM, UK, INTERNATIONAL)

Winging it

Long derided in the UK as the lonely practice of sad, solitary Northern working men, pigeon racing has a surprising history as a favoured pastime of European royalty. Step forward Elizabeth II, British monarch and prize-winning pigeon racer. The Windsors' involvement can be traced back to Congo-exploiter King Leopold II of Belgium, who donated some pigeons to Queen Victoria when the Flemish were actively pioneering the growing sport. A royal pigeon loft, based in Sandringham, was established and HM remains the patron of the Royal Pigeon Racing Association, which annually stages a show attracting up to 25,000 fanciers. In the sport, pigeons are taken from their lofts and then timed, with the speediest to return home being the winner – the distances ranging from about seventy miles to marathons nearer one thousand. It is still unclear how the pigeon knows its way back home but navigation by the Earth's magnetic fields, and by the sun, appear to be two parts of a complex picture.

Technology has transformed pigeon racing, and now automatic timing has replaced for many the lonely pigeon fancier's late evening vigil. Such was the intensity of men's passion for pigeon racing that divorces were said to be common as a result up until the 1980s. Now inclusiveness is the fashion. "Attendance of the 'little lady' may contribute to harmony back home", says the website of the International Federation of American Homing Pigeon Fanciers. Though participation numbers are declining and increasingly elderly, affection for the pastime is unlikely ever to die out soon. Pigeons have carried off a whopping sixty percent of the UK's Dickin medals for animal valour, whereas South Africa's Sun City Million Dollar Pigeon Race boasts a top prize of a staggering $200,000 in one of its many events.

PUNKIN CHUNKIN (USA, UK)

Mind the lumina

For the past 25 years, engineering sportsmen have met at the annual Punkin Chunkin Championship, in Sussex County, Delaware, where they compete to see whose machine can hurl a pumpkin the farthest. At heart, it is no more than a mechanically assisted spitting contest, yet the event recently drew a crowd of seventy thousand to watch over a hundred entrants across a dozen machine classes, and has increasingly gained the attention of media networks with a science agenda. The machines are massive constructions, cobbled together from salvaged girders and telephone poles, the best being blended together with a sculptor's attention to detail.

While there are prizes for style and design, the big blue ribbon is reserved for distance. Trebuchets and catapults, machines that find torque by releasing the potential energy stored in counterweights and coils, send their payload downfield somewhere between two and three thousand feet. Centrifugal machines reach a similar range, though are reliant on heavy diesel motors to whip an arm fully around a pivot before releasing the pumpkin into the air. But the real show stoppers are the pneumatic cannons, which can generate upwards of three thousand pounds of pressure and are coming ever closer to shooting a pumpkin a full English mile. With all that force exerted on what is no more than a common garden squash, it's imperative to choose the proper pumpkin. It must be intact upon leaving the device, and for that reason the familiar orange variety is right out. Instead it's the white-shelled lumina that is favoured. Hard and dense, luminas are home-grown and constantly monitored for water weight. All the effort pays off when thousands cheer the vegetable as it flies to its death.

REAL TENNIS (ENGLAND, INTERNATIONAL)
The real thing

It's not entirely clear why real tennis has such an uppity name. Some say it's to distinguish it from the upstart game of lawn tennis (which is what the rest of us call tennis). Others think it derives from an old French word for "royal" tennis – and it's certainly true that the sport was popular at the French court in the sixteenth century, where it developed out of the ancient jeu de paume, or "hand game". In the US it's called court tennis, which hardly clears the matter up. Real tennis was also

The robots are even smaller than real jockeys.

played enthusiastically by English monarchs from the Stuarts to Edward VII and George V – and it's in England where it has remained most alive today.

As a sport, it lies somewhere between squash and tennis: there's a net across the middle, dividing the players, but you can bounce the ball off the side and end walls. The kookie bit is that you can also play wily shots onto the projections – known as the penthouses, for their sloping roofs – and win a point directly by knocking the ball into three holes or hatches in the walls, alluringly called the "Grille", "Dedans" and the "Winning Gallery". All this might sound desperately antiquated, what with its handmade balls and courts found at aristocratic piles such as Hatfield House and Hampton Court Palace. But the sport is enjoying a modest resurgence, with new courts being built around the world – notably the swish Millennium Court of the Middlesex Real Tennis Club. Real tennis still has a way to go before it makes the Olympics again, though. The last time was in 1908, in London.

ROAD TENNIS (BARBADOS)
Racquets of fire

In the relatively quiet streets of Barbados in the 1950s road tennis was born. With neither the access to a lawn tennis club or table tennis equipment, locals invented a hybrid with wooden paddles for racquets and a bald tennis ball the object to be hit. As the net is a low eight-inch-high piece of wood stretching across the middle of the court, the game is played in a somewhat crouching position very like table tennis with the same scoring system, but on a 21ft by 10ft area.

Barbados has embraced road tennis as a national treasure and the Professional Road Tennis Association – slogan "Racquets of Fire" – has since ensured it a higher profile with courts, tournaments, prize money and sponsorship now the roads have got busier. Efforts to internationalize the sport have not got much further than other islands of the Caribbean and in the US the existence of paddle tennis, a similar but not identical game, has muddied the waters. But, if you had any doubts about the seriousness with which Barbadians take the sport consider this: no fewer than four line judges and a referee are required to adjudicate games.

ROBOT CAMEL RACING (KUWAIT, QATAR)
Do android jockeys dream of electric camels?

Qatar is the home of the most improbable but successful soccer world cup hosting bid. It is also a pioneer in the burgeoning world of robot camel racing. In traditional camel racing (see p.24) the lightest jockeys are the most prized. Until the recent introduction of robot riders, they have traditionally been young boys, sold into bondage by impoverished parents in India, Sudan and Pakistan. The ill-tempered camels are known to throw riders, and the boys' tiny frames were no match for their thundering hooves. From 2005 the charmingly named Robotics Academy of Qatar for Bright Inventions has been one of a few pioneers of android jockeys with models ranging from the vacuum-cleaner lookalike Raqbi-bot w/CD 1.0 to the mannequin-esque Kamel-bot F.10 – via the alarmingly blue Raqbi-bot w/CD 2.0 which resembles nothing so much as a giant version of that children's favourite floor toy, the crazy bone.

Human operators control the robots via handheld radio units as they follow the race in SUVs. But the jockeys have additional powers that human jockeys never had: they can measure the speed and heart rate of the camel and figure out mid-race a projected finishing time for the beast. With the weight issue in mind the robots have now been slimmed down with the lightest now a featherweight clocking in at less than three kilogrammes. Shortly after the introduction of robots UNICEF reported that over a thousand child jockeys were able to return to their families. Notwithstanding the animal rights lobby, it is thought unlikely that camels will ever be relieved of their duties in such a fashion, and they will still have to endure the occasional whip from their lightweight midget riders.

ROLLER DERBY (US, INTERNATIONAL)
Derby days

Roller skates were introduced roughly 250 years ago, and boys and girls spent the next years gleefully gliding across dry land the way they might blade over a frozen lake. The first professional races were staged about a hundred years later, travelling spectacles hyped as trials of endurance. Then the 1960s came and went, taking with them so much blissful innocence, and leaving behind roller derby. Many of us may have first encountered roller derby in the form of the 1975 movie *Rollerball* starring James Caan, a sort of less realistic *Running Man* (the Arnold Schwarzenegger movie set in a dystopian future where convicts fight for their lives on a televised game show – you get the point).

For a time, it looked like the sport may actually head in that most absurd of directions, with the 1980 US television competition *RollerGames* introducing a figure-eight track to encourage collisions, a giant launching platform, and a tank of alligators rolled out for tiebreakers. It's settled down some since then, but only in the sense that the rules are more straightforward. The most visible leagues are all-female, and there's a serious bad-ass edge to the competition. Each team consists of five players, who skate round an oval track trying to impede the opposition's progress with a series of elbows to the head. One player, called a jammer, attempts to lap the pack, and in doing so earns her team a point; then for every subsequent player she passes she earns another point. There are no lucrative TV deals, and matches often take place in illegally converted warehouses, meaning competitors play for the love of the game and even as a spectator you feel like you're putting one over on the man.

SALTO DEL PASTOR (CANARY ISLANDS)

Shepherds leap o'er their flocks at night

Many sports like football or hockey are part of big families. Others stand nearly alone but the Canarian island shepherd folk sport of salto del pastor (shepherd's leap) is a reminder that the minority sport of pole-vaulting is not alone. The volcanic Canary Islands set a long way south of Spain off the coast of North Africa, are a veritable hot bed of folk and indigenous sport ranging from *jeugo del palo* (stick fighting) to *lucha canaria* (wrestling) and from *bola canaria* (boules) to such macho pastoral activities as *levantamiento y pulseo de la piedra* (stone lifting and pushing).

The pick of the bunch is almost certainly salto del pastor which has developed into a fully fledged folk sport after starting life amongst the local Guanche population prior to Spanish colonization as a useful means of transporting shepherds across gaps in the landscape and down the many steep inclines on these volcanic islands. Vaulting techniques using the stick, called *astia*, are pretty spectacular and more exciting to watch than the golf played by many of the area's visitors. With a funky website and sponsorship for one of its events from Red Bull the sport seems to be leaping forward in the twenty-first century with regular competitions and outreach events. A similar sport, fierljeppen, in East Frisia, Holland, arose from the need to leap over water channels and there are still regular competitions mostly focusing on distance (the record is over 21 metres) rather than techniques.

SEPAK TEKRAW (MALAYSIA, THAILAND)

Look: no hands

A close relative of *jiànzi* (see p.46) sepak tekraw is related to a variety of keepy-uppy games that use a shuttlecock. It differs, however, in its use of a woven rattan ball (recently replaced with plastic) within the framework of a volleyball style game that utilizes high-kicking acrobatics and dazzling levels of balance and energetic reaches.

You can't use hands or lower arms to propel the ball over the net in this three-a-side game, but any other part of the body is okay. Several countries claim to have had something to do with the game's origins, but a net version appears to have emerged in Thailand with a volleyball-style contest taking place to celebrate the country's constitution in 1933. Similar developments took place in Malaysia, who contest with Thailand the battle for supremacy in the sport. Together they agreed in 1965 the rules and compromise name, which the sport now bears. It has subsequently been made part of the school curriculum and the annual King's Cup has become the most prestigious event along with the Asian Games and is dedicated to the King of Thailand. The game is popular in several other countries including Laos under a variety of different names.

In Laos, sepak tekraw is called *kataw* but is no less spectacular.

The most spectacular part of the game is the equivalent of the basketball "spike" performed via a bicycle-kick and usually defended close to the net in the same way. Western interest and competence in the sport is still quite limited though Canada has introduced sepak tekraw to five hundred schools. The suspicion remains that the agility of Southeast Asians bequeathed by widespread practice of martial arts will give their players the edge for decades to come.

SLAMBALL (US)
Hitting heights

This hyper-andrenalized version of basketball on trampolines comes with all the artisan pedigree and subtlety of a double caramel chocolate marshmallow cookie dough cheesecake fudge ice cream. And yet despite its overtestosterone calculated-to-the-max profile it is impossible to deny it is an arresting spectacle. Teams with names such as Mob, Maulers, Hombres and Slashers and players described on slamball's official website in such terms as "a 245lb wrecking ball of sinew and gristle" (LaMonica Garrett for the curious) aren't going to convince any sport traditionalists, but it's not exactly going to discourage the merely curious, either.

Yet if videogames-inspired creator Mason Gordon, who has successfully pitched slamball to US man-channel Spike TV, could get folk to play the game more generally outside this carefully controlled franchise then he might be on to something more lasting than a sugar-coated sporting fix. Four trampolines are situated in front of a basketball net. There are three points for a slam-dunk, two for another score. Slamball is played full contact – that's where the American football influence comes in - and there are "face-offs" for offences where shooters and defence contest a penalty shot on trampolines, a nice innovation that gives extra oomph to what in basketball can be a slightly anemic test of nerve. Slamball got off to a great start in 2002 and 2003 but since has stuttered with Gordon blaming sponsors for wanting to steer the game towards a professional wrestling style (non)contest. Slamball is set to bounce back in 2011 with another season and "camps" for interested players to help spread a game with an intense if not yet mass following.

SWAMP SOCCER (FINLAND, UK)
Football for stuck–in–the–muds

Those lucky enough to have been weaned on Lancashire soccer pitches before the advent of plastic balls and health and safety considerations will probably think there is little new about the invention of swamp soccer. And yet the guarantee of a muddy thrasharound in conditions unsuited for "total football" has a clear appeal. Now a popular event in several countries, it was in the bogs of Hyrynsalmi, approximately six hundred kilometres north of Helsinki, Finland, that the ball was set sloppily rolling by Jyrki Vaananen (aka "the Swamp Baron") in 1997. The idea apparently arose when cross-country skiers were looking for an interesting way of staying fit during the summer. They may have been onto something. Swamp soccer is nothing if not exerting.

The game is essentially one of five-a-side played over two halves of thirteen minutes by mixed teams with unlimited substitutions and (optional) fancy dress. There's a tongue-in-cheek sensibility that can be discerned in team names such as Sporting Abeergut, Unathletico Madrid and Mudchesthair United. Sweden, the Netherlands, Iceland and Scotland, which hosted the 2011 Swamp Soccer World Cup in Edinburgh, have also got down and dirty, and teams from across the world now compete.

TCHOUKBALL (SWITZERLAND, INTERNATIONAL)
"Building a harmonious society."

The 1960s and 70s inspired many an innovation in politics, art and music. Less well known is the handful of sports that reflected the spirit of that age and its progressive instincts. Biologist Hermann Brandt from non-aligned Switzerland takes the credit for tchoukball (pronounced "chukeball"). His invention had two clear ambitions: "building a harmonious society" (no easy task there then) and devising a sport that minimized injuries. This second aim was to be achieved by forbidding physical contact – a by-product of this being that the traditional sports advantages of strength and size count for less in tchoukball, thereby favouring inclusiveness and mixed teams.

The sport has elements of handball and volleyball, with attackers aiming the ball at either of two small frames or trampolines. Teams consist of nine players with three substitutes. Points are scored when the ball, after hitting a trampoline, lands outside a "D" surrounding it. Defenders obviously try to catch the ball before a score but can't really prevent attacks; they just defend immediately after an attack. Put like that, tchoukball sounds inoffensive in the extreme – but the game is very, very fast. Passes have to be completed in three seconds. The ball can't be passed more than three times before shooting and all the diving around on the floor required to prevent a score suggests a game that can't be as injury free as intended.

China, Switzerland and the UK are three countries that figure high on the game's roll call of honour, but bragging about victories in this sport is for losers who cannot see the true purely participative joy of the collective activity. The tchoukball charter that promotes the spirit of the game is the epitome of this high-mindedness. Take for example this statement about the aim of the game: "the avoidance of conflict, with one main goal in mind: fair play that does not compromise the level of play but rather links the two teams together in common activity. The beauty of one team's play makes possible – and reinforces – the beauty of play by the other team." Mike Tyson couldn't have put it better. Irrespective of whether or not any game could live up to this billing, tchoukball has become a popular schools sport in all continents including Africa.

TEJO (COLOMBIA)
Going off with a bang

Most national sports don't involve gunpowder. But then Colombia isn't just any old country. Tejo (pronounced "tay-kho") is a throwing sport consisting of pitching small metal discs from sixty feet at a single metal ring. Before the Spanish arrived something similar was played, called turmeque, by the Muisca people of Colombia's central highlands: the introduction of gunpowder may have followed on from the introduction of mining to the area. Around said ring (*bocin*) are pouches (*mechas*) of gunpowder – all of which are embedded in clay plastered into a two-sided box. Hitting a mecha (three points) should trigger a minor explosion though the big points (six) are given for getting your disk within the bocin.

If the former wasn't alarming enough for the health and safety crowd, the addition of booze to the mix would surely provoke them to a fit: the game is normally undertaken with the assistance of copious beer, encouraged by beer company sponsorship. There are often half-size children's courts to keep the young ones occupied during a big game. But despite the "crazy Colombians" schtick that wafts from the game like freshly detonated explosive, it is not especially life threatening and is popular throughout the country. Other uses of gunpowder in Colombia remain a much bigger concern than this much-loved pastime.

TROBRIAND CRICKET (TROBRIAND ISLANDS, PAPUA NEW GUINEA)

Syncretism not cricket

Some sports make money, others help people pass the time: only the select few are hailed as case studies in anthropological theory. When locals adapted the cricket English missionaries had taught them back in 1903, it was not long before community rituals and customs refashioned the English game for the Trobrianders, in what anthropologists have called a textbook case of syncretism ("melding together different systems of belief or religion"). At Lords or the MCG there is precious little dancing during or before innings.

Not so in Trobriand cricket, in which the bowling is underarm and coordinated exit and entrance dance routines for the teams are *de rigueur*. Potential sponsors may also be dismayed to find no opportunities for logos on shirts: the gear for

Sport as festival: cricket in the Trobriand islands.

players doesn't get much beyond a few feathers and a pouch. Having said that, putting off the batsmen with taunts and moves is acceptable. Teams are equal but can consist of more or less any number of players and the umpire is always from the batting team. In a surprising twist he is also a specialist in magic, weaving spells to protect his batsmen from the opposition's bowlers during the game. So much for impartiality. The score is kept on a palm frond.

Trobriand cricket is also part food festival, gift ceremony and fertility dance and its rules are said to be constantly evolving, though probably the most important aspect is that which the colonialists intended. Trobriand cricket helped turn deadly village fighting into mock warfare, transforming dissent into amiable rivalry, whilst retaining some ceremonial elements of real battle.

TRUGO (MELBOURNE, AUSTRALIA)

"A true-blue Aussie game."

The suburb of Yarraville is the home of one of the world's supremely localized sports – its following restricted essentially to a pocket-hanky square of northwest Melbourne, Australia. In the 1920s, an inventive railway worker named Tom Grieves improvised a working-class version of croquet at the nearby Newport Railway Workshops, using rail-yard tools and parts such as mallets for driving in rail spikes and rubber rings from carriage couplings.

It was decided that the length of the pitch (or "rink") – nowadays a grass lawn – should be roughly that of a 1920s railway carriage (ninety feet) and the goalmouth similar to a standard railway gauge. To play the game, four players in a team each face away from a two-post "goal" and swing a mallet between their legs hitting a rubber ring ("the wheel") towards the goal – though in the ladies' version of the game ("GoTru") the more dignified "side swiping" not the "tunnelling" stance is usually preferred. Each player is allowed 24 attempts to get the wheel between the posts, with a perfect score termed a "possible". A goal was called a "true go" – hence the game's name.

In a city dominated by the behemoth of Australian rules football, most Melbournians remain oblivious to this home-grown treasure. Once a thriving league, trugo now struggles in the rapidly gentrifying inner-city suburbs. The game often arouses wistful, nostalgic and protective feelings but may need a PR blitz to younger generations to let them know it even exists, let alone getting them to carry the torch. Until the mid-1990s you weren't even allowed to play until you were about retirement age and, with fewer than sixty registered players in total, only a few trugo clubs remain. They are all secret gems, with old-fashioned gates, clipped rinks and tiny shed pavilions with corrugated tin roofs – little oases waiting to be discovered by a new generation of punters, or eventually "redeployed" by local councils.

ULAMA (SINALOA, MEXICO)

Sporting spirit

Starting with the Aztecs, and persisting through waves of war and colonization across 3500 years, ulama stands as one of the oldest sports in the world. Still played today in the traditional manner, players don loin cloths and attempt to bat a nine-pound solid rubber ball past their opponents' end line using only their hips. There are two modern versions as well, one using a paddle, the other using the forearms instead of the hips, but neither requires as much skill or takes as much courage as the original.

The sport brings new meaning to the term "full-contact". Notes from a sixteenth-century monk document Aztec ballplayers needing a cutman to drain the blood from huge welts caused by the heavy ball. And the games weren't always about sport for its own sake: human sacrifice was not unheard of, and there is a particularly gruesome Mayan rendering (yes, they played ulama too) of a ritualistic decapitation carved into an unearthed court in the Yucatán. At first not privy to its religious significance, Spanish conquistadors thought the sport highly entertaining before realizing it was an important spiritual event. Aztecs compared the parabolic flight of the ball to the sun's journey to and from the underworld, and priests officiated at ceremonial matches staged to ensure the continued ebb and flow of the seasons.

Even the human sacrifice had its place; the thought being through ritualistic death would come an injection of fertility for the upcoming harvest. Needless to say the Spanish Catholics didn't think highly of such practices, and stomped the game out as they swept through South and Central America. It now remains alive only in the small Mexican province of Sinaloa, where it is in danger of extinction from a combination of poverty and disinterest.

ULTRAMARATHONS (INTERNATIONAL)

Keeping on keeping on

If running a mere 26 miles doesn't seem like much of a challenge, you're not alone (slightly mad perhaps, but there's comfort in numbers). Competitive distance events that extend beyond the traditional marathon finish are more common than you may think, with every continent on the planet holding at least one major race. Sadly, the race from London to Brighton, dating back to the turn of the twentieth century, has been recently discontinued. Ultramarathons take a surprisingly varied number of shapes. Some are double the length of the traditional variety, some are team-based relay races across hundreds of miles, some are spaced out over a number of days, some are staged in bitter cold, some in extreme heat, some over flat land, others through mountainous terrain – think of a distance, climate and terrain, and chances are there's an ultramarathon to match.

X-GAMES (USA)

Sports channel ESPN first made a name for itself by broadcasting the kind of events that US network television channels typically wouldn't touch: Australian rules football, regional pro wrestling, and collegiate-level athletics from marginal universities. It's now an international behemoth in sports TV. But it never lost its appreciation for edgy sporting outliers, and their X-Games franchise is living proof of the value of going out on a limb.

Before the introduction of the punchy "X" branding, the inaugural 1996 competition went under the moniker of Extreme Games, and included then-popular bungee jumping, inline skating, rock climbing and street luge. For the first few years, it was strictly a summer affair. Fifteen years later the events are significantly more mainstream (due in no small part to the efforts of the cable giant), though counterculture music, fashion and styling lend a note of underground authenticity to proceedings. Stars of skateboarding, snowboarding and BMX have been given worldwide exposure, influencing a whole generation of children to grow their hair long, wear ill-fitting trousers and spend their allowances on grip tape and sex wax. Skateboarder Tony Hawk has become a million-dollar franchise thanks to his X-Games exposure, while snow 'n' skate boarder Shaun White's multiple endorsements saw him listed among *Forbes*' top sports earners.

The games are undeniably impressive. Whether on board, skis, bike or vehicle, the motto is go big or go home. Flying off a ramp and somersaulting a couple of times before landing is standard practice for most events. (Only cart racing and snowcross, on snowmobiles, don't require such acrobatics… for now.) Dropping into a half-pipe on a bike or board and being propelled thirty feet in the air is par for the course, though the slightest slip can cause serious injury: Dave Mirra, nineteen-times X-Games medallist in BMX events, had to have his spleen removed after an injury sustained from a poorly landed pipe launch. Aside from the obvious seasonal change, there is very little difference in the summer and winter versions of the games. Snowboarding is to skateboarding as snowmobiling is to motocross, though freestyle skiing doesn't match up so easily with freestyle BMX riding, and there's no truly appropriate analogue for surfing. Consistent through both is the thrill of cheating death, and fame and glory is won by consistently performing faster, bigger and more technical manoeuvres every year.

Nineteen-time X-Games medallist Dave Mirra holds a pose for the camera.

Runners participating in these challenges require a different mindset and technique than is used for shorter races. Increasingly, runners are adopting the traditional "toe-strike" style of the Tarahumara Indians, renowned for their barefooted long-distance running abilities. And finishing under a certain amount of time is often less important than merely completing the often gruelling routes. Heart attacks and heat stroke seem par for the course, while unpredictable conditions can throw off the most prepared participants. Take for instance the case of Italian runner Mauro Prosperi, who became disoriented by a sandstorm while running across the Sahara during the Marathon des Sables. He was found after nine days of searching, having managed to stay alive by drinking his own urine.

UNDERWATER RUGBY (GERMANY, INTERNATIONAL)
Unter der Wasser

Though enthusiastic participators in virtually any sport going, particularly from the European mainland, the list of homegrown cult sports in Germany is surprisingly thin. There is Bürostuhlrennen (office chair racing) for one, which somehow seems more likely to have been invented by discontented office workers in the US. Even more surprising is the discovery that rugby's aquatic cousin is a German invention. The sport began in Duisburg in the 1960s as a new fitness regime for swimmers, with a net, before becoming competitive shortly afterwards, with goals and streamlined rules. Differences to rugby are more evident than similarities except for one: grappling for possession for the ball and physical contact are vital, hence the two underwater referees need to look out for snorkel grabbing, flipper pulling and that old rugby favourite – the elbow. A basket at the bottom of the pool is used for scoring and a water polo ball is weighed down with salt water to both give it momentum for passing and prevent it heading upwards. Depending on specific game rules, eleven or twelve players are required on each side but only six are underwater at the same time. Big lungs are needed and quite a high level of fitness. A few countries, mostly those closest to Germany, have taken up the sport that has a regular student following and there is an enthusiastic underwater video and photography scene.

However, to the uninitiated, much of the action is a blur resembling a complicated and slightly more amiable subaquatic James Bond fight. Big fish sponsors are thus likely to stay away.

WIFE CARRYING (FINLAND, SCANDINAVIA)
Over the threshold and off you go

Some sports are what they say on the tin. All wife carrying essentially amounts to is a 278-yard dash across an obstacle-strewn course, in which a man has to carry a woman – not even his wife. In one Finnish version of the event, he can win a prize

Underwater sports: six of the best

Underwater rugby is not alone. Here are six more cult pastimes from the aquatic and sub-aquatic world

Apnea (dynamic and static)

Holding your breath underwater is something everyone has probably tried. Competitive apnea is a subset of freediving that has turned it into a contest. No breathing apparatus is permitted and there are different disciplines which involve swimming (dynamic apnea) or don't (static).

Other variations utilize weights and fins. Excitement surrounds records for distances and times. New Zealander Dave Mullins' distance feat of 265 metres with fins in 4 minutes 1 second compares with Stéphane Mifsud (France) holding his breath for an astonishing 11 minutes 35 seconds in the static category.

Aquathlon

Swimming followed by running. From one point of view, it is simply a poor man's triathlon, one which leaves out the cycling. From a different perspective, it is a sport with a pedigree that can be traced back to coastguard training, in which the no-frills combination of running and swimming makes a lot of sense. World championships are held annually.

Octopush (underwater hockey)

Southsea, England, 1954 was the birthplace of this "supreme aerobic sport" in which players push a puck into their opponents' goal with the aid of a stick. Adored by devotees the sport has grown large enough to have two names and even two rival global governing bodies. Probably the most popular of underwater team sports.

Underwater golf

Golf but not as we know it. Players try to hole a weighted ball in an aquariam. Scorecards record time, not number of strokes. Zuohai Aquarium in the city of Fuzhou, China, hosted the first game in 2007. It hasn't caught on: even standing upright posed problems for the players in Fuzhou.

Underwater ice hockey

Played on the undersurface of a frozen water surface it is a game that requires a lot of pluck. Two players a side compete to manouvre the floating puck goalward. Less a case of "where is the goal" than "where is the air hole" as players surface every thirty seconds for air as oxygen tanks are not permitted. Finland won the first world championships in Austria in 2007.

of an amount of beer equal to the weight of his "wife" for finishing in the fastest time. There are options on carrying techniques but the clear favourite is the "Estonian" hold, whereby the woman wraps her legs around the man's head, top of the head pointing towards the floor, face towards his rear end. Health and safety considerations oblige the women to wear helmets which makes sense, as ladies can all too often be dropped.

All ancient pastimes need a creation myth and wife carrying has three. One legend has it that wife carrying came from a traditional brigand custom of err... stealing wives and then forcing them into marriage. Another version has it that a band of thieves led by one Herkko Rosvo-Ronkainen practised their pillaging techniques using big, heavily weighted sacks so that they were well prepared for removing real loot at top speed during a raid. A third has it that Rosvo-Ronkainen's crew were behind the wife stealing and that was also part of his shtick.

Whatever the truth, between the 1800s when Rosvo-Ronkainen was in his prime and 1997 when championships emerged in the Sonkajärvi area of Finland, wife carrying had something of a low profile. In the twenty-first century Estonian couples have dominated the event though the Finns can console themselves that they invented not only this sport but also the world mobile phone throwing championships, which got going in Savonlinna just three years after wife carrying and in which they sustain a fine record of achievement.

If he crosses the finish line first, he wins her weight in beer.

WOOD CHOPPING (TASMANIA, AUSTRALIA, INTERNATIONAL)
Knock knock on wood

Agricultural shows and fairs have included wood chopping competitions for centuries but it is only since the late nineteenth century that it has become an established sport in several countries. Not surprisingly the hacking has been the most relentless in forestry-dominated regions, though none has picked up the axe with quite so much relish as the island of Tasmania in Australia where the locals claim to have inaugurated the sport in 1891. Pride of place at Latrobe's Australian Axeman's Hall of Fame and in wood chopping annals goes to moustachioed 28-stone Tasmanian icon David Foster who, with various members of his family, has dominated wood chopping for decades, taking 21 consecutive cross saw titles from 1978.

Axemen (as choppers like to style themselves) compete in several disciplines. There is "underhand" where they stand on logs they splice in two with a razor-sharp axe, single and double sawing and "tree felling" which is actually a carefully prepared pole to be cut down in the shortest possible time. Handicapping is a big part of the sport, which also varies a lot according to type of wood used, with the premier event still being the Sydney Easter Show which Foster dominated in his prime. Tasmania's boast to be the birthplace of competitive wood chopping is countered by numerous other wood chopping traditions from North America to Slovenia and from the Basque country to near-neighbour New Zealand who boast champions in several disciplines, but Tasmania probably still shaves it for sheer enthusiasm.

YAK RACING (TIBET)
Racing on the roof of the world

A Tibetan horse festival might strike anyone familiar with the Scottish Highland Games as not all that far removed – not in spirit, at least. Horse festivals mix dancing and folk singing with games of skill and strength. The focus, obviously, is on the horses, and the traditional highlights are archery from the saddle and colourful, headlong dashes on horseback.

Yak racing, when it takes place, is a half-comic, half-competitive sideshow. The comedy comes from the yaks' nonplussed attitudes and cartoon expressions. Some are unwilling to start, others get lost en route, but the majority bound along chirpily, looking absurdly small for the job of carrying a rider, and appearing faintly absurd, what with their bouncy gaits and general shaggy friskiness. Over a short, flat stretch of dusty Tibetan plateau, however, a yak can have a surprising turn of speed, and falling in the vicinity of a horn would be less than amusing. You've got to admire the participants' hardiness, too: these races are run at altitudes that can send spectators scurrying for the oxygen tent.

Twenty Cult Sports

Epic contests of heroism, heartache and horsepower

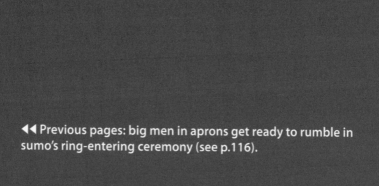

◀◀ Previous pages: big men in aprons get ready to rumble in sumo's ring-entering ceremony (see p.116).

Twenty Cult Sports

"If you drink, don't drive. Don't even putt."

Dean Martin

What makes a cult sport? All sorts of things. And that's kind of the point: any cult worth the title defines itself. So any sport can become one for any number of reasons – each of which pushes players or spectators into a place where sensible behaviour is left at the door. It's all a matter of faith, an irrational, barely explicable, often impenetrable world where things simply *are as they are*. Thus what is cult in sport cannot be fitted into orderly boxes or, most of the time, even be talked about to non-believers without frustrating both sides of the conversation. There is no formula for cult, because if there were then every sport and sportsperson would be one.

Cult sport, as it is played, bends rules, unnerves sponsors and delights observers by refusing to be confined by regular boundaries. Cult sport heroes speak to something larger than simply victory: the joy of technique or just the urge to confound expectations. Cult sport can be about participating as a player, devotion as a spectator or even simply embracing a lifestyle that an identification with a sport implies. Connections may be such that it's just the *idea* of something – possibly something that isn't really that much to do with the physical game at all – or maybe even nothing more than a brilliantly executed marketing strategy but it still forms that bond.

As it is watched, cult sport means seemingly sane individuals jettison conventional good sense and, frequently, take proceedings more seriously than the players. Cult sport also creates the kind of communities civic leaders can only dream about, as the obsessional qualities form strong bonds between unlikely individuals. What follows are twenty of the top sports to which the idea of "cult" can be applied and what it is about each which might be the key to unlocking the nature of their cult appeal.

ANGLING

It was never just about the fish

If the sole purpose of trying to catch fish with a rod, a line and a lure was to put food on your family's table, then we'd all have starved to death generations ago. In fact, if you set the hours put in against fish caught, there is probably no more vivid an example of a sport in which the process so greatly outweighs the result. Then because so much of that process involves doing not very much while surrounded by some of the most spectacular natural scenery on the planet, or simply gazing out to sea, it's hardly surprising angling, or its popular subsection fly fishing, has assumed spiritual properties. It's not unusual for the most macho of anglers to admit the reason they do it is to be able to watch the sunrise without having their manliness questioned.

This notion of having time and, literally, the space to think, to self-examine and to connect with nature, has seen it acknowledged as the philosopher's sport, and it is far from unusual to see the words "fly fishing" and "the meaning of life" in the same sentence. As a result, fishing has become a handy vehicle in fiction for male/familial bonding, escapism or ruminative coming of age – witness *A River Runs Through It*, *The River Why* or *Under Cottonwoods: A Novel of Friendship, Fly Fishing and Redemption*. It makes good cinematic subject matter too, thanks to

Angling: scenery; contemplation; self-discovery; and maybe even some fish.

fabulously photogenic vistas and plenty of moody brooding looks – well, too much dialogue would frighten the fish. Unsurprisingly these movies (the first two of the above titles have been filmed) have sold themselves on their human relations sub-texts – "It's not really about fishing at all" crops up regularly in reviews. This is an aspect that is now making quite an appearance in the journey-through-life section of the bookstore. *Blood Knots* is about "angling, friendship, honour and coming of age"; *Against the Flow* travels through Communist Eastern Europe with a rod and reel; *On the Mother Lagoon* is feminism, yoga and fly fishing; *Fly Fishing Through the Midlife Crisis* is pretty self-explanatory.

Of course it's not all spirituality and deep multi-tiered thinking. Angling, in its many forms, is one of the most popular participation sports in the world, and the vast majority of week-end fishermen don't use it to work out their inner conflicts, don't join clubs or enter competitions: they just do it for a bit of bone idle peace and quiet. It's not exactly easy either, as the skills involved and the demands made on your physical coordination keep it firmly in the realms of a proper sport. Casting is never as straightforward as it appears; keeping your balance on a river bed of smooth stones while wearing waders is not for the faint hearted.

> "To him, all good things — trout as well as eternal salvation — come by grace and grace comes by art and art does not come easy."
>
> **Norman Maclean, *A River Runs Through It***

AUSSIE RULES FOOTBALL

G'day!

For many Australians, this is the most popular sport there is, both as spectators and participants. The record crowd for an Australian Football League cup final is 121,696 at the Melbourne Cricket Ground, while, according to government fig-ures, over seven million people per year attend AFL matches. Weekly televised matches get around 1.5 million viewers, with the AFL final usually attracting twice that, as the country's largest TV audience. The sport emerged from the state of Victoria – which remains its cultural heartland – in the mid-nineteenth century, but has never registered outside of Australia. The only people who play it are ex-pat Aussies and foreign television companies have no interest in trying to break it internationally.

This may be because, unless you've been schooled in it practically since birth, it is a fiendishly complicated sport to get into, which puts off overseas TV companies – not unlike baseball, where initial incomprehension means it's not seen on televi-sion outside countries that play it. To a native, Aussie rules is a highly disciplined, rule-ridden sport with strict codes, but to the casual observer it can appear an unregulated, violent free-for-all. The truth is somewhere in between. This combi-

To many, Aussie rules is an incomprehensible mix of rugby and Gaelic football.

nation of Gaelic football and rugby is played on an oval pitch (it began as a way for cricketers to keep fit during the winter), with two sets of goal posts at each end, by teams of eighteen, with precise regulations for punching, kicking and slapping the ball, but no offside rule. It can look like mayhem, but the rules have been developed with the spectator in mind to keep it fast moving, high scoring and hard tackling. Such physical commitment is hugely appreciated by fans, although on-field violence did at one point reach such levels that police prosecution was commonplace; one prosecution ended with a jail sentence. While the Australian masses love this hardcore attitude from the players, it is putting off international interest as overseas teams have opted not to host tours because of it. Equally off-putting abroad is the seemingly endemic racism among the players – there are a large number of indigenous Australian players in the AFL – which got so bad the league recently brought in something called the Racial Vilification Code, handing out stiff penalties and bringing it under control.

Match days are like carnivals, at which barbecues are lit in the car parks beforehand, with the party vibe getting going as beer flows from kegs and coolers. Such feasting continues during the matches with meat pies and beer being dispensed by strolling vendors calling out, "Hot pies… cold beer! Hot pies… cold beer!" Before the game, players come on to the field by leaping through a crepe paper banner, but the most remarkable sights take place once a game has finished and the crowd rushes on to the pitch to start their own games of Aussie rules. Although this whole experience sounds like fun in the sun, it's a health and safety nightmare, which is probably why Aussie rules doesn't travel too well.

BASEBALL

Cards, caps and fantasy leagues

Baseball has long been hailed as the US's blue-collar sport, so essential a part of proletarian life that when Americans speak of "the ball game" or "the ball park" they are invariably referring to baseball. Such widespread working-class enthusiasm turned it into a participant sport so popular it became a cultural icon along with mom's apple pie. Astonishingly, it wasn't always like that, as when the National League was established at the end of the nineteenth century, it was to be promoted specifically as a spectator sport for wealthier Americans. The game had developed partly as a home-grown alternative to imported cricket which was still popular among East Coast gentry, and in order to keep baseball for the middle and upper classes – removed from American football and ice hockey – baseball stadiums were built outside of the cities. Importantly, though, the game's universal entrance fee of fifty cents was much higher than any other sport and the scheduling of so many games on weekday afternoons precluded most working folk.

However, such was the appeal of baseball as a participant sport – especially among children – as it needed so little equipment or facilities, its popularity quickly spread and as other sports sharply increased their admission prices, it became good value. Another factor was the stadium locations. As cities had to expand, stadiums now found themselves adjacent to newly built working-class suburbs or

> "A hot dog at the ball game beats roast beef at the Ritz."
> **Humphrey Bogart**

low-income housing projects. Baseball's almost total demographic shift was epitomized by record-breaking batsman Babe Ruth in the 1920s (see p.184), who as the spearhead of baseball's mass popularity, had risen from a Baltimore slum to become the sport's first bona fide superstar.

Baseball's massive cultural impact is probably best measured by what the sport has given to the world at large. Most obviously the cap, this now ubiquitous head-wear, which started its quest for cross-cultural global domination in the 1980s, thanks in no small part to hip hop, can be traced back to the Brooklyn Excelsiors, a nineteenth-century amateur baseball team. It was in the 1850s when they adopted a rounded, stiffened cap of black canvas with a long white bill, to set off their black bow ties. Following their championship-winning season of 1860, it began to get adopted by other teams.

> "I believe in the Church of Baseball. I tried all the major religions and most of the minor ones. I've worshipped Buddha, Allah, Brahma, Vishnu, Siva, trees, mushrooms and Isadora Duncan. I know things. For instance, there are 108 beads in a Catholic rosary and there are 108 stitches in a baseball. When I learned that, I gave Jesus a chance."
> **Ron Shelton, writer/director of classic baseball movie *Bull Durham*, 1988.**

Baseball cards, which gave rise to all manner of sporting-related cards, were introduced towards the end of the nineteenth century. Originally they were used to advertise a local business, with photographs of popular local baseball players reproduced on wallet-sized cards, with details of the business on the reverse. The cards proved so popular as artefacts, tobacco companies picked up the idea to include them in cigarette packs as gifts but with the players' details and statistics on the back. It didn't take long for such giveaway cards to spread to other products, sports and countries, eventually evolving into sticker sets. The first sporting fantasy league was Rotisseries League Baseball, founded by a New York writer in 1980 for his friends with, notebooks and pencils to keep records – the sport's seemingly limitless statistics being ideal for this purpose. Adopted by print media, these games quickly took off among sports across the board, and the Internet has made them part of everyday life for so many fans.

BOCCIA
It's not for everyone

In a game of boccia, players pitch blue or red leather-covered balls down a 12.5 metre-long course to try and land them as close as possible to a smaller ball covered in white leather, the jack, that has already been tossed down the course. This is not unlike the French game boules, and both are derived from an Ancient Greek game, which involved pitching smooth stones towards a smaller one. However, boccia has one huge difference: it is one of the very few sports designed wholly for the disabled. It is one of only two Paralympic events that has no equivalent in the

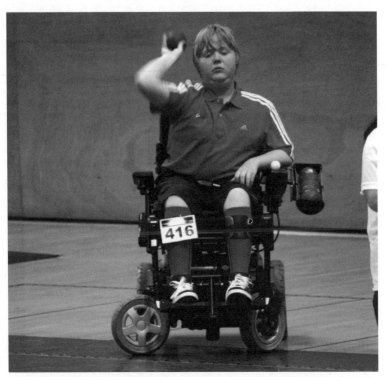

Boccia: one of only two Paralympic sports with no able-bodied equivalent.

main Games (the other is goalball), and its governing body is the Cerebral Palsy International Sports and Recreation Association.

Boccia came to the UK in the early 1980s and became part of physical therapy for cerebral palsy sufferers, which is where the CPISRA spotted its potential as a competitive or recreational sport because it required skill, accuracy and strategy rather than strength, size or speed. It was developed with the size of the court designed to accommodate wheelchairs, and rules evolved to include the use of hands, feet or a ramp, meaning the ball can be kicked, rolled or thrown as long as it is propelled solely by the player themselves. Official competition boccia is open to all athletes with severe disabilities who are confined to wheelchairs, so this is not limited to cerebral palsy but includes muscular dystrophy and other neurological conditions. Competitors are split into four classifications, two of which are eligible to use assistants to help them position their wheelchairs, but who must keep their backs to the jack at all times. Boccia is played in sixty countries world-wide, with a world cup and a world championship and was introduced to the Paralympics in 1984.

BOXING

All human life

It's been a while since the art of boxing suggested any notions of "noble". Indeed while the basic rules might be much the same as in 1881, when John L. Sullivan became the first gloved heavyweight champion, what is quaintly called the boxing game has changed beyond all recognition. Since the sport prostrated itself before television pay-per-view dollars and became a promoters' playground where the deal is more important than the fight, it's become almost meaningless for the fan. Fragmented into a bewildering number of world governing bodies, it's virtually impossible to know who is champion that week. Then as "challengers" are carefully selected to provide a lack of precisely that – challenge – you'd have to go back to the late 1980s and Mike Tyson to experience the traditional spirit of pugilism. Unless, of course, you're going to the movies.

> "I was nobody. But that don't matter either, you know? Nobody's ever gone the distance with Creed, and if I can go that distance, I'm gonna know for the first time in my life, see, that I weren't just another bum from the neighbourhood."
>
> **Rocky Balboa,** *Rocky*

Boxing has long found favour on the silver screen, as a straightforward metaphor for manliness – a wimpish Buster Keaton posed as a boxer in the 1926 film *Battling Butler* in order to impress a girl – while the gladiatorial combat aspect provided an obvious alternative to the "man's gotta do…" Western. As times and social attitudes have changed, however, the boxing movie has vastly expanded its horizons and offers itself up as a handy hook on which to hang all manner of moral and relationship issues. As well as basic rags to riches (*Rocky*) and good versus evil (*Champion*, *Rocky II* and *III*), we get honesty versus corruption (*The Set Up*, *On the Waterfront*, *Let's Do It Again*), tradition versus modernism (*Fat City*), the passing of time (*The Champ*, *Requiem for a Heavyweight*), being a man (*The Quiet Man*), personal redemption (*The Harder They Fall*, *Somebody Up There Likes Me*, *Cinderella Man*), justice being served (*The Hurricane*), father–son conflicts (*Broken Noses*, *The Champ*) and even father–daughter conflicts (*Million Dollar Baby*).

> "Boxing is drama on its grandest scale."
>
> **Howard Cosell, the voice of American sports broadcasting**

It's in these epic films that boxing is more than merely allowed to regain its tattered dignity and preserve its honour. They remind viewers that it used to be something really important in so many people's lives. After all, it wasn't so long ago that a heavyweight championship bout was watched by literally everybody and

Six bigger picture boxing movies

(That aren't *Rocky* or *Raging Bull*)

The Champ (Wallace Beery, Jackie Cooper, 1931)
Not a great deal of actual boxing, but as a struggling, alcoholic, ex-heavyweight champion ends up back in the ring to do right by his son, there won't be a dry eye in the house.

Body & Soul (John Garfield, Lilli Palmer, 1947)
This straightforward story of a talented young boxer caught in the realization that the world he is making his fortune in is seedy, corrupt and soul-destroying, offers up some beautifully choreographed fight sequences, setting the standard for future boxing movies.

On the Waterfront (Marlon Brando, Karl Malden, 1954)
Marlon Brando plays a former boxer turned docker who attempts to fight corruption outside the ring – this Oscar-laden boxing-without-the-fights movie made him a cinema legend.

Fat City (Stacy Keach, Jeff Bridges, 1972)
Gritty *film noir* about a young, dumb up-and-comer who meets an over-the-hill former champion who should've quit years ago. The film examines the small-town, unglamourous end of boxing and the advance of time for us all.

Million Dollar Baby (Clint Eastwood, Morgan Freeman, Hilary Swank, 2004)
When veteran boxing trainers Freeman and Eastwood reluctantly take on Swank as a professional fighter, Eastwood's nonexistent relationship with his estranged daughter is brought to the fore.

Cinderella Man (Russell Crowe, Renée Zellweger, 2005)
True story of the rise and fall and rise of Depression-era heavyweight champion James J. Braddock, who balanced his wife's abhorrence of boxing with a need to feed his family. His comeback after serious injury became a metaphor for the American people's resilience.

would be a topic of general conversation for days to come. Now, these films appeal beyond sports fans and take boxing back into that realm of day-to-day life. In this respect it's interesting that not every boxing movie enjoys the traditional happy ending. Most importantly, the genre itself remains emotionally engaging enough to make us think about what goes on around boxing and connect with it on a deeper level than the fights themselves. As long as Hollywood continues its fascination with boxing, the sport will hang on to its perceived nobility and, therefore, its cult status.

CRICKET
Anything else just isn't

If Hollywood has boxing on which to hang so many metaphors for the human condition, then the literary world has cricket. In English literature, cricket probably features more than any other sport, and has done so for a couple of hundred years. Dickens' *The Pickwick Papers* features a hilariously observed account of a cricket match; the game is central to *Tom Brown's Schooldays* – Brown's nemesis Flashman goes on to be a cricketer; A.J. Raffles, the thinking man's jewel thief, would burglarize the country houses he played cricket at; Tennyson, Blake and Byron all featured the game in their poetry, as did Tom Stoppard in *The Real Thing*; A.G. Macdonell's satirical classic *England, Their England* centres on a cricket match; James Joyce alludes to cricket in *Finnegan's Wake*, likewise Douglas

The very essence of Englishness. Or so we've been told.

Adams in *Life, the Universe and Everything*; the game became the foundation for *Netherland*, Joseph O'Neill's grim tale of post-9/11 New York. It will hardly be surprising to learn that Samuel Beckett – the man who wrote *Waiting for Godot*, a riveting drama in which hardly anything happens – played first-class cricket.

It's the idea of cricket being both civilized and civilizing, that made it such a popular subject during the colonial era when cricket-based writing was in its hey-day – among the literary players were Arthur Conan Doyle, A.A. Milne, H.G. Wells, Jerome K. Jerome and P.G. Wodehouse. Peter Pan's creator J.M. Barrie even had his own cricket team, the Allahakbarries, for which fellow authors regularly turned out. In the literature of this time, the game established itself as so strong an illustration of the essence of Englishness, it made substance of the nation's cultural statement. Cricket became synonymous with all things even-handed and virtuous – rules, fair play, patience, fortitude, skill, team work, individual flair, camaraderie… This was exactly how the nation and the Empire wanted to see itself, and the idea of taking those values, through the game, to the West Indies, India, Africa and Australia imparted a degree of benevolence to colonialism. It gave rise to the perception of cricket as a metaphor for life, and such sayings as, "On a sticky wicket" , "Played with a straight bat", "Bowled us a googly" and "It's just not cricket" passed into everyday parlance around this time. Remarkably, the long-term effect of this has meant the greatest cricketing writer of the modern era, C.L.R. James, was Trinidadian, while Indian film is starting to use cricket as a colonial metaphor, but from a colonized point of view – witness *Lagaan: Once Upon a Time in India*.

> "Reading poetry and watching cricket were the sum of my world, and the two are not so far apart as many aesthetes might believe."
>
> **Donald Bradman**

However, in a world of ball tampering, betting scandals, cynical fast bowling and the game evolving to better fit television's requirements, this may not be the case today, and cricket is more a metaphor for a way of life than for life itself. However, in terms of cult status, the mere notion that cricket retains such strong associations with good manners, unhurried afternoons and above all fair play is more than enough to be going on with.

CURLING

Dem stones, dem stones…

Sandra Schmirler was captain of the Canadian curling team that took home gold from the Nagano Winter Olympics in 1998, the first time the sport was in medal competition. Less than two years later she succumbed to cancer; nearly twenty thousand people attended her funeral, which was broadcast live on Canadian television. The remarkable thing here isn't the turnout to say goodbye to a national sporting hero – after all, Canada has over a million regular curlers, about two thirds of the world's total – but that it took the Winter Olympics authorities until 1998 to introduce it as a fully fledged event. It's been with us since at least the mid-sixteenth century – the sport features in a painting by Bruegel the Elder from that period – and anybody who has so much as glanced at it on TV will be well aware of its hypnotic qualities. Each Winter Olympics it becomes almost a guilty secret as thousands of apparently sensible people all over the world hastily leave wherever they might be, mumbling all manner of excuses, to get home in time for the curling. And woe betide anybody who might attempt a conversation with them once the stones start sliding. Either that or, like most American comedians on TV during the Games, you'll be sufficiently moved to make mildly bemused "how dull is curling?" gags. It's no coincidence that curling became the most searched for sport on the Internet during the 2010 Games.

Although we suspect the American jokes about shuffleboard on ice, cleaning skills and scarcely believable trousers might be provoked by the US team's abject failures in the event, the enthusiasm is much more explainable. Virtually unchanged for over four hundred years, since Scottish textile workers slid flat river stones across frozen ponds, it's the perfect antithesis to modern life: serene, genteel and positively polite. While the frantic activity of the broom work causes just enough excitement to keep it on the right side of soporific, the obvious teamwork involved as the skipper plots the course and barks orders to the broom handlers appeals to an inherent spirit of cooperation. Any warm spectator glow is enhanced by curling being one of the very few sports in which players call their own fouls – if you burn (touch) an opponent's stone with your broom, shoe or body part it would be unthinkable if you didn't own up and take the penalty. The clearly discernible tactics being employed as the house (target area) begins to fill up will draw you in further, while probably the greatest armchair attraction lies in the notion that men and women who obviously aren't highly trained, finely tuned athletes – i.e. are

The Fab Four curl

In what was one of the very few onscreen – or off screen, for that matter – examples of The Beatles playing sport, they opted for curling in a memorable scene from *Help!* George sends the stones down, while John and Ringo work the brooms – regular household items – and Paul stands in the house. George, however, fails to notice when the baddies hand him a stone loaded with explosives and plays it anyway. As he spots the smoke coming out around the handle, he warns the others by shouting that it is, in fact, a "fiendish thingie". The lads escape, a hole is blasted in the ice and a bewildered swimmer emerges asking for directions to the White Cliffs of Dover. Who said curling was dull?

Everybody's favourite Winter Olympic event.

people much like you and me – are winning Olympic medals.

Interestingly, in spite of curling's ostensible comedy gold, those TV gagsters would seem somewhat out of step with Americans in general – virtually unnoticed, and certainly not owned up to, the event's underground following is growing in the US. During those last Olympics, TV network CNBC reported a seven hundred percent increase in the Games' viewing figures when curling came on.

CYCLING

A wheeled world of imagination

The cool thing about cycling is just about all of us can do it and pretty much most of us have at one stage or another, even if that experience dates back to the tricycle with the pedals attached to the front wheel. Then when you have been riding a bike it's not at all difficult to imagine you're somewhere else: as a kid, when you charged through woods you were in a World Mountain Bike Championship, or hurtling round a circuit in your local park was like being on some sort of velodrome – and don't mention that frequent arm and collar bone breaker the downhill pursuit. This sort of fantasy cycling doesn't stop when you get older either. There can't be many cyclists who haven't pretended they're on a particularly tricky stage of the Tour de France during their ride to work.

Indeed, riding a bike, whether for sport or otherwise, was just something everybody seemed to do, and that has long been the case – film footage of factory workers or miners coming off shift in the 1950s usually shows many more cycling than walking and hardly anybody driving a car. While this in itself ought to be enough to preclude cycling from any sort of cult status, in recent years its standing in the world has changed radically. It's no longer just something you do but has assumed "social statement" proportions. Men and women who used to simply own or ride bikes are now *cyclists*, a title uttered as if bestowed in the New Year's Honours List. In these days of limited natural resources and global warming, cycling has become a lifestyle choice the rest of the world understands and will quite rightly applaud – cycle to work and you're likely to receive acclaim for being thrifty, keeping yourself fit and saving the planet, as well as instant camaraderie from others who have taken to two wheels. Remarkably, while cycling can barely pedal under the weight of its green credentials, if you ran the same journey all the above would apply, yet colleagues would be perpetually asking you what you're training for while quietly assuming you're a bit nuts. Especially if your journey is over ten miles.

Perhaps the most remarkable thing about cycling as a cult sport, though, is the distance by which the cult is separated from the sport. In spite of there being so many different branches of competitive cycling available – road racing, hill climbing, cyclocross, track racing, BMX-ing, time trials, to name but a few – it's a miniscule proportion of cyclists who actually compete. Except in their heads, of course, as there won't be many who haven't looked up at the entrance to the office car park and seen the Arc de Triomphe at the end of the Avenue des Champs-Élysées.

DARTS
Oche, oche, oche!

The professional darts world circuit isn't quite on the same level as golf or tennis, but as well as the UK it takes in several European countries, Canada, the US, South Africa and Australia, while television broadcasts the bigger events all over the globe. With millions on offer in prize money and appearance fees, and the TV audience demanding some sort of spectacle, darts in the twenty-first century has come a long way from its humble beginnings in public houses' public bars. Yet the only concession professional darts appears to have made to its glamorous new status is that players drink water instead of lager as they wait their turn to throw and nobody in the hall is smoking. But what seems most

Why oche?

The idea of "stepping up to the oche" (pronounced like a cockney version of "hockey") to take your throws from behind a line that is 2.37 metres (7 feet 9.25 inches) from the board, is one of darts' great mysteries. It came into official darts use when, in the late 1920s, the News of the World newspaper used it to describe the throwing distance in the published rules of the darts competitions it sponsored. Since then, everybody has accepted the term and will happily bandy it about, but nobody seems to know what it means.

The most popular, and somehow most appropriate explanation, is that it comes from Hockey & Son, a West Country brewery, because the first officially prescribed distance was three of their beer crates laid end to end – exactly nine feet. Then, when the size of the crate changed to two feet several years later, so did the distance of the oche from the board as it became eight feet, or four crates. This well-established tale has been discredited by the fact nobody can find any evidence of a Hockey & Son brewery. Another erstwhile "clarification" is that it comes from the Old English word "hocken" meaning to spit, and was carried over from the spitting contests that used to be a part of pub life, in which contestants had to stand behind a line. Another theory is that it comes from the Flemish word "oche" which means groove and was applied to a line drawn in the dirt for throwers to stand behind. West Country historians claim the skittles-style game Aunt Sally, when played in that part of the country, always had a "hockey" to mark the throwing distance.

astonishing about post-Sky Sports darts is that it never really left the back bar of your local boozer – it just took that situation with it, increasing the ambience exponentially as the championships and the venues got bigger and bigger. Indeed, the substitution of water for lager was pragmatic rather than image-conscious because the heat in the big venues was causing players to dehydrate, and smoking was simply outlawed.

Darts crowds at big events are like pub outing conventions, with a beery jamboree atmosphere as they sing songs, chant in football match style and wear fancy dress, either in support of their favourite player or just for a laugh. The players themselves remain, in spite of all the cash washing round the world of darts, the

Six cult comedies

Horse Feathers (The Marx Brothers, 1932)
Groucho is dean of Huxley College. Harpo and Chico are bootleggers, who he enrols in the school in order for them to play on the football team. The big game climax involves a makeshift chariot.

The Fish That Saved Pittsburgh (Julius Erving, Stockard Channing, 1979)
This very 1970s basketball comedy revolves around astrological signs (the fish – Pisces), features an abundance of afros, a disco soundtrack and Dr J. in the lead role.

Caddyshack (Chevy Chase, Rodney Dangerfield, 1980)
Somewhere there was a plot about a golf caddy trying to earn a college scholarship, but it's submerged in the scattergun gags and Bill Murray hunting a gopher.

Happy Gilmore (Adam Sandler, 1996)
An ice hockey star with anger management issues turns golf pro with a hockey stick shaped driver – admit it, you've tried to take a run-up for a tee shot after seeing this.

Kingpin (Woody Harrelson, Randy Quaid, Bill Murray, 1996)
Quaid's naïve Amish tenpin bowling prodigy is upstaged by Harrelson's prosthetic hand and Murray's spectacularly badly behaved hair.

Blades of Glory (Will Ferrell, Jon Heder, 2007)
Ridiculously funny ice skating film, that redefines the notion of pairs and involves a routine so dangerous the last time it was performed heads rolled. Literally.

same bordering-on-middle-aged, decidedly unsporty-looking, tonsorially unfashionable types you'd find in any public bar in Britain. The difference now is they make their entrances to the arenas to dry ice, strobe lights and heavy metal-ish theme songs, usually flanked by spangly costumed "leggy lovelies". Then there's the nicknames. In true pub regular style, any darts champion worth his arrows will have something awe-inspiring embroidered on the back of his custom-made bowling shirt – The Spanish Assassin (Carlos Rodríguez), The Milky Bar Kid (Keith Deller, see p.264), Bobby Dazzler (Bobby George), The Viking (Andy Fordham) or The Power (Phil Taylor). It's said that in terms of crowd support and psychological advantage, a good nickname is worth an extra throw.

> "My nickname the Crafty Cockney was an accident. There's an English-owned pub in Santa Monica, California, that all the darts lads go to, and I bought a souvenir shirt from there. I started wearing it back in London and everyone assumed it was my darts name, and it just stuck."
> **Eric Bristow, the Crafty Cockney (obviously).**

It's meant World Darts, as it remains dominated by UK players, is a raucous, flashy carnival that really has remained true to its roots. But then these British pub roots go so deep. In the early twentieth century, darts was banned from licensed premises as part of a crackdown on games of chance, but in 1908 a Yorkshire publican went to court to prove it was a game of skill. He set up a dartboard, stood the regulation distance away, threw three twenties and challenged the officers of the court to do the same. A few tried but none managed it and the judge was forced to rule darts as a game of skill. As a result it quickly established itself as being one of the very few games people were legally allowed to bet on in licensed premises.

FOOTBALL

Not always just for kicks

As the most popular spectator and participatory sport in the world, the general public's interface with football is an astonishing state of affairs. It seems to operate on that sort of level whereby if you're put in a room with a bunch of people you went to school with the intervening years count for nothing and you all become fourteen years old (or whatever) again. The chances are you started supporting your team as a little kid, thus you won't grow up in its presence, and the majority of football fans never develop an adult relationship with their club. Hence the arguments, the grumpiness, the euphoria, the irrationality involved in being a fan. But sometimes it can go even further than seeming to take over your life on a regular basis. Supporting a football team can sometimes cause behaviour so mind-boggling it might even be beyond cult. Witness the examples below.

Iglesia Maradoniana: The Church of Maradona

"Our Diego, who art on Earth/Hallowed be thy left foot/Thy magic come/Thy goals be remembered" is the chant that, er, kicks off a service at La Iglesia Maradoniana, in a rented hall somewhere in Argentina. The priests, who all wear number 10 on their backs, enter as the altar boys hold aloft symbolic footballs wreathed in crowns of barbed wire and dripping fake blood. At least the chanting congregation assume it to be fake. Part of each service involves new congregation members being "baptised" by having a photo taken of themselves wearing the pale blue and white of Argentina performing a raised arm jump against a lifesize poster of a hapless Peter Shilton, on which Diego himself has been digitally removed. It's your own personal "Hand of God" moment . It symbolizes that you too can be like Diego, and that, therefore, he remains a humble man of the people.

The Church of Maradona was founded by a group of friends in Rosario, Argentina, in 1998, as part idolatry, part tongue-in-cheek and total football fan logic – one of the founders said at the time, "If football is our religion, then we had to have a God." *D10S* – the idea that Maradona's shirt number already existed within the Spanish word for god, "dios" – was all the encouragement they needed. Today, they claim the church has over a hundred thousand members worldwide, as it has no permanent base but travels the globe spreading the word, photographing converts and celebrating Christmas on 30 October, Diego Maradona's birthday.

In 1943, prior to Real Madrid hosting Barcelona, the Spanish dictator General Franco, a passionate Real supporter, sent a delegation of his notorious secret police into the away team's dressing room to deliver his version of a team talk. The Barca players were instructed not to forget that Catalan only existed within Spain by the general's good grace. Barcelona, who had been favourites to win, lost 11–1. Sticking with the same fixture, sixty-odd years later, when former Barcelona hero Luis Figo transferred to Real and returned to his former club to play against them, he was ready for sustained barracking and certainly a few missiles. He was less prepared for the recently severed pig's head that sailed out of the crowd to land near his feet when he went to take a corner.

Liverpudlian Danny Pierce, in 2008, had his baby daughter christened Eva-Toni-Ann Pierce, as a mark of his lifelong affection for the Merseyside club that plays in blue. Little Eva was actually his third daughter, but it had taken him that long to convince his partner to go along with the name he claimed he thought up when he was at school. In another bizarre naming incident an Italian group of direct action anarchist "art terrorists" called themselves the Luther Blissett Project and every one of their members took the name of the former Watford and A.C.

Six cult sports TV dramas

Eastbound & Down
Will Ferrell is the guiding hand of this comedy series about a foul-mouthed, obnoxious, perennially horny, mullet-sporting pro baseball pitcher, who after being sacked by his team returns to his home town and former school as a PE teacher.

Footballers' Wives
Has life imitated "art"? This ridiculously over the top soap opera of obscene wealth and total lack of taste among a group of Essex-residing professional footballers and their spouses preceded the rise of the WAG by a couple of years.

Friday Night Lights
A high school football team and its father figure coach become the hook on which to hang an examination of Smalltown US, its dramas, moral dilemmas and complicated love lives.

Jossy's Giants
Sid Waddell, the face and voice of darts on British television, wrote this 1980s knockabout comedy series centring on the boys' football team the Glipton Giants which, although aimed at children, became essential viewing for students and the underemployed.

United!
1960s football-themed soap opera followed the fortunes of Brentwich United on and off the pitch, and was the BBC's attempt to get mileage out of the sport's newfound glamour. Stadium scenes were shot at Stoke City's ground and footage of Liverpool versus Juventus sometimes used as action sequences – Juve's kit had the same stripes as Brentwich.

The White Shadow
1970s series about a white former pro-basketball player who quits through injury to take a job as coach at a predominantly black and Hispanic high school – he is their White Shadow. It avoids being totally worthy, and crackles with the kids' almost constant sharp humour.

Milan striker Luther Blissett. They never said exactly why – hey, they're anarchist art terrorists – but rumours at the time pointed to their leader being an A.C. fan and their identifying with Blissett, who is black, as something of an outsider in Italy's notoriously xenophobic and racist football culture. In Germany, Hamburg S.V. fan Lars Rehder bought up a section of a cemetery practically in the shadow of the club's ground, selling burial plots to supporters. Part of his deal involves coffins in the club's colours, genuine stadium turf over the top of the graves and terrace style steps for the placing of urns. Commentary from the deceased's favourite match is one of the service's optional extras.

Then there's the time rank outsiders Iraq won the Asian Cup in 2007, beating Saudi Arabia 1–0 in the final. The country was so overwhelmingly overjoyed that Shiites, Sunnis and Kurds celebrated in the streets together for two or three days before normal service was resumed and mistrust and hostilities resurfaced. As stated above, football can make people lose their minds.

AMERICAN FOOTBALL
Party hearty!

In spite of baseball's apple pie status (see p.89), as a sports spectator experience, it's difficult to get instantly closer to the American Way than with that country's version of football. Going to a game is like stepping into a ful-colour version of a Frank Capra movie – but with beer, swearing and a multicultural cast, obviously. And this is before you've even got near the turnstiles, let alone encountered those uniquely American delights of cheerleaders, march-ing brass bands and the enthusiastic Mexican waves inside. Killing time before an American football match is a matter of hanging out on lawn furniture, listening to music, cooking, eating, drinking, watching the kids and a few dogs run around, playing Frisbee or catching a football – all very family-oriented, all very chilled out. Whereas the British might prepare themselves for a major sporting event by slopping match day-priced drinks over each other in a hazardously over-crowded pub, across the Atlantic football fans indulge in the altogether more civilized practice of tailgating, a kind of portable party experience that is as much a part of the game as anything that happens on the field. It's not just in the NFL either; tailgating is taken equally seriously at college games, many of which are bigger events and better attended than a lot of English Premier League fixtures.

The basics of tailgating are you arrive at the ground and park up, unpack the beer and the food and while away the time before kickoff with sports-related small talk. However, in the past decade or so the scene around the US has become sophisticated to the point at which meticulous preparation is now going into what are, essentially, pre-match picnics. Serious tailgaters arrive up to 48 hours before game time. This will make sure they get a good parking spot as although

New England Patriots fans thaw themselves out outside the Gillette Stadium.

stadium car parks are big enough to accommodate most people travelling by car, the downside is you could end up a kilometre away from the ground. Choice of vehicle is important; clearly something with an actual tailgate helps, but the serious party types roll up in RVs (that's recreational vehicle) that have been customized outside with team logos and inside with just about every portable comfort known to man – armchairs, beds, toilets, fridge-freezers, televisions, hi-fi… Turning up early gives plenty of time to fire up the barbecue or smoker, and the truly committed roll out propane-powered cookers with the sort of gourmet capability that would put most household ranges to shame. It's not unusual to see full-scale wet bars set up next to these outdoor kitchens. Put the recent trend for portable smokers along with the thousands of regular charcoal grills in operation, and on a good day it's not unusual for the stadium to be obscured by a haze of meat and charcoal smoke.

Sunday afternoon football tailgating has now reached a point at which there are a number of guides available online, detailing and reviewing the different car park preferences and ambiences around the NFL: Oakland Raiders' fans have the wildest fancy dress and favour ribs and brisket steak; at Philadelphia Eagles, it's stuffed peppers, smoked Polish sausage and, of course, Philly cheese steaks; Tampa Bay Bucs' fans favour fish; unique to Chicago Bears fans are grilled Krispy Kreme Doughnuts; the beer of choice at Denver Broncos is the Fat Tire local brew; it's not unusual to find whole pigs being spit roasted outside the Miami Dolphins' stadium.

GOLF

Seldom the best way to enjoy a good walk

According to recent statistics (Sports Marketing Surveys), one percent of the world's population regularly plays golf, a figure that, apparently, rises to around one in ten in the US. Yet never has such a popular sport failed so dismally to come to grips with contemporary fashion. It wasn't so long ago a round of golf required you to dress like an Edwardian motorist, but then suddenly everyone seemed to be opting for the Las Vegas lounge lizard look – grown men in white belts *in the 1990s*? Now, thanks to those sartorial frightfests Ian Poulter and John Daly, we've seen where things could have been heading and should think ourselves lucky the diamond patterns and Miami colour palette has been reined in to a point at which Tiger's trouser pleat-bonanza or Shingo's cowboy hat are the closest anybody gets to edgy. And we've not even got on to footwear. But it's not because golf has the ability to make successful, wealthy young sportsmen dress like their dads and have permanent "hat hair" that it has cult status, but because it makes legions of seemingly sensible men and women follow suit. That's the truly spooky thing about the game of golf: there's nothing you can't sell a golfer if he or she believes it will take a couple of shots off his or her game. And this is as likely to mean cash laid out for some ridiculous, bondage-style swing-o-flex device (a trawl through the patent office is never less than entertaining) as it is to be a white roll neck jumper "just like Monty wears".

The game exerts an even greater pull over players as regards the lengths they'll go to for a chance to play a few holes, or in some cases just hit a few balls. Quite apart from the speed golf and the underwater golf dealt with elsewhere (see p.106) golf is such an obsession among many – probably fifty percent of that one percent – there are very few places you won't find a course of some description. Arctic Circle golf is a big deal, as for some months of the year you can play around the clock – the course record at Yellowknife Golf Course in Canada is 171 holes in 33.5 hours. While oil-rich sheiks have laid regular courses in the desert, less privileged Middle Eastern golfers mark out their course, play off a mat put down where the ball lies and putt on "browns" – green-sized areas of sand held together with used engine oil. This has even led to sand golf becoming a recognised sport.

Urban golf takes it to city streets using soft balls and, literally, mapping out routes to target "holes". There are Urban golf associations in most of the world's major cities. Rooftop golf is the same sort of thing but shots go from roof to roof, while golf simulators bring practically every famous course to a medium-sized room near you – South Korea has over five thousand of them. If you can't get to even a virtual course, bigger cruise ships feature driving ranges into the ocean using balls made of eco-friendly compressed salt; a game has been developed in New York where floating balls are driven at targets in the Hudson River; and astronaut Alan Shepard famously took his clubs to the moon.

The really worrying aspect of the Cult of Golf, though, is its effect on players' truth gene: according to his country's state-controlled media outlets, North Korean dictator Kim Jong II carded a world record-busting 38 under par 34 at the Pyongyang Golf Club. The score apparently included five holes in one, slightly better than the three or four he usually gets per round, and, clearly to the relief of the PGA, he had a country to oppress and didn't have time for the Tour.

Six insane golf courses

Kabul Golf Course, Afghanistan
Expect to be accompanied by an AK47-bearing security guard and to tee off in the shadow of Afghan tanks. The rough is strewn with debris from explosions, bunkers have nothing to do with sand traps and don't even ask about a shot index.

La Paz Golf Club, Bolivia
The world's highest playable course is 10,650 feet above sea level, where the rarefied air means it's possible for even the most ham-fisted Sunday hacker to drive over 400 yards.

Legend Golf & Safari Resort, South Africa
This has an extra hole with a 630-yard par three. The reason it's possible is because the tee is 1500 feet above a green that is shaped like a map of Africa and you have to be choppered up there.

Nullarbor Links, Australia
Eighteen holes played on a course that measures 1300 kilometres around the coastline of Southern and Western Australia, with around eighty kilometres between each one. Local hotels offer discount rates for players.

Skukuza Golf Course, South Africa
Situated in a wildlife park and originally built for the wardens' use, it is now open to the public. There are no fences, thus hazards include lions, leopards, rhinos, elephants, warthogs and zebras.

Uummannaq, Greenland
Just outside the Arctic Circle and home to the World Ice Golf Championship, in which 36 holes have been created from the ice floes and glaciers and can involve pitching from one to another across freezing water. Natural shifting of the ice patterns means the course is constantly redefining itself.

KARATE

Those kids were fast as lightning

If ever there was a prime candidate for sporting culthood it has to be karate. Or kung fu, or tae kwon do, or whatever your style of choice. Nowhere else in the sporting lexicon will you be able to find such a degree of philosophy, symbolism, theory, etiquette, tradition, patience and attention to detail. Couple that with rigorous conditioning and training regimes, and the notion that you'll probably never be quite as good as you could have been if you'd spent time in a mountain top monastery. Then remember that most people seemed to have "learned" karate simply by watching the films, which were some of the most hilariously violent and atrociously dubbed films you're ever likely to see at the late night pictures. Add this all up and you've got something that is part sport, part ancient tea ceremony, part SFX and totally cult.

For centuries, martial arts in the Far East had flourished in semi-secrecy and utter seriousness, as the degrees of contemplation, inner focus and mental tuning required tended to preclude casual interest from the West. Enter the 1970s, and a wave of Hong Kong produced low budget kung fu films hit British and European cinemas – traditionally screened late night on Friday – substituting plot, acting and production values with simple stories of revenge and honour and as much acrobatic, impossibly fast, ludicrously high-leaping, bone-snapping martial arts fight

> "If you plant rice, rice will grow. If you plant fear, fear will grow."
>
> Kwai Chang Caine, from the TV series *Kung Fu*

sequences as could be crammed in. They turned Bruce Lee into an underground then a mainstream hero and suddenly martial arts were on everybody's agenda. Every church hall, school gym or rentable space became a makeshift dojo at least once a week, as teaching kung fu became a nice little earner for anybody with a degree of flexibility and a nifty line in perplexing, cod-Zen philosophizing. It seemed everybody could do a fighting stance and a passable *kiai!*, while playground arguments previously about football teams now centred on which style was more effective. To top it all off, the portly, balding, perennially pyjamaed Carl Douglas got to number one in the UK charts with the single "Kung Fu Fighting".

Central to karate's place in the mainstream was a man who had a background in theatre and dance rather than gruelling martial arts regimes, actor David Carradine. He starred in the TV series *Kung Fu* as Kwai Chang Caine, a mixed race Shaolin monk who roamed the Old West, dispensing Buddhist-ish wisdom and righteous butt-kicking in equal amounts – he'd frequently play a wooden flute. Carradine's ability to perform kung fu-type moves in the regulation fight scenes came from his training in modern dance – at least Steven Seagal and Chuck Norris could actually fight. *Kung Fu* ended in the second half of the decade, and although the BBC tried to keep things going into the 1980s with *The Water Margin* and

Monkey, the karate craze was more or less over by then. One resounding legacy, among the broken bones, torn muscles and dislocated joints from that period is that Great Britain produced a world-beating karate team, winning five consecutive world championships between 1982 and 1990.

Six late night specials

Vintage kung fu films that never quite made it into the mainstream

The One-Armed Swordsman (1967)
The first to make an impact in the UK (it arrived here in the early 1970s), it's a classic tale of a school under attack and a former student returning to seek vengeance, having developed a deadly one-armed sword style in the meantime.

Fist of Fury – aka The Chinese Connection (1972)
Bruce Lee's biggest pre-Hollywood film is all about his murdered master being avenged and the Chinese fighting Japanese oppression, but is fondly remembered for introducing nunchucks to an appreciative UK audience.

King Boxer – aka Five Fingers of Death (1972)
More Chinese–Japanese rivalry and vengeance for slain teachers (regularly recurring themes) in a movie that features a blind man fighting in a darkened room and climaxes with a tournament, thus maximizing the number of fight scenes.

Lightning Swords of Death: Shogun Assassin 2 (1974)
Ogami (the shogun assassin) wanders the beautifully photographed countryside pushing his young son in a pram, despatching potential killers with stunningly choreographed violence. Easily the best of the six *Shogun Assassin* films.

Drunken Master (1978)
Jackie Chan's first starring role brought a degree of comedy to the genre, and introduced drunken boxing, a style that imitates a drunkard's movements, using momentum and fluidity.

The Shaolin Temple (1982)
Not to be confused with the 1976 film *Shaolin Temple*, this one made Jet Li a star as a youngster who learns kung fu in a Shaolin monastery before returning to the palace to kill the tyrannical general that murdered the emperor and assumed the throne.

KAYAKING
Making a splash

Three or four decades ago, if you went kayaking it was probably for one of two reasons: upper body strength development or a serene paddle across a lake or around a fjord. More recently though, kayaking has gone extreme and participation in the sport has been steadily climbing as a much younger age group takes it up. Advances in materials and construction processes have allowed for all sorts of different types and shapes of kayak, which are stronger, lighter and less expensive. Boats can be plastic, inflatable, folding, fibreglass or self-constructed from a wooden kit, while the new, sit-on-top designs are good for beginners. It's now not such a huge investment you can't keep a kayak tucked away in the cellar for occasional use, and it has become far more attractive for the less-dedicated kayaker to get involved with the relatively specialist, potentially dramatic aspects of the sport.

Variations of kayak size and shape have radically redefined the sport's boundaries, allowing traditional aspects to become more exciting and new styles to develop. Increases in strength mean white-water kayaking can now be a more hazardous proposition, leading to a rise in popularity that saw it become an Olympic sport in 2004. Likewise sea kayaking has a greater element of danger, as boats can be built to withstand greater battering, allowing kayakers to take more chances. Slalom kayaks are stable, manoeuvrable, catamaran-type hulls. Sprint kayaks are much harder to keep upright, but, as the name suggests, cut through the water like torpedoes. One new, very popular variant is surf kayaking, in which small boats are ridden on waves like surfboards, but the most exciting development is freestyle kayaking, also known as "rodeo boating". It's done in what are called squirt kayaks – flat, low volume, designed to flip end over end and run while completely submerged. The idea is to pull off as many spectacular tricks and stunts as possible, which include cartwheels, spins and loops which might be performed completely underwater. It's turned kayaking into the aqua equivalent of skateboarding, giving it huge teen appeal.

And what's happened to the sedate paddlers? They're going on the other recent development – kayaking tours and holidays, on which iceberg, coastlines, mountains, rock formations and all manner of natural vistas are viewed from the water.

MARATHON RUNNING
Only the beginning

Running marathons is much like joining a club. Or maybe that should be running *a* marathon is like joining a club, because the vast majority of people who run one do exactly that – run just the one – as they don't do it again. This isn't because they're particularly difficult – it would take most able-bodied people less than six months to reach the point at which they could run a four-hour-something mara-

Freestyle kayaking – or rodeo boating – is not for the faint-hearted.

thon. Also, they get much easier after you've done the first, because you know how to run it and you'll always have a certain level of residual running fitness. "One and done", as the saying goes in the runners' world, happens for two reasons – the process leading up to the event is far more engaging and enjoyable than the event itself; therefore that end becomes little more than a running rite of passage.

It is virtually impossible for anybody who ever gets halfway serious about their running not to think about those 26.2 miles and wonder if they could run them or not. Then people seem to always assume that's what you're doing, and you get asked, "Are you training for the marathon?" so often you end up being almost talked into it. But once you are, it makes a real difference to your approach to your running. Suddenly it has a sense of purpose as you're not just jogging round the streets: you're "in training", for a marathon no less – yes, there's an audible swagger in your voice when you answer, "Sure am!" to the above perennial question. You have an attainable goal that will be reached in a series of achievable steps, clearly charting your running progress and improvement – there are all manner of down-loadable training logs and charts out there. Three or four months of constant improvement, obsessing about things like recovery periods, carb intake and pro-nation will lead up to a punishing day out with a terrific camaraderie, followed by no small sense of achievement and enormous pride as you sit on the tube wearing your medal and your silver space blanket (of course you finished). But then what?

You've done a marathon, enjoyed it as much as you can enjoy running nonstop for four-hours-something, you know you can do it now, when there was always a degree of doubt driving you on through training, you've joined that elite group… so why do it again? The thing to do now is take up ultramarathoning, sometimes called "adventure racing", where races are 50 miles, 100 miles, 150 miles or maybe

After you've run an urban marathon, try a fifty miler. In the Namibian desert.

How to run for miles and miles and miles

"To run marathons, or ultramarathons, it's not a case of psyching yourself up, but freeing your psyche not to stop yourself from doing it. You simply have to lose the mentality that this is some kind of punishment – too many people look on exercise as a punishment for eating, it's not. At all. You don't see little kids saying 'Oh. I ate a donut, I'd better go out and play kick the can for another hour.' That's the difference, they just get on with it.

Runners should have the mentality, go out there with no expectations, do what you want ... do what feels good and the opportunity to push a little bit further to explore a little bit more becomes your incentive to run a little further. Pretty soon you'll be covering the big distances, but you'll be enjoying it too."

Chris McDougall, barefoot ultramarathoner and author of *Born to Run*

24 hours in duration and take place across landscapes like Namibian deserts, South American mountain ranges, Scottish Highlands or Iceland's volcanic terrain. To keep things interesting these races often go through the night and most of the serious ultra runners don't wear shoes.

SKIING

Not so exclusive any more

For a long time, skiing was viewed more as a sporting culture than a cult sport, existing as much as a glittering merry-go-round of fashion parades, nightlife and mountainside après-ski as anything else. It was an image made global in the 1960s and 70s as ski resorts with their dramatic scenery peopled by shapely ski bunnies and suave polo-neck wearing playboys became a lazy movie-world metaphor for wealth and sophistication. The Saint, James Bond, the men from U.N.C.L.E., the Persuaders… would all regularly take to the slopes. If you did actually go skiing while you were, er, going skiing, it was usual for men to imagine they were glamorous 1970s downhill daredevil Franz Klammer, a state of affairs as likely to end with a broken leg as any sort of exhilaration and women being suitably impressed. Then, come the 1990s, budget airlines and snowboarding happened, meaning the whole perception of going on the piste shifted considerably. The influx of younger, noisier, less conventionally cultured individuals, with their baggy clothes and unusual woollen headwear effectively revived the European and American snow sports, by making them something accessible and contemporarily hip.

Ski culture and ski resorts' determination for exclusivity had been suffocating them as, below the snowline, fashions and attitudes were changing and the idea of this louche exclusivity began to look about as relevant and attractive as the Playboy

Mansion or Miss World. It's a mark of how out of touch the ski industry had become that many resorts and runs banned snowboarders. It got to a point, however, where they simply couldn't afford to turn away paying customers, but more than simply new money and a new discipline, it brought a new sensibility that spread over into skiing itself, reinventing the sport for this upstart, adrenaline-fuelled generation. To go along with the three or four types of snowboarding, skiing has developed a similar series of judged, freestyle disciplines that involve twists, tricks and somersaults being performed during jumps, either from ramps (aerial skiing) or on steep, tight runs with man-made bumps in them (mogul skiing). Increasingly, though, resorts are building special terrain parks for freestyle skiers, with routes that include jumps, banked turns and half pipes and decorating them with such urban-associated obstacles as burnt out cars, shells of buildings and food stands.

Evolving out of these parks, as skiers search for more excitement, is the backcountry end of newschool or freeskiing, which takes them on to terrains with natural drops and bumps and obstacles to be negotiated at terrifying speed. Where it sets itself apart from traditional off-piste skiing is these new arrivals will be performing tricks as they hurtle down. There's even an urban version of it, which, similar to skateboarding, involves flights of stairs, roofs, handrails or any other sloping surface. While this may not be recognizable as the skiing of thirty years ago, at least it offers a much bigger choice for après ski carryings on.

Forget the idle rich: these days it's the slacker generation you'll find on the piste.

Six cult sports books

Beyond a Boundary by C.L.R. James (Yellow Jersey)
A beautifully written work that combines Trinidadian James's personal memoirs with sharp social and political commentary and allows his love of cricket to become the vehicle for the break up of the British Empire.

Born to Run by Christopher McDougall (Profile)
This fascinating immersion in the little-known world of ultra-running, courtesy of a lost tribe in Mexico and a handful of American nutcases, contains a clinical dissection of the running shoe industry – apparently they create the problems they go on to solve.

Dancing Uphill by Frances Holland (M&N Publishing)
Put together by Holland's two daughters from his detailed and charmingly written diaries and extensive collection of memorabilia, this is a riveting account of pre-technology competitive cycling, when the hills were just as steep as they are now.

The Boys of Summer by Roger Kahn (Harper Perennial)
A touching, often quite sad, but never less than absorbing fan's story that follows Jackie Robinson's Brooklyn Dodgers to their World Series success in 1955, then meets the same players again in the 1970s and their collective middle age.

The Golf Omnibus by P.G. Wodehouse (Bonanza Books)
Fabulously funny and brilliantly written collection of golfing and golf club stories from the 1920s and 30s, recounted by "The Oldest Member", combining the author's obsession with the game with some of his sharpest character observations.

The Life and Crimes of Don King by Jack Newfield (Harbor Electronic Publishing)
Tracing the rise of the boxing impresario from stomping a man to death in a Cleveland street to out-negotiating African dictators, this paints such a detailed and complex picture of King, there are times when you find yourself rooting for the man who did so much to destroy professional boxing and several boxers.

SUMO WRESTLING
The bigger they are…

There are very few sports in which participants could be instantly identified away from their arena – basketball has its two metre tall short guys, not all darts players have beer bellies, surfers often aren't blond… but there's no mistaking a sumo wrestler. Quite apart from the massive girth and topknot of hair, a professional sumo wrestler will be dressed in a traditional Japanese ankle length robe and sash, and you'll probably hear him coming because of the wooden sandals (*geta*) on his feet. Don't expect this to be any different in the depths of a Japanese winter either: at the risk of a fine, professional sumo's code of behaviour precludes wearing an overcoat.

Dress codes are just one example of an activity that, essentially, hasn't changed for centuries and remains bound by so much Shinto (ancient Japanese belief system) tradition and ritual it seems as much performance art as sporting endeavour – indeed sumo was first developed as entertainment to please the gods thus ensuring a bountiful harvest. The sumo ring (*dohyo*) is made of clay covered with spiritually purifying sand, the canopy above it is styled as the roof of a Shinto shrine, while the four different-coloured tassels represent the seasons, and the purple bunting around it symbolizes clouds. Kelp, cuttlefish and chestnuts will be placed in a new ring (rings are built from scratch for every competition) as offer-

There's a great deal of etiquette involved, which is probably just as well.

ings to the gods for safety. For the ring-entering ceremony, contestants arrive wearing decorative aprons over their loincloths (*mawashi*), and the lowest ranked wrestler comes in first and walks a full circuit before stopping. The others follow, according to rank until the ring is completely encircled, at which point they turn to face inwards, clap once and raise each hand in turn to show they are unarmed.

As the two contestants prepare for a bout, they liberally sprinkle salt on to the ring, for purification, and on their own bodies for protection. Before any actual wrestling can begin, they face off, and spend several minutes lifting their legs as high as possible and stamping down on the ring's surface to scare off evil spirits. The two wrestlers then grapple, and a winner is declared as soon as one man pushes his opponent out of the ring or forces him off balance so something other than the soles of his feet touch the ring, thus the bouts themselves can be over in seconds. All that's left then is *Yumitori-shiki*, the bow-twirling ceremony that closes a contest – a sumo dressed in an ornate ceremonial apron enters the ring from the same side as the winner departed and twirls a longbow, cheerleader style, over his head and around his body. It's a gesture of appreciation to the gods for a successful tournament, and it is considered a great honour to be selected to perform it.

With all this honour, tradition and symbolism, though, comes great pressure to do well, and in a world as introverted as sumo this will only intensify. It's, therefore, not altogether surprising that sumo is currently embroiled in a corruption scandal of a massive scale (see p.237).

SURFING
Come on safari with me

Few sports could even dream about being cultier than surfing. It continues to produce its own fashions and haircuts; has more documentary and drama films made about it than far more popular sports such as, say, football or angling; has given rise to all manner of jargon that has passed into common parlance – "radical, eh dude?" There is also a genre of music called "surf" and it revived the fortunes of hitherto horribly unfashionable wood-trimmed station wagon type cars. Almost uniquely, surfing is a sport driven by the culture that surrounds it, rather than the other way around. You've watched enough California-set detective dramas to hear suspects described as a "surfer type", used as police shorthand for suntanned hippies with strings of beads and long, straggly blond hair, waxed-down board strictly optional. This remarkable state of affairs came about because surfing was introduced to American youth on a wide scale as desirable social experience rather than a serious sport. In fact such is the pervasiveness of the cult on offer here, many become surfers long before they learn to surf, if indeed they ever learn to surf – of the world's most famous sons of the surf, the Beach Boys, only one of them, Dennis Wilson, had ever been on a board.

Surfing had been practised in Peru, Polynesia and Hawaii since ancient times, and when Captain Cook returned from Tahiti on the *Endeavour* in the late-eighteenth century he wrote of witnessing what we now call surfing. It was introduced to California at the beginning of the twentieth century, but remained of little interest until the film *Gidget* in 1959, starring the seventeen-year-old former model Sandra Dee in the title role. An archetypal beach movie, telling the tale of young love in and out of the Californian surf, it sold the idea of a surfer lifestyle to cinema audiences all over the US as the ultimate exercise in teenage glamour. The cult of the surfer was up and riding.

Beach movies became a genre in themselves, with a remarkably straightforward shopping list: music; clear blue skies and balmy nights; good-looking youngsters doing pretty much what they liked while wearing dangerously few clothes; surfboards as an underarm accessory or stuck in the sand as set dressing. A slacker's

The man who showed America how to surf

Or, to be perfectly accurate, how to be a part of surfing without necessarily going in the water. Photographer LeRoy Grannis totally understood the relationship between surfing as a lifestyle and surfing as a sport, and turned his camera inland as frequently as he captured the on-wave activities. As he once told the *Los Angeles Times*: "The Gidget movies struck a chord, suddenly everybody wanted surf – or at least look like surfers."

Grannis had been surfing since he was a teenager, but at age 42, in 1959, he was advised by his doctor to find a less strenuous hobby. Sticking to what he knew, he began photographing both surfers on the waves and on the beach. He was an accomplished and creative photographer (his other hobby – at the time he worked for a telephone company), and developed a waterproof box to allow him to use his cameras and change film in the surf, keeping him close to the action. But as part of the surfing movement himself, he understood the cultural phenomenon and was able to take it seriously as art. This was the first time this had happened, and his pictures were seized upon by newspapers and magazines. These iconic black-and-white pictures had a depth and texture to them that captured every nuance and emotion of the lifestyle. He shot the shacks, the campfires, the cars, the board workshops and, of course, the boys and girls. He recorded everything that went on as it really was, photos that provided substance for the surfing songs that were being written, recorded and proving very popular all across the US.

LeRoy Grannis died in 2011 aged 93. He had been photo editor of *Surfing Illustrated* magazine and co-founded *International Surfing* magazine, he was elected to the International Surfing Hall of Fame as the sport's number one photographer and documentarian. In the early 1970s he retired from surfing and surf photography, and took up the more sedate sport of hang gliding.

Six sick surfer films

Blue Hawaii (Elvis Presley, Angela Lansbury, 1961)
Being an Elvis film, this was as much about the girls as it was about the surf, and it is believed to have given rise to the term "board babe".

Beach Party (Jackie Shannon, Bobby Vinton,1963)
Pretty much what it says on the tin, with the bonus of a Dick Dale sound-track. So successful it heralded a series of similar Party films – *Ski Party*, *Pyjama Party*… you get the idea.

The Endless Summer (Michael Hynson, Robert August, 1966)
To a soundtrack by The Sandals, this documentary feature follows two surfers' journey around every top surf spot on the planet and a few that had not yet been discovered.

Big Wednesday (Gary Busey, Jan-Michael Vincent, William Katt, 1978)
Angst-ridden, metaphor-happy, John Milius-written and directed ode to lost youth epic as three friends reunite to ride that perfect wave.

Point Break (Keanu Reeves, Patrick Swayze, 1991)
Reeves is an FBI agent chasing Swayze and his gang of sky-diving, wave-riding bank robbers, who do their dastardly deeds wearing masks of former US Presidents.

Surf Ninjas (Rob Schneider, Ernie Reyes Jr, 1993)
Family fun as surfing meets martial arts when two L.A. teenagers reclaim an Asian kingdom they never knew they were entitled to.

paradise that, into the 1960s, presented a much cooler, more obviously pleasure-oriented and less ethically encumbered approach to dropping out than following the hippie trail. Surfing as a way of life took on such magnitude in some quarters, that it gained spiritual significance, and one former world champion, Australian Nat Young, attempted to register it as a religion in the early-1970s. With such devotion and promotion came clear cut marketing opportunities and within a decade or so surfing and being a surfer had grown into the multi-million dollar international leisure industry it is today. One in which, at the mere thought of the possibility of perhaps a reasonable wave, apparently sensible individuals will leave the comfort of the landlocked bosoms of their families and drive two hundred miles to the coast. "Let's go surfing now", indeed.

ULTIMATE (FRISBEE)

Pie in the sky

Think American football with a dinner plate-sized plastic disc instead of the actual football and you've got what used to be called ultimate Frisbee – it's now officially known as "ultimate" because Frisbee® is a trademark of the toy company that first marketed the discs. Teams of seven players have to pass the disc between themselves to score touchdowns by having it caught by a team member in the opposition's end zone. When a player receives a pass (catches the disc) they cannot move and have ten seconds to throw a pass; handoffs or running with it are outlawed. A league regulation ultimate field is 100 metres by 36.5 metres, but the game is informally played on the beach, in parks or even in the street (urban ultimate).

But also think American football without the violent behaviour and the pumped up jock attitude. Ultimate is a strictly non-contact sport, indeed so gentle in its ideology the rules go as far as outlawing "win at all costs behaviour", viewing it as contrary to the spirit of the game, and there are no referees as players are entrusted to announce when they have committed a foul. As a result, while the sport is played by men and women, it's a hugely popular mixed activity, with the only stipulation being there must be at least three members of each gender on the field for each team at all times.

Ultimate's relaxed approach to sporting competition comes from its 1960s hippie background. The aerodynamically developed disc had been a hit with college

Ultimate, a sport so well mannered you call fouls on yourself.

students throughout the 1950s in the US, but had a huge marketing push in the following decade after acquiring the brand name. It was sold as the ultimate in serene sporting activity as it sailed languidly through the air and was far more likely to be caught than a hurled baseball or football. The enduring image from this time was positively soothing, as, usually against beautiful Californian skies, hippies at rock festivals or in parks, or surfer types on the beach – men and women – looked ultra laidback as they floated the disc back and forth. There was a point in the US in the 1970s, that ultimate players became an accepted quasi-hippie social type, whose defining sartorial signifier was a headband. The ultimate game was born on a college campus in the late-1960s, and the original leagues and competitions all took place between American universities.

> The name "Frisbee" came about because, in the 1950s, American college students would throw aluminium pie dishes to each other, and the favoured flyer was made by the Frisbie Pie Company of Bridgeport, Connecticut.

Today there's reckoned to be five million regular ultimate players in the US (although no official figures exist), with a growing international popularity that stems from, unsurprisingly, universities all across Europe and in Australia – in the UK, in 2006, ultimate became officially recognized by British Universities and Colleges Sport. Alongside this expansion, an organization called Ultimate Peace uses the game to promote understanding in divided communities around the world: "We focus on fun and education, not politics, using the exhilarating and character building sport of ultimate as our tool."

WRESTLING
The world's a stage

There is probably no other sport, cult or otherwise, in which the notion of Olympian ideals and one contestant pitting themselves against another in a trial of skill and strength is currently so resolutely ignored. And the remarkable thing is professional wrestling seems not to care about this to such a degree it has become an oblique selling point. Once televised wrestling removed the necessity to even *appear* a genuine contest, it could concentrate on hyping up the drama by concentrating on the most spectacular throws, falls and acrobatic moves. It's got to the point at which wres-

> "Wrestling is ballet with violence."
> Jesse "The Body" Ventura, former pro wrestler turned actor turned politician.

tling in the US now refers to itself as "sports-entertainment" rather than simply sports and is talked about alongside the music business and Hollywood as a significant part of the entertainment industry. Indeed it's hardly surprising so many former pro wrestlers go on to acting careers (see opposite) as they've already been acting for years in the ring.

Really though, partly due to such brazenness, it's impossible to knock the pro wrestling industry. It has refined its output to become a modern day equivalent of a pantomime, as the mainstay of the cartoon-like violence perpetrated by men with cartoon names and cartoon costumes is audience participation on a massive scale. Major wrestling events are held in huge arenas, with the crowd surrounding the ring and making the kind of noise that communicates a sense of excitement to the armchair viewer far better than just two blokes grunting and grappling. Of course the audiences are whipped up to responses that are as choreographed as anything that goes on in the ring, with fighters clearly delineated into baddies and goodies as part of ongoing dramas built up over time by promoters and broadcasters. The former are roundly booed and hissed during their introductions, then will ramp that up by performing dastardly deeds before the bout begins – breaking stuff, roaring, chasing people, that sort of thing – and this persists during the contests as they try sneaky foul moves which the ref contrives not to see. The good guys' names and costume designs are much less aggressive, and it's basically their job to get flung about a bit, maybe even get hurt, to elicit as much sympathy as possible before they somehow find the strength to overcome the odds and win the fight. There's a long-term aspect to this too, as organizers promote feuds between fighters in magazines, online and in trailers, with those concerned threatening all sorts of mayhem for slights incurred, building up audience expectation to fever pitch. While ongoing storylines are commonplace, rematches for good guys who have been on the wrong end of beatings guarantee a good turnout. This can be extended over several bouts.

> "It's beating a dead horse if you're talking about saying wrestling's fake. People don't want to hear that. Wrestling's an art – going out there and performing. I'd like fans to remember me as a guy who would go out and entertain them."
> **The late Owen Hart, former World Champion wrestler, who was killed when the harness lowering him in for his entrance failed and dropped him 24 metres into the ring.**

It's pure theatre, but remains so successful because it's very well-produced theatre – wrestlers at bigger bouts have made entrances lasting several minutes and turned up on zip lines, motorcycles, up through the ring in a lift or even in a low-rider car bouncing on its hydraulic shock absorbers. But really, though, when you strip away the big venues, the pay-per-view cable technology and all the special effects, it's not evolved at all from the chap with the megaphone in front of the fairground tent, enticing you to come in and watch a carefully rehearsed "fight".

Six actors with grunt and grappling CVs

André the Giant
All 2.24 metres (7 feet 4 inches) of him stole the show as Fezzik in *The Princess Bride*, but he died in 1993 before getting the chance to build on it.

Dwayne "The Rock" Chambers
Now confident enough about his acting career to have dropped "The Rock" from in between his names. Proved his action hero worth in *The Scorpion King* and showed considerable comedic potential in *Be Cool* and *The Other Guys*.

Hulk Hogan
Probably the smartest wrestler-turned-actor, as he's never done anything other than play his ring persona – friendly tough guy – with no attempt whatsoever to "bring" anything to his roles, which include *Mr Nanny*, *Suburban Commando* and *3 Ninjas*.

Jesse "The Body" Ventura
Was making a name for himself with roles in *Predator*, *The Running Man*, *Demolition Man*, *Batman & Robin* and *The X-Files*. Then, in 1999 he was elected governor of Minnesota. Yet another style of acting?

Rowdy Roddy Piper
Made a name for himself with a substantial role in John Carpenter's cult classic *They Live*, but hasn't done a great deal since.

Stone Cold Steve Austin
Was very funny in *The Longest Yard*, the Adam Sandler remake of *Mean Machine*, and gave a more than creditable account of himself in *The Expendables*.

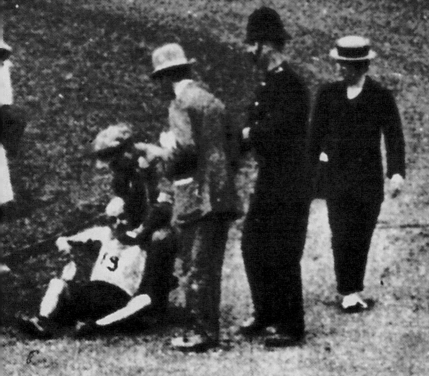

Never Mind
the Olympics

It's really not all about the winning

◄◄ Previous pages: A helping hand to disqualification: Italian Guiseppe Pietri stumbles just metres from the finish of the 1908 marathon (see p.132).

Never Mind the Olympics

"The Olympics – a lifetime of training for just ten seconds."

Jesse Owens

For most of us, the Olympics goes off without a hitch. We watch on television as sporting giants – nations and individuals – come together and provide spectacle as well as proving themselves on the track, field, in the pool and arena. However, there's often more to the Games than gets put on public display...

Huan Huan (child of fire), symbolizing the Olympic flame – one of the five official mascots for the 2008 Bejing Games.

SPORTS THAT NEVER MADE THE OLYMPIC CUT
For demonstration purposes only

At nearly all Olympics there will be one sport that is of demonstration status, inasmuch as the International Olympic Committee has been convinced they should try it out. Usually it is something particular to or popular within the host country, who will use this as an opportunity to sell it to a worldwide audience. Although medals are awarded for demonstration sports, these will not be counted within that Games' medal table. The reason for that is whatever nation proposing the event – usually the host – is seen as having an unfair advantage. The trials fulfil a number of purposes for the IOC, allowing them to establish how popular a sport will be among countries, competitors and spectators, and what are the logistics and costs involved in staging it – as demonstration sports are usually already played in the host country, the infrastructure is there, but would it be practical elsewhere? But the big question, as far as the very modern Olympics is concerned, will be "Is there an international television audience for it?"

> The only time animals have suffered in an Olympic Games was in Paris in 1900, the sole occasion pigeon shooting has been part of the programme.

American football, Aussie rules and boules have all been demonstration sports in the countries where they are virtually a way of life – the US, Australia and France respectively. Likewise such lesser-known events as glima, korfball and pesäpello – all of which can be found in "Around the World in 80 Sports", see p.7 – are huge in their respective countries or regions of Iceland, the Netherlands and Scandinavia and, somewhat understandably, were demonstration sports where they had the deepest roots: glima was paraded at the 1912 Stockholm Games, korfball at the 1920 Antwerp Games *and* the Amsterdam Games of 1928, while pesäpello was demoed at the 1952 Games in Helsinki, Finland. In the aftermath of a Games, the IOC meets to discuss and decide the success of any demonstration. If a sport fails to satisfy any of the above criteria – i.e. it's not practical, economical or doesn't attract sufficient interest from competing nations or viewers – it will never be seen again.

American football was rejected twice, in 1904 and 1932, Aussie rules in 1956 and boules in 1900. Other high profile sports that failed to get taken up include tenpin bowling (1988), motor racing (1900), water skiing (1972) and roller hockey (1992). If events such as those didn't find favour, it is therefore relatively easy to see why the following didn't make it either.

Budo (1964)
A modern Japanese martial art rooted in lifestyle, philosophy and sport rather than aggression or self-defence.

Gliding (1936)
Yes, with planes with no engines.

Kaatsen (1928)
A version of handball, played on grass with teams of three players, that is popular in the Dutch province of Friesland, where the annual tournament is the world's oldest regulated sports event.

Budo: mostly it's the "art of fighting without fighting".

La canne (1924)
A French martial art, in which opponents fight with walking stick-type instruments. Its roots are in the nineteenth century, where it was developed as self-defence for Parisian city gents.

Longue plume (1900)
An outdoor version of Jeu de Paume – the original French version of Real Tennis – that is played on a court of indefinite length.

Savate (1924)
Now known as boxe francaise, a French kickboxing style that evolved from eighteenth century street fighting, employing kicks and punches but not against the shins and knees. Contestants wear padded boots, hence the original name which translates as "old shoe".

Surf lifesaving (1900)
It's about the conventional saving of lives in high surf rather than anything that involves surfboards – the competitive element is very popular in Australia.

Swedish Ling gymnastics (1948)
Developed by a Swedish fencing instructor Pehr Henrik Ling, this was very popular in the US in the late nineteenth century. It was a system designed to promote health, fitness and general wellbeing, with a series of pushing and pulling movements that used no equipment and had their emphasis on callisthenics and posture.

SOMETIMES THEY JUST GET IT WRONG
It's not all fun and Games

Although most Olympic Games and the build-up to them appear to to the world to go off totally smoothly, the people that organize them, the athletes taking part in them and the cities that host them are as prone to mishaps as anybody else.

Take Denver, Colorado, whose administration completely misread the mood of its people. In 1970 the city won their bid for the 1976 Winter Olympics, but rather than celebrate such an award the good citizens feared massive local tax rises would be levied to pay for the event and went into revolt mode. It was objected to with such widespread strength of feeling officials withdrew the bid and the Games were moved to Innsbruck in Austria. Such a rebuttal was completely without precedence, and has never happened again since. The good people of Salt Lake City, Utah, however, were much more accepting when they were awarded the Winter Olympics in 2002. In fact they were so proud the city's administration ran off hundreds of official posters proudly proclaiming the event *THE FIRST*

OLYMPIC WINTER GAMES OF THE MILLENIUM, completely failing to realize how to spell *MILLENNIUM.*

In Nagano, Japan, in the 1998 Winter Olympics, American Ross Rebagliati won the first ever snowboarding gold – it was a new event that year – then had it promptly taken away from him when he tested positive for marijuana. Hey, he's a snowboarder, what did they expect? Remarkably though, his gong was just as quickly handed back to him when officials discovered that nobody had actually put THC (the active ingredient in the cannabis plant) on the official list of banned substances. It probably hadn't crossed anybody's mind to do so as the wacky weed could hardly be considered a performance-enhancing drug in conventional athletic competition, but then they'd never had snowboarders at the Games before.

Not that all competitors needed any help to behave dopily: at the 1972 Munich Olympics, American sprinters Eddie Hart and Rey Robinson were watching the

They've only won one Olympic medal... ever.

Country	Medal	Event	Games
Barbados	bronze	men's 100 metres	Sydney 2000
Bermuda	bronze	heavyweight boxing	Montreal 1976
Cote d'Ivoire	silver	men's 400 metres	Seoul 1988
Djibouti	bronze	men's marathon	Seoul 1988
Guyana	bronze	bantamweight boxing	Moscow 1980
Iraq	bronze	men's lightweight weight lifting	Rome 1960
Kuwait	bronze	mens double trap shooting	Sydney 2000
Netherlands Antilles	silver	sailboard	Seoul 1988
Niger	bronze	heavyweight boxing	Munich 1972
Senegal	silver	men's 400 metre hurdles	Seoul 1988
Tonga	silver	super heavyweight boxing	Atlanta1996
Virgin Islands	silver	sailing	Seoul 1988

How baseball didn't get past first base

Baseball for men and softball for women (underarm pitch, shorter bat, smaller diamond) were voted into the Olympic programme for the 1996 and 1992 Games, respectively, but were unceremoniously removed as events from the 2012 schedule. In the first poll of the International Olympic Committee, squash and karate were elected to replace them from a shortlist that included golf, rugby sevens and roller sports. However, in the second round of voting, both those proposed events failed to gain the required support from two thirds of the 205 National Olympic Committee members, and were subsequently dropped. The IOC then voted not to replace softball and baseball at all.

Baseball was vetoed as an Olympic sport (and softball followed) because, according to International Baseball Federation president Riccardo Fraccari, the International Olympic Committee felt "it needs to change the perception it is solely an American sport." Remarkably, for the five Games that baseball was included Cuba was far and away the most successful nation, taking gold three times and silver twice

Games on a TV in a shop window as they waited for a bus to get to the stadium. Imagine their surprise when their heat came on the screen. They claimed they had been given the wrong start time for their race, and they completely missed it.

Tardier still were the Russian rifle shooting team in 1908. They arrived in London for the Games a week late because Russia still used the Julian calendar instead of the relatively modern Gregorian version and there was a twelve-day discrepancy. Or Soviet rower Vyacheslav Ivanov who, after winning gold at the 1956 Melbourne Olympics, got so excited he threw his medal up in the air. It landed in Lake Wendouree and was never found.

When Princess Anne competed as part of the British equestrian team in the 1976 Olympics in Montreal, the Queen's daughter became the only female athlete not to be given a gender test.

Sometimes the kindness of strangers can do more harm than good to a faltering athlete. When Italian runner Guiseppe Dorando Pietri entered the White City Stadium to finish the marathon in the London Games of 1908, he was way out in front but was so exhausted he got confused and turned the wrong way on to the track. By the time he turned round he'd added two hundred yards to the distance, which proved too much for him as he collapsed just before the finish line, only to be lifted to his feet and helped across it by two officials. As a result of this good deed he was disqualified for taking assistance.

SPORTS THAT GOT IN ONLY TO BE DROPPED
Now you see them, now you don't

Getting past that tricky demonstration stage isn't necessarily the end of it. What follows is a list of sports that were deemed to have made it only to be dumped from the programme at a later date.

Bandy (see p.12)
This event is unusual inasmuch as it was accepted by the IOC after being demonstrated at the Oslo Winter Olympics of 1952, but wasn't actually put on the programmes of subsequent Games because there were no more countries entering than Norway, Finland and Sweden who took part in the demo. It is currently under consideration for inclusion in the 2014 Winter Olympics in Sochi, Russia. This is appropriate as the sport is also known as Russian hockey.

Basque pelota (see p.62)
This was part of the 1900 Games, but as only Spain and France entered there was only one match and, understandably, Spain won gold. It did reappear as a demonstration sport at the 1924, 1968 and 1992 Games, but was never much better subscribed thus has never made it back on to the programme proper.

Cricket
When the Belgian and Dutch teams pulled out of the 1900 Olympics, it left only Great Britain and France. Devon & Somerset Wanderers, who were representing Britain, took gold after a two-day, two-innings, twelve-a-side match, and cricket was never seen at the Games again.

Golf
Individual women's and men's matches and a men's team event were played at the 1900 and 1904 Games, with the US, Great Britain, Greece and Canada competing at the former, but only the US and Canada taking part in the latter. The event is currently under serious consideration for reinstatement for 2016, involving professional golfers.

Pole dancing? Who says it's not a serious sport?

Pole-dancing-for-fitness organizations around the world are petitioning the IOC to have the "sport" included in the Olympic programme for 2016. Not all of the more traditional participants are fully onside with these efforts, though, as many believe removing its titillating essence for Olympic participation will turn it into just another branch of gymnastics, where competitors already established in that field will dominate.

Roque
US version of croquet, played on a hard, walled court (the ball can be played off the walls). In 1904 the US was the only nation to field a team and it was dropped forthwith.

Ski ballet
Pretty much what you think it's going to be – movement, to music, but on skis. Astonishingly has featured as a demonstration sport not once but twice: in 1988 and 1992.

Tug of war
Part of the athletics programme in every Olympics from 1900 to 1920, as club teams rather than national teams were entered it wasn't unusual for one nation to occupy all three podium places.

Water motor sports
Power boat racing was a demonstration sport in 1900 and made it on to the programme in 1908. Unfortunately, adverse weather conditions wreaked havoc with the event and only one boat in each of the three classes of race finished the seventy kilometre course.

MOVEABLE MARATHONS
Because the King wouldn't get out of bed

The marathon wasn't always 26.2 miles; indeed the original distance from the legendary Battle of Marathon to Athens was merely 24 miles. The first Olympic marathon, in 1896, was 40 kilometres (24.8 miles) and from then on it varied between 40 and 43 kilometres. The recognized 26.2 miles distance first came about at the London Olympics of 1908, when the course had been measured at precisely 26 miles from a start just outside the gates of Windsor Castle to the White City Stadium in West London. King Edward VII was due to start the race but because of a heavy cold his doctor advised him not to leave the castle. Which meant the start had to be moved 385 yards (352 metres) inside the grounds, so His Majesty could start the race from his bed in a doorway. However, the finishing line had to stay where it was because it was perfectly in line with the Royal Box, where his wife Queen Alexandria would be sitting.

The Olympic marathon distance changed again for the next two Games, but in 1909 a race called the Polytechnic Marathon took the exact same route from the entrance to Windsor Castle to the White City Stadium. This race became established as an annual event, gaining such prestige within the International Association of Athletics Federations that they decided it should be fixed as marathon distance, rounding it down to 26.2 miles. It's a decision that has lasted much

A right royal cold means they'll run for 26.2 miles.

longer than the White City Stadium. Built for those 1908 Olympics, what was London's premier sporting arena was closed in 1963 and demolished in 1965 to make way for the BBC Television Centre.

AMERICA'S OLYMPIC ANTHROPOLOGICAL DAYS

All in the name of science, apparently

The Berlin Games of 1936 have been roundly condemned for the host government's inherent racism (see p.247). Less frequently discussed but no less abhorrent were the 1904 Olympics, held in St Louis, US. Included on the programme were two Anthropological Days, which were shameful by today's standards and, somewhat ironically, spoke volumes about the so-called civilized society of just over a century ago.

The St Louis sports-meets-science proceedings, gathered men from some of the world's indigenous peoples – pygmies, native Americans, Philippinos, Mexican tribesmen, Patagonians, Japanese Ainu, Syrians… "savages" from all over – who were already in the city as exhibits at the World's Fair. The idea was to have them compete against each other in such allegedly appropriate events as tree climbing, mud throwing and greased pole climbing, in order to document an accurate hierarchy among the world's different races. Then, on the second day, they would compete against white men in various Olympic events to determine exactly how superior the Caucasian race was.

It all began to go wrong when the indigenous people refused to take part, not because it was so potentially humiliating but because they were mostly professional actors and tableau artists with agents who set about negotiating fairly hefty fees. Then once the mixture of cash and coercion had been applied, participation was half-hearted and non-competitive, especially on the second day when the majority thought there was little point in putting too much effort into competition with specialised athletes in events they had no previous experience of.

> At these 1904 Olympics, the crowds attending were segregated into Whites Only and Coloured areas, yet they were the first Games in which an African-American athlete won a medal – George Poage took bronze in the 200 and 400 metre hurdles.

These were the only Games to feature Anthropological Days, and it is believed to have prompted the birth of the modern Olympics as it was so obvious attitudes needed to be dragged out of the Victorian era. However, that didn't stop the founder of the Olympics, the French aristocrat Baron de Coubertin, from shooting himself in the foot with the somewhat prophetic statement that such human rights travesties "will of course lose their appeal when black men, red men, and yellow men learn to run, jump, and throw, and leave the white men behind them."

UNDER THE OLYMPIC FLAG
When is a nation not a nation?

Twice during the history of the Games, athletes have been allowed to compete as individuals rather than as part of a nation's team. In the Barcelona Games of 1992, teams from the Republic of Yugoslavia – Macedonia, Serbia and Montenegro –

And we thought "women weaken legs".*

There are always rumours of all sorts of nocturnal carryings on in Olympic villages – athletes have, in the past, claimed there is status attached to the squad that demands the most condoms to be provided. In Munich in 1972, however, nookie was recommended as part of the British athletes' training regime. One of the team's medical advisers stated that to "maximize the quantity and quality of sleep" before an event, competitors should have around half an hour's sexual activity before they got their heads down.

* Mickey Goldmill, Rocky Balboa's trainer, *Rocky*.

Six things you might not know about the Olympics

Girls allowed
Women competed for the first time in the 1900 Olympic Games in Paris. However, they had to wait over a decade before they could enter the swimming events. That wasn't permitted until Stockholm in 1912.

Hello sailor!
Part of the swimming events at the 1896 Olympics in Athens were two 100 metres freestyle races: the first was contested by just two swimmers, from Hungary and Austria; the second was open only to those serving in the Greek Royal Navy and was called the Greek Sailors' 100m Freestyle. Not to make things too easy for the seafarers, the racers started from a rowing boat positioned offshore in the Bay of Zea.

It wasn't always lycra
The original Olympians – the first contest was in Greece in 776 BC – performed naked in tribute to their manliness, and trained to musical accompaniment because it was as much about culture as athleticism.

Getting away from the wife
Because of the male nakedness on display, married women were banned from watching the Ancient Olympics. However, for exactly the same reason single women were encouraged to attend, as it was thought this could help their search for a husband.

The first Paralympics
These took place in 1948 at Stoke Mandeville Hospital in Buckinghamshire, UK, and were to coincide with that summer's Games being held in London – the term comes from combining the two words "parallel" and "Olympics". Originally these Games were only open to war veterans – World War II had ended three years previously – and the first time they admitted all disabled athletes was at the Rome Olympics of 1960.

You can take something too seriously
After the 1964 Tokyo Olympics, Japanese marathon runner Kokichi Tsuburaya committed hari kari, as the timing of his event in the Games' schedule meant it was his country's last chance to win a gold on the track, and he came third to only manage bronze. He felt particular shame because the Japanese were the host nation.

Just the once

Two nations have only been to the Olympics once, both in 2008. The Marshall Islands, a chain of islands in the Pacific Ocean just north of the Equator and west of the International Date Line, sent five athletes to compete in tae kwon do, swimming and track. And the fourth smallest country in the world Tuvalu, situated halfway in between Hawaii and Australia with a population of 12,000 and an area of only 26 square kilometres, sent three athletes to compete in weight lifting and the men's and women's 100 metres.

were prevented from competing because of UN sanctions against that nation. The International Olympic Committee allowed the athletes affected to participate without representing a country, as Independent Olympic Participants, parading under the five-ringed Olympic flag, which was also raised for their medal presentations (between them they won a silver and two bronzes).

At the Sydney Games of 2000, four competitors from the formerly Indonesian island of East Timor were also admitted as Independent Olympic Participants, again under the Olympic flag. This was because their nation was so newly independent, they hadn't yet formed a National Olympic Committee, although the athletes themselves had been preparing for this for years and were ready to go.

There was another precedent set in 1992 at both the winter and the summer Games, because the Soviet Union had been broken up very late in 1991. While the Baltic nations of Lithuania, Latvia and Estonia competed as their own national teams, the twelve newly created republics of Armenia, Azerbaijan, Belarus, Georgia, Kazakhstan, Kyrgyzstan, Moldova, Russia, Tajikistan, Turkmenistan, Ukraine and Uzbekistan competed as the Unified Team or EUN, which stood for the French language Equipe Unifiée. At the opening ceremonies they paraded as a group under the Olympic flag, but on the podium the flags of the respective medallists' nations were raised.

London is the only city to host the Olympics three times – 1908, 1948 and 2012.

THE TRUE OLYMPIAN SPIRIT
The Cuban who just wouldn't quit

At the 1904 Games in St Louis, in the US, Cuba's marathon representative, Felix Carvajal, was so poor he had to beg for the money to pay his passage to New Orleans, then left himself six months to cover the 1100 kilometres (700 miles) to the Games by running, walking and hitchhiking, doing labouring work for food and lodging along the way. Mostly sleeping rough and eating fruit from trees, the 21-year-old, who spoke no English and had never previously left his rural Cuban community, arrived at the stadium in St Louis quite literally as the marathon was about to begin. He lined up at the start in woollen trousers, a long-sleeved shirt, work boots and a beret – he had no running kit – and the race had to be delayed while, in a concession to the 35 degree heat and on the advice of a fellow contestant, he cut his trousers off at the knees and tore part of the sleeves off his shirt. Carvajal led the field for much of the race, only losing ground when he stopped to eat some apples from a route-side tree, yet he still managed to finish fourth.

Felix Carvajal, St Louis, 1904, modelling his unconventional running kit.

The Legends

Making this sporting life a little
more entertaining

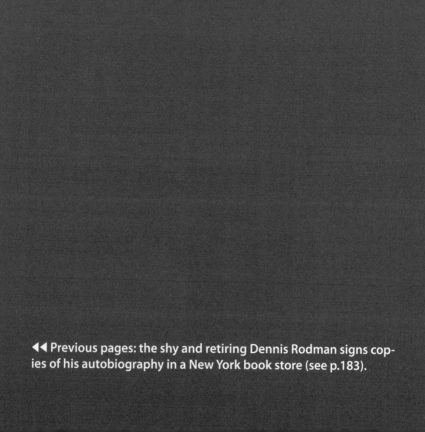

◄◄ Previous pages: the shy and retiring Dennis Rodman signs copies of his autobiography in a New York book store (see p.183).

The Legends

"It's hard to be a diamond in a rhinestone world."

Dolly Parton

There's a world of difference between a Sporting Great and a Sporting Legend. Obviously both need to be very good at what they do, but it's at that point a Great will stop, get an early night and be first to the nets or the driving range or practice courts in the morning. Following that, they'll vanquish an opponent or two, getting the job done with a minimum of fuss – after all, it's the winning that counts. But not in a Legend's world it won't be. Over there, it's as much about how you win as whether you win, and what you had to get past to do it. Even to lose with panache will be its own reward. Then, right after that, there's a good chance a Legend will do pretty much what his or her fans would've done, and blatantly enjoy their time at the top in the only way anybody who's getting paid shedloads of money to do something they enjoy ought to. And sometimes it helps if you're clearly a bit bonkers. Hence this section's selection process, and why Eddie "The Eagle" Edwards, Dennis Rodman, Martina Navratilova, Viv Richards and Eric Cantona are all Legends, and Phil Mickelson, Michael Vaughan and Sebastian Coe will forever be confined to mere greatness.

MUHAMMAD ALI
He ain't got no quarrel with them Vietcong

For a large part of the 1970s, Muhammad Ali's was the best known face on the planet. And quite deservingly so. Irresistible as a boxer; charismatic, charming and wonderfully photogenic as a media subject; morally bold; inarguably humanitarian; and politically committed, he was "the Sixties" a good few years before the social revolution properly got going, and he seemed to mean more to most people than most of the world's elected leaders. Rising to prominence at the same time as the establishing of worldwide telecommunication he became the first global superstar, reaching places even The Beatles and Elvis couldn't get to. Unlike so many sportspeople or entertainment types who take up a cause, Ali remained completely dedicated to his – Islam and opposing the Vietnam war – without letting his day job suffer. He was always shrewd enough to realize that without Muhammad Ali the Greatest, Muhammad Ali the Activist would not gain nearly so much traction. Yet, with the notable exception of the Rumble in the Jungle (see p.196) and his recapturing the world heavyweight title twice, Ali's biggest achievement in boxing is often overlooked – he not only ushered in, he virtually created boxing's modern era.

> "When it comes to ballyhoo, Ali made Barnum and Bailey look like non-starters. He had the incandescent quality of the real star which would have made him famous, even if his gift was knitting not fighting."
>
> Michael Parkinson, legendary UK television chat show host

Just before he renounced the name Cassius Clay, the epic battle he went through with Sonny Liston (see p.271) to take the title for the first time in 1964 was the new world vanquishing the old. Brutally brilliant, Liston represented everything that was wrong with boxing as the US changed along the Kennedy-era guidelines: illiterate, ex-convict, mob-controlled, totally powerless when it came to his career and his finances, discouraged from any dialogue with the media and with hardly any options once he'd finished fighting. The challenger, on the other hand, wanted complete control of his own destiny, picked his own team, made sure the public knew who he was first hand and rode the Civil Rights momentum to promote black pride and self-awareness in a way the white US had to take notice of, but weren't automatically scared by. Here was a boxer, who all people could not only relate to but wanted to engage with. This shone a glamorous spotlight on to the sport, bringing it into everybody's consciousness around the same time as television technology was bringing it into every living room. While Ali became an anti-war icon and a race spokesman, he was also the man who gave boxing respectability.

> "It's not bragging if you can back it up."
>
> Muhammad Ali

"I'm the prettiest thing that ever lived." Would you argue with him?

Importantly, though, he was good enough and canny enough to make sure it kept it. Ali's fights were always events, sucking an entire world in with humour and panache and such a building sense of excitement they became impossible for anybody to ignore – *everybody* had an opinion on or a desired outcome for an Ali fight. Then once he had the millions tuning in, he was skilled enough to put on a show that would always be far more entertaining than the gory slugfests that so often made up heavyweight fights. Much of this new public would have been put off by overt displays of violence: they'd much rather have had a good show instead. And with Muhammad Ali they were guaranteed to get that. He was, and remains, quite simply, The Greatest.

LANCE ARMSTRONG
Tough in the saddle

In 1996, the outstanding young cyclist Lance Armstrong began the year as he'd ended the previous one, by winning races. However, as the year progressed gold medals and podium finishes were turning into sixes and sevens in events he was expected to win. When he finished as far back as twelfth in the Atlanta Olympics road race – an event he was favourite to win for more than just his home crowd support – Team Armstrong knew something was seriously wrong. In October, just two months after those Games, the cyclist was diagnosed as having testicular cancer so advanced it had spread to his lungs, stomach and brain. In the aftermath of the surgery to remove a large tumour from one of his testicles, Armstrong's survival chances were rated at no more than forty percent. He had further surgery to remove a tumour from his brain, and three months of ground-breaking chemotherapy that offered a new cocktail of drugs to avoid the potentially lung-damaging bleomycin. The idea was he'd need all the lung capacity he could get when he resumed his cycling career.

Before the end of 1997 he was training again and the following year, with the cancer in remission, he was back on the international racing circuit, a comeback trail that had one specific goal – the 1999 Tour de France. That Armstrong, the poster boy of American cycling, had completely beaten testicular cancer was a story in itself, but it was nothing compared with the next chapter. He finished first on that Tour, winning four stages and beating his nearest rival by nearly eight minutes. Much more than that, though, this was the first of Armstrong's seven consecutive Tour de France wins, two more than the previous record. After the last of them, in 2005, he promptly announced his retirement from professional cycling.

> "Yellow wakes me up in the morning. Yellow gets me on the bike every day. Yellow has taught me the true meaning of sacrifice. Yellow makes me suffer. Yellow is the reason I'm here."
>
> Lance Armstrong on how seriously he takes the Tour leader's jersey

Self-inflicted idleness didn't seem to suit Lance Armstrong much though. After three years campaigning to raise awareness for testicular cancer and squiring such glamorous women as Sheryl Crow, Tory Burch and Kate Hudson, he realized he was at his most effective in the saddle. In 2008 he began another comeback with one eye on the 2009 Tour, and he prepared for it by taking part in the Australian event, the Tour Down Under. Although he finished way back in the field, the turnout to the race – to see Armstrong – was huge, and as a result many got to hear the cyclist's campaigning message. The Australian government pledged A$ 4 million to build a cancer research centre. Armstrong came third in that 2009 Tour de France and was clearly no longer the force he once

Lance Armstrong in that coveted yellow jersey on the 2004 Tour de France.

had been, but he continued to compete, using international events as a platform for his work raising consciousness as regards testicular cancer. He has stated an intention to retire for good after the 2011 Tour Down Under.

SIR IAN BOTHAM

All round good guy

In the 1970s and 1980s Ian Botham was a cricketing bad boy, upsetting the Establishment and a fair amount of the UK media; in 2007 he became Sir Ian Botham, the knighthood adding to the OBE he received in 1992. And it's the circumstances of these two situations that made him so popular among not just cricket fans but people in general – he was, and probably still is, the first English cricketer to have a widely recognizable profile outside the game and continue to enjoy a non-cricketing fanbase. Here was a cricketer gloriously unhindered by tradition. He did and said much of what those looking on would like to have done and always took responsibility for his actions, even if that wasn't always the sensible option.

> "So you want to play sport; fine. Everyone wants to play sport, but what are you really going to do?"
>
> Sir Ian Botham's careers teacher.

If Ian Botham had a problem with a colleague he seldom held back, and made his displeasure with plodding England opener Geoff Boycott very public; when Somerset, his county, sacked Viv Richards (Botham's best friend) and Joel Garner, Botham rowed mightily with captain Peter Roebuck, and walked out to join Worcestershire. And his feud with Ian Chappell was as long lasting as it was legendary. The former Australian captain was as forthright as Botham himself and they clashed – physically – in a Melbourne bar when Botham took offence at the anti-English remarks Chappell was making to his friends, and knocked him off his bar stool. Years of animosity followed, most recently with the twosome sharing a commentary box but refusing to speak to each other. Then it kicked off again during the 2010 Ashes series, when the pair squared off in an Adelaide car park to be separated by their respective production teams. Add this to the suspension for smoking dope, much-publicized adultery and his playing professional football for lowly Scunthorpe United – his local team – during the winter and it's no wonder he became the country's best-loved sportsman. What sealed his knighthood were the very Bothamesque contributions to charity. Over the last 25 years he has walked ludicrous distances – the 1,407 kilometres (874 miles) from Land's End to John O'Groats a mere stroll – showing how fit and strong he remains, while raising huge amounts of money in aid of Leukaemia Research. To date his walks have earned the charity over £12 million.

Of course none of this would have counted for very much if Botham wasn't probably the best all-round cricketer England has ever produced. In an era when the national side seemed to be more about not losing rather than actually winning, Botham crashed into the team with an all-or-nothing mixture of sheer power and magical inspiration, grabbing games by the scruff of the neck, determined to put the opposition on the back foot – like the 1981 Test series against Australia, which became known as Botham's Ashes (see p.285). He finished his Test career with 5200 runs, at an average of 33.54 and including fourteen centuries and 383 wickets, at an average of 28.4 and including 27 five-wicket innings and four ten-wicket matches. While these wouldn't be brilliant figures for a specialist bowler or batsman, from the same person they were phenomenal. But the real achievement was that interest in cricket went through the roof every time "Beefy" Botham stepped on to the pitch.

Sir Ian Botham's international statistics

	Tests	ODI*
Matches	102	116
Runs	5200	2113
Batting average	33.54	23.21
100s	14	0
50s	22	9
Highest score	208	79
Wickets	383	145
Bowling average	28.40	28.54
Five-wicket innings	27	0
Ten-wicket innings	4	0
Best bowling	8 for 34	4 for 31

* One day international

ERIC CANTONA

Seagulls… trawlers… kung fu fighting…

The single act for which most football fans will remember Eric Cantona will be his leaping into the stands at Crystal Palace's ground, having just been sent off for violent conduct, to launch a flying kung fu-style kick into the chest of supporter Matthew Simmons. He then followed it up with a flurry of punches and was fined £30,000, stripped of the French national team captaincy and banned from playing any sort of organized football anywhere in the world for eight months. Years later Cantona referred to it as his favourite memory from English football, and nothing about it should have surprised anybody, given the midfielder's history before he arrived at Leeds United in 1992. He had served bans in France for, among other offences, fighting with team-mates, kicking the ball at a referee, throwing his boots at a team-mate's head and tearing up his shirt after being substituted. At one French Football Federation disciplinary hearing, he got a one-month ban increased to three, after calling each member of the panel, in turn, an idiot. He

Eric Cantona: an artist off the ball as well.

managed to get himself barred indefinitely from the national team after giving a post-match interview in which he famously described the team's coach, Henri Michel, as a "sack of shit".

In truth, however, once he arrived in English football, Eric Cantona's transgressions only serve to put his on-field achievements in a sharper perspective by allowing us to contrast both Leeds and Manchester United with and without him. In his only year with Leeds, 1991–1992, they won the old First Division title; then upon moving to Manchester United, Cantona's addition to a lacklustre side brought them consecutive championships in 1993 and 1994. It is equally significant that in 1995, when he was suspended, they didn't win the titles, but were back on top when he returned in 1996. It's during the next season as Manchester United's captain that Cantona made his most significant contribution to the club: he took responsibility for the group of youngsters that had come in to the team – David Beckham, Paul Scholes, Gary Neville and so on – and schooled them in the notions of hard work, never giving up and maintaining discipline.

He retired after that season, turning his hand to acting – mostly bit parts and TV commercials – directing a short film, contributing spoken word soliloquies to an album by French rock group Dionysos and getting serious about the painting he had dabbled in when in Manchester. An eccentric artistic bent wasn't exactly unexpected from the man whose unique philosophizing included such ramblings as, "I am searching for abstract ways of expressing reality, abstract forms that will enlighten my own mystery" *and* "I am mistrustful of people who are constantly over-intellectualizing."

Thankfully, Cantona also developed a passion for beach football, captaining then coaching the French national team and taking them to third place in the 2006 FIFA Beach Soccer World Cup. He returned to football proper in 2011 by joining New York Cosmos as director of soccer – kind of head coach and strategist – and is no doubt stalking their training pitches with a ramrod-straight back (he'd done national service in France), shirt collar standing proud underneath a foreign legion-style haircut, crashing volleys past hapless American goalkeepers.

BOB CHAMPION & ALDANITI

A genuine win double

There was a degree of determination and refusal to be written off about this pairing of man and horse that overcame apparently insurmountable odds to win the biggest prize in the English National Hunt calendar. Two years before their 1981 Grand National triumph, Champion had been given no more than a few months to live and the horse was virtually waiting outside the knackers' yard. In 1979, after returning to Britain from a successful period riding in the US, Yorkshire jockey Bob Champion went to see his doctor. Not that he felt ill or anything – the day before he had ridden a winner – but he wanted a diagnosis on a suspicious testicu-

John Daly's gut may be gone, but the strides remain the same.

lar lump which turned out to be a fairly well-developed case of cancer. Treatment was not nearly as advanced back then as it is now, and the jockey was given a less than fifty percent chance of living beyond three or four months, with his only hope being an aggressive cocktail of very new drugs. And he had to start taking them that day.

Champion signed up for the chemotherapy, and, even if he survived, nobody gave him a chance of riding competitively again, but rather than convalesce, he threw himself back into training. His plan was almost to pretend nothing was wrong, so he set himself the goal of the 1980 Grand National, a race he'd ridden in eight times previously, but had yet to make it into the winners' enclosure. He never made it to that race, as the rigours of training proved too much for his recovering body – one of the side effects of the drugs was damage to the linings of the lungs – but it was during this period, at a meeting in Leicester, that he was paired up with Aldaniti, a chestnut gelding that had been similarly discounted as a contender. The horse had been rejected by its mother, was chronically undernourished until learning to drink milk from a bottle, then when eventually he started racing, he suffered a series of leg injuries, including a broken hock bone that would have finished most horses. Indeed, unable to even train at one point and getting weaker by the day, Aldaniti's owners seriously considered having him put down. Champion, however, immediately recognized a kindred spirit in the horse and was quoted as saying, after that first race together, "This horse will win the Grand National one day."

He wasn't wrong. After a bad start, it was as if Aldaniti sensed this was his one big chance, and the two came together in a near faultless display of running, riding and jumping that saw them streak past the strongly backed favourite Spartan Missile, to take the race by four and a half lengths. This historic victory turned the two of them into instant celebrities, which Champion used to raise millions for The Bob Champion Cancer Trust, although the horse was every bit as big a draw as he was for personal appearances. Bob Champion retired from racing in 1983, having ridden over five hundred winners, while Aldaniti died of old age in 1997.

JOHN DALY
The blue-collar golfer

Amid the eating, the drinking, the divorcing, the gambling and the fearsome trousers, it's sometimes easy to forget that John Daly is actually a very good golfer. His unique backswing – bringing the club so far past parallel to the ground it can look like his head is on back to front – has brought him eleven Driving Distance titles, and frequent tee shots of over 350 yards. His delicate short game and subtle touch around the greens are surprising for such an oafish individual, but his skills have been sufficient to win him the US PGA Championship in 1991 and the British Open in 1995. The former he won at age 25, after only gaining entry when somebody dropped out and the other eight reserves couldn't make it. He drove all night to get there for the start, had no practice round, yet shot 69 on the first day, from where greatness beckoned. He opted instead for the route marked Legend.

As professional golf began trying to convince the outside world its players were "athletes", a three-hundred-pound Daly would stride the fairways puffing on snouts, wolfing down McDonalds and chasing the burgers down with the seemingly ever present economy-sized Diet Coke. Indeed, it was this constant sipping that came to define John Daly as much as what he achieved on the course, when in 1993 he confessed to drinking a bottle of Jack Daniels a day. Nearly twenty years later, after a succession of alcohol-fuelled misdemeanours – including teeing off from a beer can at a Buick Open – some hefty PGA penalties and several spells in rehab, he claims to be off the sauce for good. However, an NFL footballer he met in rehab told him giving up drinking would be relatively simple once he found something else he could devote himself to. John Daly found gambling and where other golfers measured their careers against what they'd earned, Daly's yardstick seemed to be how much he'd forked out in casinos, which is estimated at between $50 million and $60 million. The single most spectacular illustration came after he lost the 2005 World Golf Championship in a play-off against Tiger Woods: he flew to Las Vegas, where he converted his $750,000 prize money into a $1.65 million deficit in less than five hours. Then after the casinos have finished with him, there are the four ex-wives and the three children they have between them to be considered, and it will come as no surprise that on Daly's first album there's a song called "All My Exes Wear Rolexes". Yes, that's right: John Daly has released two albums of "semi autobiographical" country songs, entitled *My Life* and *I Only Know One Way*. They feature guest appearances by Darius Rucker and Willie Nelson and other tracks are "I'm Drunk, I'm Broke", "Hit It Hard" and "Blue Collar Golfer".

Currently considerably slimmer after gastric band surgery, the now teetotal John Daly has his own reality TV show. The Golf Channel's *Being John Daly* followed him, fly-on-the-wall-style, as he plotted his 2010 comeback and the first episode was described by *The New York Times* television critic as being "haphazardly organized".

EDDIE THE EAGLE

He changed the rules. Literally.

It's not difficult to think of Eddie the Eagle as little more than a bespectacled buffoon, with a comedic, ironic nickname, who became a metaphor for the heroic loser. And it's just as easy to forget – or to never have realized – that Michael Edwards ("Eddie" was merely an abbreviation of his surname) would never have reached the position from which he came to epitomize the Plucky British Loser, had he not been British ski jumping record holder, which was what qualified him for those 1988 Calgary Winter Olympics in the first place. Eddie was also ranked

Six other singing sports stars

Mark Butcher
England cricketer Butcher used to take his guitar on tour with the team and hold singalongs in his hotel room. On retirement in 2009 he cut an album entitled *Songs from the Sun House*.

Joe Frazier
The heavyweight boxer had a soul group called Joe Frazier & The Knock-outs through most of his boxing career, and although his vocals left plenty to be desired, they were seldom without a gig. Can't imagine why.

Hoddle & Waddle
Billed as Glenn & Chris, their performance of their sole single "Diamond Lights" will never be forgotten by anybody who's ever seen it. If for no other reason, than because Hoddle (Glenn) clearly didn't want to be there.

Carl Lewis
Never the shrinking violet, record-breaking athlete Carl Lewis recorded the soft funk album *Modern Man* in 1987. The video for one of its singles, "Break It Up", regularly features on Worst Ever lists.

Andy Murray
A quick trawl of YouTube reveals the Scot needs little encouragement to start singing, but his rapping on fellow tennis pros the Bryan Brothers' single "Autograph" is on the same level as footballer John Barnes' unfor-gettable "Anfield Rap".

Jacques Villeneuve
His album of mellow, largely acoustic rock, *Private Paradise*, reveals a surprisingly sensitive singer/songwriter with a moody, moving voice.

in the world's top ten amateur speed skiers, and held the world ski stunt jumping record for clearing ten cars and six buses. But it was always the circumstances of his competitive life that were far more interesting.

A keen amateur speed skier, when he failed to make it into the British men's downhill team for the 1984 Winter Olympics in Sarajevo, he turned his attention to ski jumping simply because he'd have more chance of getting to the next Games. He wasn't wrong in this respect. At the 1987 World Championship, he finished 55th, but as Britain's sole representative in this event he qualified to become the nation's first ever Olympic ski jumper. It hadn't been an easy four years up until then. With no sponsorship whatsoever, Eddie's journey had been a combination of improvization and kindness from ski jumpers around the world, plus whatever plastering jobs he could get wherever he happened to be. He moved to Lake Placid in the US, where he had to wear several pairs of socks to stop his borrowed boots from flapping about; he slept in a scout hut while training in Switzerland; he worked in the kitchens of the hotel he stayed in with the US team when he trained with them in Colorado; at one international competition the Italian team gave him a new helmet because his was held on with string; at another the Austrians fur-

Six inspiring sports films

Rocky (Sylvester Stallone, 1976)
Stallone's greatest talent was that he knew how to keep things simple and here he wrote a touching tale that pushed audience emotion in uncompli-cated directions that were impossible not to go along with.

Chariots of Fire (Ian Charleson, Ben Cross, 1981)
A textbook example of how music should work in a movie – without the Vangelis soundtrack, this inspiring epic would be not much more than a straightforward film about two athletes running for different religious-based reasons.

Field of Dreams (Kevin Costner, James Earl Jones, 1989)
Ray Kinsella (Costner) finds himself as he turns one of his cornfields into a baseball diamond to attract a team of ghostly baseball players. It's impossible not to be swept along.

Any Given Sunday (Al Pacino, James Woods, Cameron Diaz, 1999)
Director Oliver Stone at his most bombastic, and anybody who fails to be moved by Al Pacino's locker room speech ought to check they've still got a pulse.

Bend It Like Beckham (Parminder Nagra, Keira Knightley, 2002)
Totally enjoyable hokum, that has brilliant footballer Jess (Nagra), taking on the boys, her parents and her emerging sexuality to hit the back of the net on all fronts.

Seabiscuit (Jeff Bridges, Tobey Maguire, 2003)
Depression era saga of three men, whose associations with each other through unfancied racehorse Seabiscuit bring redemption from their very different difficulties. And, of course, the horse becomes a winner.

nished him with new skis; but the most bizarre episode was when a Finnish coach put him up in a functioning lunatic asylum in Kuopio. He had been invited to Finland to train with their squad, and one of the trainers was a painter and decorator working in the high security hospital. Eddie helped out plastering in return for his own cell – apparently not padded.

He arrived on the world stage in Calgary sporting glasses thick enough to correct his chronic long-sightedness – they would mist up at altitude, meaning he frequently jumped blind – nine kilos heavier than anybody else in the field and with a £7000 bank loan. By the end of the Games he'd come last in both the seventy-metre and ninety-metre jumps, acquired the enduring epithet and won over TV audiences everywhere, also, it seems, Olympic president Frank King who appeared to be breaking protocol and alluding to a particular athlete when his closing speech mentioned "soaring like

> "I had a number of marriage proposals, all that stuff. Women used to write to me and say: 'If you are ever in the Birmingham area, pop over.' Weird. Sadly my sister used to run my fan club, so I never saw a lot of those. She whisked them out!"
>
> **Eddie the Eagle thinks back to 1988.**

an eagle". The huge crowd responded with a spontaneous chant of "E-ddie! E-ddie!" He returned to the UK to a life of celebrity, a book and a video – *On the Piste* – a number two hit in Finland with the phonetically learned song "Mun Nimeni On Eetu" (My Name Is Eddie) and a small fortune made and lost.

Today, the Eagle still skis, has a law degree, a radically altered appearance following corrective optical surgery and a jaw realignment operation, runs a building restoration firm and remains in demand on the minor celebrity circuit. But he never made it to the Olympics again. Following his Calgary "triumph" organizers decided such a thing shouldn't reoccur and changed the qualification rules: entrants had to be placed in the world's top fifty or in the top thirty percent. Try as he did for the next three Olympics, he didn't make the cut, and in the US these qualification requirements are still known as the "Eddie the Eagle Rule".

BOBBY FISCHER
Grandmaster, check faster

It is still very likely that Bobby Fischer is the only chess player most people could name, and twenty years after his last high profile match, he remains the best player the world has ever seen. Yet at the time of his death in 2008, this supremely gifted individual was almost as well known for his bizarre behaviour than his way with the kings and queens.

Born in Chicago, in 1943, but raised in Brooklyn, Fischer took up chess at the age of six, became totally engrossed in it, and by thirteen he was the youngest ever

US Junior Champion. It was in the following year, 1957, that he really began to make his mark, achieving a Chess Master rating – then the youngest American to do so – and retaining his Junior title. He then became the youngest player to win the US Open Chess Championship, a competition he made his own by winning eight times between 1957 and 1967. In the 1964 tournament he achieved the perfect score of 11–0, the only time this has ever happened. The only reason he didn't win the 1961/62 tournament was because he didn't enter.

> "When I was aged eleven, I just got good at it."
> Bobby Fischer on the secret to his chess success.

At the age of fifteen Fischer became the youngest ever Chess Grandmaster, and by the time he was sixteen he had dropped out of school to play chess full time, was living by himself and had his first chess book published. But as he moved out of his teens and was starting to dominate world chess, his behaviour was becoming increasingly odd away from the board. In spite of his standing and the prize money he must have accumulated, Fischer rarely spent anything on clothes and was once refused entry to the prestigious Manhattan Chess Club for looking too scruffy. When he didn't win the 1962 Candidates Tournament (the World Championship eliminator), he accused the Soviet participants of colluding against him – his refusal to compete in it again actually led to a rule change. That same year he renounced his Jewish background and joined the cult-ish Worldwide Church of God. In later years he would deliver vitriolic anti-Semitic rants in radio interviews, became fascinated with Hitler and linked with white supremacist movements.

> "Chess is life. All I want to do, ever, is just play chess."
> Bobby Fischer on the secret to maintaining that success.

By 1971 he was at the top of the world rankings by the biggest ever margin, (remaining there for a total of four and a half years) and was gearing up for his epic 1972 tussle with the great Boris Spassky and the World Chess Championship crown. After that things began to go seriously downhill. Fischer never defended

Bobby Fischer raises the game

In 1996 Fischer attempted to launch a variation of chess he'd named Fischerandom Chess in which the back row pieces are not placed in their regular positions, but each player can shuffle them so they could start from anywhere behind the pawns. He claimed it meant a far more skilful game, as much less depended on rehearsed opening gambits. It failed to catch on, because, many in the chess world believe, it made the game too difficult for all those without Bobby Fischer's genius for it.

his title, being stripped of it in 1975, and played only one more high profile competitive game. This was a lucrative but unsanctioned rematch with Spassky, held in the then Yugoslavia in 1992, for which he is said to have earned $3.5 million. By now Fischer was in serious trouble with the the taxman and never returned to the US, moving all over the globe. He was finally arrested in Japan in 2004 as he tried to board a plane with a US passport that had been revoked in response to his tax debts and his regular anti-American radio broadcasts from different countries. After eight months in jail – he was stateless so couldn't be deported – the Icelandic parliament voted to give him full citizenship, and he lived there until he died in 2008.

MAURICE FLITCROFT
His first ever round of golf was at the 1976 Open

Crane operator and sometime comedy high diver Maurice Flitcroft used to announce himself as "Golfer Extraordinary", and in many ways he was exactly that. In 1974, after watching a match play contest on television, he became enamoured with the sport, bought half a set of clubs by mail order, found a battered red vinyl golf bag in a second-hand shop and would thrash around in open land near his family home in Barrow-In-Furness, Cumbria. Two years later, having never played an actual round of golf anywhere, he entered the Open – UK golf's most prestigous competition – completely unphased by the prerequisite that every amateur present their handicap certificate at the qualifying round, and the chain-smoking 46-year-old simply ticked the box marked "professional" and nobody thought to challenge him.

Astonishingly, Flitcroft made it on to the first tee, by virtue of the fact he got lost on the way to the course and arrived too late for a practice session that surely would have raised a few eyebrows. A cigarette ever-present in his mouth, he was wearing a fishing hat and plastic sandals and, having acquired a few more clubs, had one over the maximum of fourteen in that red bag. In spite of his first drive being, as he said afterwards, "not a total disaster, it could have hit an official on the head", it only travelled a few metres and he

> "It weren't a fair reflection of my play."
>
> **The ever-optimistic Maurice Flitcroft looks back on his record breaking 121.**

carded a horrendous 121 – 49 over par, the worst score in the history of the Open. It made newspaper front pages the next day. "British Open Chump" was one headline, and earned him a lifetime ban from all Royal & Ancient golf courses. Some professionals playing that day demanded their entrance fees back to compensate for this mockery of all they held dear.

Not that any of this seemed to worry Flitcroft. He may have been thrown off the course, but it was far from his final appearance in the competition. In fact he saw the R&A regulation change to introduce regional qualifiers was seen as a bit of a

The truly amazing Bethany Hamilton.

challenge. He continued to enter the competition under increasingly bonkers pseudonyms including Arnold Palmtree, James Beau Jolly, Count Manfred Von Hoffmenstal and Gene Pacecki (both a pun on pay cheque and a tribute to US postal worker Walter Danecki who had bluffed his way into the Open in the 1960s and achieved the previous highest score). He'd often turn up in disguise, favouring curious headwear and droopy moustaches coloured with food dye, as R&A secretary Keith Mackenzie became obsessed with keeping him out and at one point hired a handwriting expert to analyse entry forms.

Flitcroft made it into the competition a few times, but never completed a round: in 1984 he was banished after a 63 over the first nine holes caught Mackenzie's attention, and in 1990, at a mere three over par after two, he was chased off the course after being rumbled thanks to his ludicrous American accent. But while the Royal & Ancient may not have been too impressed with his efforts, he was an international celebrity and the Blythefield Country Club in Belmont, Michigan, has an annual prize named after him. The Maurice G. Flitcroft Member-Guest Tournament is so named because the club believes more of their golfers can relate to this chancer from Cumbria than they can to, say, Phil Mickelson. In this spirit the event uses one green with two holes and another with a twelve-inch diameter cup.

BETHANY HAMILTON
Gnarly, or what?

In October 2003, thirteen-year-old Bethany Hamilton was already building a reputation for herself in the surf competitions around her native Hawaii. At around 7.30 in the morning on the last day of that month, after paddling out from Kauai's North Shore, she and some friends were idling on their boards waiting for a wave. Bethany had her left arm trailing in the ocean. She noticed a shape in the water next to her, felt a sharp tug and watched the water around her board turn red. It was then she realized the "shape" was a fourteen-foot tiger shark, that had severed her arm about five inches above her elbow and bit an enormous semi-circular chunk out of her board. She called to her friends, who pulled her back to shore, and it was only after they'd tied off the wound with a tourniquet from a surfboard leash that Bethany fainted.

Her friend's father drove her to hospital, where, by coincidence, her father was being prepped for knee surgery. His daughter took quite literally his place on the operating table, where the remains of her arm were amputated to just below the shoulder and she was given a series of blood transfusions after losing approximately sixty percent following the attack. After a mere six days in intensive care, she was strong enough to leave the hospital and go home.

More remarkable than simply surviving the attack and the relative speed of her recovery, though, was that within four weeks, Bethany was back in the same waters relearning how to surf. Rather than appearing in any way traumatized, her biggest obstacles were coming to grips with her balance on the board – an arm is a significant amount of the body's weight – and with how paddling out now meant much greater use of her legs. Initially she used a longer, thicker and slightly wider board for greater stability. Within four months she was back on a competition-style short board, and two months later she was competing again.

Faced with enormous demand from the US media, if the Bethany Hamilton saga had stopped there it would have been an inspirational story, but that wasn't what she was about. She'd surfed since she could walk and she saw no reason why she shouldn't continue her dream to become the best in the world. By 2005, she had won the US Junior Championship and in 2008, at age eighteen, she turned pro and set off on the World Qualifying Series. This was a punishing schlepp around the world's surf competitions, trying to rack up enough points to become one of the sixteen surfers taking part in the following year's Association of Surfing Professionals World Tour. She finished just three places outside qualification, while her friend Alana, the girl who was out with her at the time of the attack, made it into the elite sixteen. At the time of writing, Bethany is still competing, still just outside the World Tour, but confident qualification is only a matter of time.

TONY HAWK
Chairman of the board

If anybody asked most people to name two famous skateboarders, and Michael J. Fox wasn't to be counted, they'd probably get no further than "Tony Hawk, and, er…" This is because Hawk is the man who took the marginal, almost deliberately exclusively cool sport of skateboarding, and introduced it to youngsters everywhere as mass market and accessible, yet still somehow left-field and the epitome of cool. He was shrewd enough to recognize the *idea* of skateboarding was as important as actually getting on a board, and promoted it as much as an urban youth culture as a sport in itself. His clothing and footwear companies promoted skateboarding style; his boards were a "must have", even if you were just going to carry one around under your arm; his show reel DVDs presented skateboarding like a rock video and let you rewind the tricks and stunts; the Boom Boom HuckJam stage show (and later TV extravaganza) further reinforced the music and skateboard connection with punk or heavy metal bands providing a live soundtrack for choreographed stunt riding by skateboarders, BMXers and motocross bikers. Most of all though, he was

> "I love the fact that there is now a skate park in almost every city, but it will always have a rebellious or underground edge to it because it is based on individuality."
> **Tony Hawk**

the first to seriously develop skaters' point of view video games allowing all the thrills of riding without the danger of falling off on to concrete. It all established an international *prêt-à-porter* skateboard lifestyle for kids of all ages.

Of course none of this could have counted for too much if Tony Hawk hadn't been very, very good at skateboarding. Tony Hawk was simply the best skateboarder the world has ever seen. So good, in fact, his first sponsorship deal came in when he was just twelve years old. By fourteen he'd turned professional and during the thirty-odd years before he retired from competition, he amassed an astonishing haul of gold medals, championship titles, trophies and X-Games triumphs. He took skateboarding into new dimensions, thanks to a relentless drive to improve every performance and stretch the boundaries of the sport by dreaming up and then perfecting a vast array of new tricks, both on the vert ramp (the large U-shaped ramp which has high sides that go straight up into the air) and on everyday objects like steps, hand rails, walls, tables and rubbish bins. He'd then give them names – Stale Fish, Backside Pop Shove-It, Madonna, Frontside Hurricane, Saran Wrap and Indy 540 are all Hawk's. But the one that ensures his place in skateboard legend is the 900, a trick that involves coming off the vert ramp and spinning two and a half times (900 degrees) before landing. It's so difficult it was said it could never be done. After years of practice, during the 1999 X-Games Hawk became the first skateboarder to nail one in competition, on his eleventh attempt of the afternoon. It was a full five years before anybody else managed one.

GIL HERON
You may have heard of his son

There's a reason why jazz poet, musician and writer Gil Scott-Heron's Scottish gigs have always been so enthusiastically attended, and fans are given to turning up wearing the green and white hooped shirts of Celtic FC: his dad, Gil Heron, is one of Celtic's most vividly and fondest remembered players. Although his time at the club was relatively short – just one year – he made a huge impression among not only those supporters but on Scottish football fans in general.

Born in Kingston, Jamaica, in 1921, his family moved to Canada when he was very young, and it was in the Royal Canadian Airforce during World War II that he began to take sport seriously. Not very big, he was extremely fast and blessed with lightning reflexes. He excelled at boxing and sprinting before concentrating on soccer, at which by demonstrating superb ball control – at speed – he began to make his mark as a winger. Following demob in 1945, he turned professional with the Detroit Wolverines in the newly established North American Professional Soccer League – yes, the USA tried to get serious about soccer at the end of the war – and won the title, with Heron as the league's top scorer with 28 goals. The league collapsed during the following season, it was never that secure: and had only been set up as a response by a miffed millionaire when turned down in his application for a franchise in the existing American Soccer League. Which is where Gil Heron ended up, as he was seized upon by the Detroit Corinthians, and spent three years with them as their top goal scorer in each season. It was while playing for them that he was scouted by Celtic FC, who were on one of their regular close season tours of North America, during which it wasn't unusual for them to come home with a new signing or two.

It's testament to Heron's abilities that Celtic weren't actually playing Corinthians, simply that they had heard about this outstanding talent and the scouts had made the journey up to Detroit to watch him in action. They weren't disappointed, invited him to Scotland for a trial and he made his debut in Glasgow in August 1951, as the club's first black player. He immediately won the fans over with a goal in the 2–0 win over Morton and very soon his speed earned him the nickname the Black Arrow. Less impressed were referees and linesmen, who would often rule him offside simply because they didn't believe anybody could cover the ground he could in the time he did. Opposition defenders too, when confronted with the Black Arrow's pace and trickery, usually let him know that tackling in Scotland could be far more, er, full-blooded than in the US leagues.

In spite of a dream start, as the bruises added up he began to lose his taste for life at Celtic and was transferred to Third Lanark A.C. at the end of his first season. The same situation prevailed, so he left after one season to join Kidderminster Harriers in England where he stayed for two years before returning to the Detroit Corinthians.

Although Gil Heron only spent one season at Celtic he left a profound impression on the city of Glasgow, where he was a regular, dapperly dressed fixture around town, always having the time to stop and chat. When he died in 2008, every major Scottish newspaper ran a sizeable obituary.

CHARLES HOLLAND
Britain's original Tourist

When Charles Holland decided to enter the 1937 Tour de France, he'd already been to two Olympics and had won Best British All-Rounder. He'd met Continental riders who had ridden the Tour, and figured if they could, he could. He entered as an individual, because there was no British team; in fact until that point no British rider had ever taken part. Although regulations put him as part of a hastily conceived British Empire Team – himself, another English rider, Bill Burl, and a Canadian – this was merely a flag of convenience, and as both the others had dropped out by the end of the second day, Holland was riding as an individual. In Tour terms, this meant no manager or route strategist, no support personnel or vehicles, no sponsorship other than the basic food and lodging provided by the organizers, and after the Canadian had retired, not a word of French. Carrying his own spare tyres, food and drink – a marshal's car transported his pyjamas, tooth-

Charles Holland (front) out for a spin with his brothers Jack (centre) and Alf.

brush and toothpaste to each hotel – Charles Holland was taking on the world's most gruelling road race completely alone.

Through equal parts phenomenal riding ability and sheer grit he stayed in touch with the leaders, making friends with other riders and becoming the star attraction for spectators as he did so. The French press quickly became aware of this lone Englishman, giving him instant respect, meaning he got cheered the loudest by the crowds lining the route and was soon receiving sack loads of fan mail at the hotels, from all over Europe as well as the UK. He remained within the first fifty riders, covering unfamiliar terrain and experiencing conditions ranging from freezing on the Alps to so hot the tarmac in the road was melting

> "Tour fever was rampant in Paris in the two days before the race started. Everywhere we went cameras clicked at us and we both developed cramp from signing autographs."
>
> Charles Holland describing his and Bill Burl's build-up to the Tour de France.

near the Mediterranean. Then after approximately 2000 kilometres of the 2500-kilometre race, disaster struck, illustrating just how heroic Holland's efforts had been. On the eighteenth day his back tyre was wobbling, so while he enjoyed lunch at a roadside café, a local mechanic taped his wheel. He caught up with the stage leaders, but got a puncture and after fixing it himself was unable to inflate his tyre because his pump had warped in the heat. He borrowed a replacement from a reporter, but after two more punctures that pump had broken and he'd run out of spare tyres. Villagers tried to help, providing him with beer, and eventually a tyre was donated by a passing holiday-maker. It fell off. Another was found, which fitted a little better and a disconsolate Holland wobbled off to the next control point, only to find they'd packed up and gone. He took off his number and the first Briton to ride in the Tour de France retired from the race. It was eighteen years until the next British entrant, and then that was as part of a properly supported and sponsored team.

BILL LEE

Baseball's space cadet

Back in the early 1970s in the US, it was rare that the emergent counterculture interacted with anything as staunchly blue collar as baseball, on the field of play, that is. When it did, the chances are its name was Bill "Spaceman" Lee, the constantly smiling, dedicatedly nonconformist left-handed pitcher who became a legend during his ten years with the Boston Red Sox. Laid-back to such a degree he was almost horizontal – Lee was an enthusiastic marijuana advocate, claiming it helped him deal with Boston's traffic fumes while road running – it's hardly

Bill Lee, still pitching "super slow" in the senior leagues.

surprising his trademark pitch was the frequently unplayable "Leephus", a super-slow version of the eephus ball, a high arcing pitch that travelled at about fifty miles per hour, almost half the speed of a regular pitch. In his time with the team, he won a remarkable seventeen games in a season (twelve would be considered very good) three years running, and was integral to the team, which narrowly lost one of the most exciting World Series ever, against the Cincinnati Reds in 1975.

What really endeared him to the tough Boston crowds though was his passionate hatred for the New York Yankees, his team's bitter rivals – he and fellow pitcher Reggie Cleveland dubbed themselves, "the Yankee Killers", much to the fans' delight. His career statistics proved he did actually raise his game against the Yankees, a fervour that boiled over in a 1976 match against them when he suffered permanent damage to his left arm during an on-field fight. Which only made him dislike them even more.

In spite of his proven abilities and crowd popularity, Lee found himself on a collision course with Red Sox management when Don Zimmer was appointed head coach in 1976. A disciplinarian of the old school, Zimmer's first task was to break up Bill Lee's Buffalo Head Society, a group of similarly free-spirited Red Sox players, who would meet at legendary Boston sports bar the Elliot Lounge for an evening of beer, merry-making and the planning of outrageous practical jokes. As a demonstration of who was in charge, Zimmer would drop the pranksters from the starting line-up, a tactic which brought him into escalating conflict with Lee, who would refer to his coach as "the Gerbil". Although the Red Sox were enjoying a successful spell under Zimmer, fans sided with the players as the quarrels became increasingly public. In 1978, the coach began to get rid of the players concerned and when Lee was traded to the Montreal Expos, the Red Sox's Fenway Park stadium was daubed with anti-Zimmer graffiti the next day.

Lee's three years with the Expos were among the club's most successful, but he left in 1982 after a disagreement with management. Since retirement he has taken to farming in New England, but as one of the most popular players in Red Sox history, he remains close to the fans by continuing to turn out for the semi-pro New England team known as the Grey Sox, made up of former Red Sox players.

VINCE LOMBARDI

It was more than just football

"If you aren't fired with enthusiasm, you'll be fired with enthusiasm" was just one of the pithy quotes attributed to Vince Lombardi, possibly the greatest coach in the history of American football. His reputation for no-nonsense sound bites, delivered to the media as well as his players, was matched only by the rate at which the no frills methods of his teams despatched their opposition. When Lombardi took the job as head coach of the Green Bay Packers in 1958, he took over the worst team in the club's history – they had won only one game during 1957 and not won their division since 1947. In 1967 he retired from coaching to become the club's general manager, by which time they had won five NFL Championships, including three in a row from 1965 to 1967. The football Establishment was so impressed with these achievements, following his unfortunate death from cancer in 1970, the Super Bowl trophy, which isn't actually a bowl at all but a Tiffany & Co-crafted, life-sized sterling silver model of a football, was renamed the Vincent Lombardi Trophy. Likewise the city of Green Bay changed the name of the street the club's stadium is on so the address now reads as 1265, Lombardi Avenue.

Perhaps the most remarkable thing about how Lombardi achieved what he achieved was how straightforward his methods were – his mantra in life as well as on the football field was, "Keep it simple, play to your strengths and work harder than everybody else." His coaching methods relied more on man management and motivation than detailed tactical understanding, an approach he'd learned during his five years as an assistant football coach at West Point Military Academy. There he observed the cadets being trained to put the unit above the individual, to maintain mental discipline and a sense of overall order no matter the circumstances. He underscored this with a strong spirituality and moral belief system – Lombardi was a devout Catholic. It was these principles designed for combat conditions that the football coach brought to his players at the Packers, expecting nothing less than total obedience, dedication and application from them. It was joked among the players that the only place the Spartan-like Lombardi methods could have worked was in Green Bay, because the wind-swept Wisconsin city was so devoid of metropolitan glamour there was very little to distract them. As the coach's philosophies developed, so did his sergeant major-ish approach and he was given to unexpected and violent verbal explosions of temper, most notably when he thought somebody wasn't quite giving their all for the team.

> "If winning isn't everything, why do they keep score?"
> Vincent Lombardi

His side of the bargain was he'd not only turn them into winners on the field, but off it as well. As he coached these young athletes he'd impress upon them that these were not simply the rules of the game but rules for life and that the disciplines and principles he was instilling into them could be taken into any area of business, the arts or a trade. This aspect is probably the football coach's best-known legacy, as any big US book shop's self-help or business sections will be dominated by titles such as *The Lombardi Rules*, *The Essential Lombardi* and so on.

JONAH LOMU

A brick outhouse stands no chance

In the second semi-final of the 1995 Rugby World Cup, New Zealand lined up against an England side many assumed were winners in waiting. The English were recent Five Nations competition winners, were in form, had stormed through the preliminary stages and were the team New Zealand's All Blacks had admitted they least wanted to play. Then this apparent English juggernaut ran into Jonah Lomu, or rather the 1.95-metre, 125-kilogram Maori ran into them. By this game, Lomu had scored a try against every team his side had played, yet this was nothing compared with his demolition of England. Within two minutes Lomu had received the ball, knocked Tony Underwood out of the way, put on a burst of speed that left Will Carling gasping in his wake and powered through Mike Catt to score the first of his four tries. The All Blacks won the game 45–29, a score line that somewhat flattered their opponents as the England back line had been totally destroyed by a demonstration of how rugby should be played from the man who would change both the game and the perception of it.

Six formerly sporting thespians

Vinnie Jones
Previous Wimbledon F.C. midfield hard man, he now makes a reasonable living playing underworld hard men.

Jason Lee
The prominent Scientologist and star of *My Name Is Earl* was a professional skateboarder in the 1980s and 90s – he and Tony Hawk were the first skateboarders to be given their own signature Airwalk shoe.

Ed Marinaro
Joe Coffey was a *Hill Street Blues* icon, and the man who played him was a running back with the Minnesota Vikings, New York Jets and Seattle Seahawks.

Bradley Walsh
He was on Brentford F.C.'s books before injury and a foray into stand-up comedy pushed him towards TV presenting and acting.

Estella Warren
As a teenager, the *Law & Order* star was three times Canadian national synchronized swimming champion, and a solo bronze medallist in the World Championships.

Carl Weathers
The *Rocky*, *Action Jackson* and *Arrested Development* co-star used to play as a linebacker for the Oakland Raiders.

At twenty years old, Lomu had been a fringe member of the New Zealand squad as they went into the tournament. Following this game, however, he was the most talked about player in the world. He had it all. He could run the 100 metres in 10.8 seconds; his footwork was nimble enough to bamboozle defenders without actual contact – his swerves and moves became known as the "Maori two-step"; his speed and agility frequently took him *over* opponents. Defenders who managed to get near enough seemed to bounce off, while it wasn't unusual to see would-be tacklers dragged along until they lost grip. He had a keen eye for a pass and his defensive abilities probably could have stopped trains. He changed the way rugby union was played, as back lines now had to outthink and outmanoeuvre rather than simply out-muscle, and speed and movement became far more valuable attributes in forwards. Lomu became rugby union's first global superstar and the biggest draw the sport had ever known. His exciting, attractive style of play brought new crowds to the game, and virtually single-handedly he had wrenched its image away from the commonly held notions of squat men with broken noses and cauliflower ears smashing into each other. A new perception that wasn't hindered by Lomu being articulate, charming and very photogenic.

ROCKY MARCIANO
The harder they come…

In 49 fights as a professional, the closest anybody ever got to beating Rocky Marciano was when it took a split decision verdict for him to beat Roland La Starza, some twenty fights into his career. Other than that, only five more of his bouts went the distance, meaning he won 43 of his fights – almost 90 percent – by knockout and retired in 1956 as unbeaten world heavyweight champion. It's the joint longest victorious streak for a heavyweight boxer, and he's the only one to have gone through a career without a defeat. Never a particularly crafty boxer, what made Marciano so special was his enormous heart, great physical strength and the knowledge that his continued success was the only thing standing between his family and the grinding poverty they had experienced when he was a child.

An all-round athlete as a youngster, he played semi-pro baseball before getting into boxing in the army as a way to avoid kitchen duties. He continued boxing on discharge after the World War II, but when he looked to turn professional, he was turned down by various prospective management teams as being too short, too light, too untutored and, at 25, too old to change much. He trained himself, which is how he built up his amazing strength and stamina – he worked as a labourer, ran seven miles every morning with his brother, did an hour of lifting home-made weights every evening, would regularly go swimming, punched a mailbag filled with sand, earth and pebbles and gave up the forty-a-day habit along with the beer. When he was taken on by a trainer and manager, all they had to do was turn his street-style brawling into boxing, which they did by getting him to use his left hand, to stand in a crouch in order to slip punches and, to improve his balance and mobility, making him spar with his laces tied together.

While Marciano learned his ring craft well, he was never going to be the greatest boxer and what endeared him to the public was his ability to turn a fight around with guts and determination, then finish it with a single overwhelming blow. This was usually a right cross delivered with a devastating power that came up from the soles of his feet – it helped him being shorter than most of his opponents – and few saw the punch coming because such was Marciano's strength it only needed to travel six inches. He called the punch "Suzie Q", and it was never more effective than when he won the World Heavyweight

> "What could be better than walking down any street in any city and knowing you're the heavyweight champion of the world?"
>
> **Rocky Marciano on the simple pleasures brought by being the best.**

Championship from Jersey Joe Walcott in 1952. Having been knocked down in the first round and woefully behind on points as the champ pounded him for most of the fight, in the thirteenth round Marciano's superior stamina meant he found the energy to deliver a stunningly accurate Suzie Q to knock Walcott out and take the title for himself. Until he retired four years later, his openness, friendliness and hard work ethic remained unchanged, making him one of the most popular champions of all time.

MIL MÁSCARAS
Part-wrestler, part-superhero

Such is the superstar *luchadors'* relationship with showbusiness (see p.74) they seem to spend more time in movies, comic books and TV adventure series than they do in the ring. It should, therefore, come as no surprise that Mexico's biggest wrestling star, Mil Máscaras – the Man of One Thousand Masks – was, in fact, created by a film company as a character for the silver screen. That the athletic Aaron Rodríguez Arellano turned out to be quite so good at the actual wrestling proved to be a bonus rather than a qualification.

In the mid-1960s, the most popular films in Mexican cinemas were wrestling-horror flicks: generic, knock-about-violent movies portraying the wrestler almost as a superhero – plots inevitably involved a poor community being terrorized by some sort of monster/supernatural beast with a masked *luchador* coming to their rescue. When his two established stars became unavailable, movie producer Enrique Vergara recruited the novice grappler Rodríguez, then 26, and created the Mil Máscaras character as an orphan raised by scientists and conditioned to become a super-fit, super-smart individual, dedicated to fighting injustice – a superhero without a super power. The flamboyant look, the exaggerated posturing and the garish masks were all part of the role Rodríguez played in that self-titled film, which was such a hit that it led to over twenty films during which he wrestled assorted villains including Nazis, mummies, vampires, cowboys, land-grabbers, racists and corrupt authorities.

Taking this persona into the square ring wasn't that difficult for the athletic and powerfully built Rodríguez, who, prior to his film career, narrowly missed out on representing Mexico at judo in the Tokyo Olympics of 1964. Mil Máscaras's audience followed him out of the cinemas and into the wrestling arenas, where his

A dozen or so of the Thousand Masks.

speed and ability with the high-flying moves so popular in lucha libre – wrestlers launch themselves from the ring's posts and ropes – made him an instant "face", which is one of lucha libre's pantomime good guys. Quickly becoming the most popular wrestler in Mexico, Mil Máscaras's exciting style and extravagant personality allowed him to take lucha libre to Japan, where he achieved iconic status, breaking the sport on TV in that country. He was also largely responsible for taking lucha libre beyond Spanish language television in the US, where he became the first masked wrestler to fight at Madison Square Gardens, when the World Wrestling Federation (now the World Wrestling Entertainment) lifted their ban on masked competitors for him. Mil Máscaras managed to extend his Thousand Mask screen guise to the ring, where it is customary for wrestlers to fight with one trademarked mask design – they're as unique as clowns' make-up – by entering the ring wearing a different mask for each bout, but, before the contest began, whipping it off to reveal his regular black-and-white affair with the vivid red "M" on the centre of his forehead. What did take the rigidly stage-managed world of televised pro-wrestling by surprise though was this screen idol's refusal to go along with the play acting that went on in the ring. During Mil Máscaras's career he would not "sell" opponents' moves – exaggerate their effect – or agree to bouts' pre-determined outcome, much to several high profile opponents' distress. This movie screen creation actually wanted to wrestle for real.

JIM MORRIS

The oldest rookie

It all began with a bet with the baseball team at Reagan County High School in Big Lake, Texas, and within a few months their 35-year-old part-time coach and physical science teacher found himself on the mound in the Major League, pitching for the Tampa Bay Devil Rays. Jim Morris had dreamed of this moment since he was a baseball-obsessed child, but had long since given up on that dream after an unsuccessful stint as a pro more than ten years previously. After playing American football at college with a fair amount of success, he entered the 1982 amateur baseball draft to be picked by the New York Yankees, for whom he didn't sign, but joined the Milwaukee Brewers instead. After four years with their minor league "feeder" teams, and having suffered several injuries that involved surgery to his pitching arm, they let him go, and he moved to the Chicago White Sox. Once again Morris never made it into their Major League squad and with a growing family to think about, abandoned the notion of professional baseball to return to Texas and take up teaching.

Part of his duties in his new career involved coaching the school's baseball and football teams, and as he pitched to the batters on the former, the kids would complain he was throwing too fast. With an arm like that, they said, he should be in Majors. He struck a deal with them – if they won their division championship, something that had never happened before, he'd try out for a big league club. Astonishingly, in 1999, they did just that and when the Devil Rays came to nearby Brownswood to hold open tryouts, Morris gathered up his family for moral support and went along. Twice the age of pretty much all the other hopefuls, the scouts only agreed to let him pitch because he told them about his deal with his students, and then he'd have to wait until last.

Jim Morris wound up and threw; the Devil Ray official, timing his pitch, shook his head and then shook his radar gun. It must be faulty; the old guy's warm-up pitch had been timed as 94 miles per hour. The second came down even faster and the scout changed the gun. But by then Morris had loosened up and had thrown a dozen pitches timed at a staggering 98 miles per hour. When the scouts told him his speeds, he didn't believe them and made ready to leave. By the time he got home there was a series of messages from the Devil Rays on his answering machine. He was finally on his way to the Majors.

With an arm like that, he made swift progress through their minor league ranks and by the end of the season made his first team debut, facing the big-hitting Royce Clayton of the Texas Rangers. Morris struck him out in four balls. He stayed with the Devil Rays during 2000, making 21 appearances in total, with 13 strikeouts, before age and injuries caught up with him. They let Jim Morris go at the end off that season.

Now well known as a motivational speaker, among Morris's greatest achievements as regards his brief stint in the Major League was that the only concession anybody ever made to his age was during the traditional rookie initiation. All the new boys had to travel from Anaheim in Texas to a fixture in New York City wearing full drag, but the veterans let Morris wear a long dress, while the other rookies had to wear miniskirts.

ERIC "THE EEL" MOUSSAMBANI
Something fishy

When Eric Moussambani took to the starting podiums for his qualifying heat of the men's 100 metres freestyle at the 2000 Olympics in Sydney, it was obvious something was amiss. The two swimmers lined up next to him were looking sleek and tall, in seemingly regulation drag-resistant all-over body suits, while Moussambani was wearing the sort of trunks you'd take on holiday with you. And he hadn't noticed the drawstring at the waist wasn't tied up. But the young swimmer from Equatorial New Guinea went on to win this particular race, in a manner that hadn't been seen before – struggling to complete the course for a time of more than twice the standing Olympic record, and not even quick enough to come inside the 200 metres timing. But this remorselessly upbeat Olympian – dubbed Eric the Eel by the press men that mobbed him as he got out of the pool – became one of the highlights of those games.

Eric the Eel prepares for Olympian immortality.

Moussambani had got his place in the Equatorial New Guinea team as part of the Olympics wild-card entry system, designed to encourage developing countries to participate in sports they might usually have ignored. It meant the usual quali-fication requirements were waived although beneficiaries of this ruling had to swim a preliminary heat. This was the race that Moussambani and two other wild-card entries, from Niger and Tajikistan, were lining up for. However, the IT worker from Africa had only learned to swim in January of that year, did all his training in a local hotel's twenty-metre pool and had arrived in Sydney never even having seen an Olympic-sized fifty-metre pool, and having never swum further than sixty metres. To give him his due, he did point this out to his coach, who suggested he give it a go anyway.

At the start, as he fiddled nervously with his goggles while he took his mark, the other two swimmers each overbalanced and fell into the pool. This constituted a false start and under Olympic rules they were not allowed another, meaning Eric the Eel lined up for the next start unable to lose – he was the only man left. While the 18,000-strong crowd in the aquatic centre let loose a chorus of boos in reaction to the judges' decision, as they watched the lone swimmer make painfully slow progress, they realized a star was about to be born. As he made the turn, already well outside the Olympic record, they got behind him, and when, twenty metres out, he was struggling badly and looked as if he really wasn't going to make it, the noise level escalated. As he finally touched the side, the cheers were of relief as much as they were in appreciation of this exhibition of true Olympian spirit.

He had finished in a time of 1 minute 52.72 seconds, with the world record of 47.84 seconds blissfully untroubled. It was Eric Moussambani's personal best and an Equatorial New Guinea national record. Perhaps even more astonishingly, he qualified for the Athens Olympics in 2004, after recording a sub-57 seconds time, but irregularities with his visa prevented him from travelling to compete.

MARTINA NAVRATILOVA
Grand Slam, thank you ma'am

In December 2010, when an accumulation of fluid on the lungs caused by altitude sickness forced Martina Navratilova to abandon her attempt to climb Mount Kilimanjaro, Africa's highest mountain achieved something few had managed in the past: it beat the greatest female tennis player the world has ever seen. At around 4500 metres, she was too weak to continue, had to be stretchered down by porters and then spent several days in hospital. Yet in spite of the serious risks to her health, the 54-year-old's biggest concern was that she had to quit something she'd set her mind to.

Martina Navratilova's will to win and refusal to be put down took her to a record-breaking eighteen Grand Slam singles titles, 31 Grand Slam women's doubles titles and ten Grand Slam mixed doubles titles – the last of these, the US Open, coming a few months before her fiftieth birthday. Between 1978 and 1994 she virtually owned Wimbledon, reaching the women's singles final twelve times, only losing on three of those occasions and remaining unbeaten there from 1982 to

Six second careers

Ian Botham (see p.148) and Jim Thorpe (see p.187) weren't the only multi-tasking stars.

Denis Compton
In the 1930s and 1940s, Denis Compton played 78 Test matches for England, scoring a record-breaking 5807 runs and taking 25 wickets with his slow left-arm deliveries. He also won the League and the FA Cup during his 54 appearances for Arsenal, and represented England 12 times.

John Elway
The Denver Broncos quarterback was, in 1979, drafted straight out of high school by the Kansas City Royals baseball team – fellow future NFL star Dan Marino was also in that draft. Elway went from the Royals to the New York Yankees, where he spent two years in their minor league side.

John Hopoate
This Australian rugby player was effectively kicked out of the game after accumulating so many suspensions – one for sticking his finger in three opposing players' anuses. He channelled his violent tendencies into professional boxing and became Australian heavyweight champion in 2006.

Bo Jackson
As a running back for the LA Raiders, Jackson covered 40 yards in 4.08 seconds – a record that still stands – and made the All American team twice; in the off seasons, he was a designated hitter for the Kansas City Royals, with whom he made the All American baseball team in 1989, the only person to do so in two different sports.

Roy Jones Jr
To warm up for his evening title fight with Eric Lucas in 1996, Roy Jones Jr., then the best pound-for-pound fighter the world had ever seen, played a basketball game that afternoon for the Jacksonville Barracudas, a minor league team. He beat Lucas to retain his title, and became the first person to compete in two professional sporting contests in the same day.

Michael Jordan
From 1994 to 1995 Michael Jordan "retired" and joined the minor league Arizona-based baseball team the Scottsdale Scorpions, transferring to the Birmingham Barons, feeder team for the major league Chicago White Sox, who were owned by Chicago Bulls' owner Jerry Reinsdorf.

Martina on the mountain, while she still had the beating of it.

1987. During the 1980s she put together the longest winning run in women's tennis as she went unbeaten for 74 matches. But it was away from tennis that Martina Navratilova's fighting spirit really came into its own, usually as a reaction to circumstances that had been set against her.

After joining the US professional tour in 1973, while still an amateur but as Czech national champion, the authorities in her country (the former Czechoslovakia) felt she was becoming too Americanized and ordered her to give up tennis and return home. She reacted by moving full time to Florida, gaining political asylum and, as a result, being stripped of her Czech citizenship by a regime eager to publicly score points off the West. In turn, her reaction was a lifetime using her position as a sporting icon to speak out against the Eastern Bloc's oppressive political and social systems, and to campaign for human rights and against the mistreatment of children and cruelty to animals. She is most committed to gay and lesbian rights issues, which is another reaction to a personal injustice – her coming out as a lesbian in 1980, which cost her a great deal in lost sponsorship, came about following agitation by the Czech authorities behind the scenes in the American media. She has since made it her mission to encourage others to come out and so remove the stigma.

In 2010 Navratilova was diagnosed with breast cancer, but after a lumpectomy and six weeks' radiation treatment she saw that off, and within a month had competed in a triathlon in Hawaii and played an exhibition match against Lindsay Davenport. She has also become Health & Fitness Ambassador for the American Association of Retired Persons (AARP), a powerful over-fifties pressure group. Her statement on beating cancer was pretty straightforward: "I think if you can survive the Communist system, and being gay on top of that, then you can survive pretty much anything."

HELLÉ NICE

Fast, loose and faster still.

They genuinely don't make Grand Prix drivers like this any more. Before she successfully campaigned to be able to compete in men's races – women-only Grand Prix were no real test for her – Hellé Nice had made so much money as one of the most in-demand exotic dancers in Paris in the 1920s, she owned her own chateau and her own yacht. Back then, in her late teens and twenties, she supplemented that income with modelling and fulfilled her need for speed as an impressive downhill skier. In fact she only gave up dancing and turned to motor racing, at the end of the decade, when a bad accident on the slopes wrecked one of her ankles.

As very much a part of Parisian society, Hellé had affairs with some of the city's most eligible men – not all of them bachelors – including Maurice Chevalier, Comte Bruno d'Harcourt, Baron Philippe de Rothschild, Jean Bugatti and Le Mans winner Henri de Courcelles. There was such a crossover between the French aristocracy and the motor racing scene – Paris was pretty much the hub of the Grand Prix world in the 1920s and 1930s – Hellé had no difficulty fulfilling her desire to race. During her first year in competition she won the Grand-Prix Féminin, had set a new women's land speed record and toured the US, winning races against some very experienced opposition. It was on her return to France in 1931 that Ettore Bugatti (Jean's father) installed her in their all-male team of Grand Prix drivers, driving a supercharged Type 35C. Her custom-painted baby blue model became a fixture in motor races and rallies around the world, and although Hellé Nice never actually won a Grand Prix she was always a strong competitor, frequently beating the top male drivers and finishing third in the Monza GP of 1933. Then in 1936, tragedy struck.

In the São Paolo Grand Prix, while in second place and travelling at over one hundred miles per hour, her car hit a bale of straw and flipped through the air into the grandstand, killing four spectators. Hellé herself was thrown clear to land on an on-duty soldier, who died instantly, while she recovered to return to the track the next year. But she'd lost some of her edge and would never again compete in a men's race, although she did set several records in all-female events, many of which still stand.

In 1949, she entered the first Monte Carlo rally after the war, and at the competitors' ball before the race, fellow driver Louis Chiron loudly and at length accused her of being a Nazi collaborator. Although she denied it and he produced no proof to back these claims up, Hellé Nice was instantly ruined: her friends and associates deserted her; her long-time partner left, taking most of her money; and the motor racing world shunned her. Although these post-war years were suspicious times, there had always been a simmering resentment as regards Hellé Nice for her attraction of sponsors, her often cheesy publicity courting, her readiness to employ her considerable feminine charms and the fact that she was a very good driver. Such was the reaction to the accusations, one of the most remarkable women of the twentieth century died alone and in abject poverty in 1984. No evidence as to her being a German agent has ever been uncovered.

RED RUM
"Murder" spelled backwards

If the Grand National is "The People's Race", then Red Rum was "The People's Horse", and not simply for that awe-inspiring victory over Crisp in 1973 (see p.204). For most of the 1970s he was the only racehorse most people in Great Britain knew by name, but the fact that so many of them did was testimony to the horse's strength and spirit. Even today, some fifteen years after his death and over three decades since he ran his last race, Red Rum's three Grand National wins has yet to be equalled and he remains the standard other hopefuls are judged against. His script wasn't always written that way though.

Red Rum was born in 1965 in County Kilkenny in Ireland, and began his career as a not-very-successful sprinter and intermittent hurdler. Then, at age seven, he was sold for a mere six thousand guineas at Doncaster sales, to local man Noel Le Mare. Responsible for the horse was trainer Ginger McCain, a used car dealer and sometime taxi driver, who had held a full training licence for just five years. Red Rum was to be based in McCain's cobbled yard at the back of his car showroom in Southport, a small coastal town near Liverpool, where the first thing he noticed was that the horse was lame, to be diagnosed with pedal osteitis, a painful and chronic inflammation of one of the bones in the foot. Remarkably, swimming in the Irish sea – the only place the trainer could take Red Rum for exercise was Southport Beach – rejuvenated the horse, while galloping on the sand and scrambling up and down the dunes gave him great strength and stamina. He won his first five races for his new stable at the end of 1972, prompting them to enter him for the next year's Grand National and the famous duel with Crisp. Although the handicappers clearly felt Red Rum was the underdog – he carried 23lbs (10.4 kilograms) less than his rival – the public obviously thought this plucky, disadvantaged creature had a chance and backed him all the way to joint favourite. The race itself, in which Red Rum came from a long way behind to beat Crisp by just three quarters of a length, is universally acknowledged as the Greatest Grand National Ever, but the horse wasn't content to leave it there. During the next five years Red Rum won the Grand National in 1974 and 1977, coming second in the two years in between and, in 1974, winning the Scottish Grand National as well.

Red Rum retired on the day before what would have been his sixth Grand National, in 1978, when he pulled up during a run out and was found to have a hairline fracture in one of his feet. Not that he was going to take it easy, as a life of celebrity beckoned. He led the annual Grand National parade; made personal appearances; opened supermarkets and hospitals; gave rides to children for charity; was the subject of many books – his life was even turned into a children's adventure – and was pictured on tea towels, jigsaws, tin trays and such like; had a life-size statue erected at Aintree (the Grand National's course)and countless smaller china likenesses in living rooms around the country; opened the Steeplechase ride at Blackpool Pleasure Beach; and even had a lamentable pop record made about him in 1975, "Red Rum" by Chaser, written and produced by Jolley & Swain, the duo who would later be responsible for Spandau Ballet, Bananarama and Imagination. Red Rum suffered a stroke in 1995 and had to be put down. He is buried under the winning post at Aintree.

SIR VIV RICHARDS
Batsman forever

During the late 1970s and 80s, when fast bowling dominated Test cricket, batsmen would fetch up at the crease in almost as much armour as a medieval knight.

Except Viv Richards. Pads, gloves and a box, sure, but the only thing he ever wore on his head was his maroon West Indies cap. Once asked about it, he gave a dismissive laugh and said the only protection a batsman should need is his bat. This was a vital part of the fundamental psychology of his game: it was a fight between him and the bowler, and not just one he wanted to win, but a battle he sought to dominate to the point of humiliation. Not wearing a helmet, chewing gum and gazing down the wicket with studied nonchalance while the fastest bowlers snorted and

Sir Viv Richards' international statistics

	Tests	ODI*
Matches	121	187
Runs	8540	6721
Batting average	51.00	47.00
100s	24	11
50s	45	45
Highest score	291	189
Wickets	32	118
Bowling average	61.37	35.83
Five wicket innings	0	2
Best bowling	2 for 17	6 for 41

* One day international

pawed the ground up the other end usually meant he'd won the first round. Ask the Australian pace man Rodney Hogg who had the temerity to crack Richards on the jaw with a bouncer during a Melbourne Test. Richards rubbed his face, stared Hogg down, hit the next ball for six and took the bowler apart until he was mercifully taken off having conceded ten runs per over. Or Tony Greig: after vowing to make the West Indies "grovel" at the start of the 1976 Test series, Richards hit the

English bowlers for a total of 829, and it probably would have been more had he not been ruled out of the second Test through illness.

During his international career, he captained the side from 1984 to 1991 and is the only West Indies captain never to have lost a Test series. He scored 8540 runs in 121 Tests, and 6721 runs in 187 One Day Internationals, including an unforgettable 189 not out from a mere 170 balls at Old Trafford in 1984, and the only bowler that ever came close to consistently containing him was Dennis Lillee. A frighteningly fast bowler and equally aggressive competitor, while the twosome enjoyed some riveting duels in the 1970s and 80s, the Australian rarely took this particular wicket by sheer pace. He had to use all of his craft and guile to outthink the batsman and manoeuvre him back towards his wicket, because, fearsome a sight as Lillee in full flight was, it was never enough to intimidate Sir Viv Richards.

He is a man of great principle too, the strength of which was tested in 1982 with the recruitment of West Indies players for an unsanctioned series of rebel "Tests" in apartheid South Africa. As most of the players who toured down there (from Australia, Sri Lanka and England too) were either fringe players or over the hill, to include the greatest batsman in the world at that time would have given the series massive credibility and Richards was offered, quite literally, an open cheque compared with the $100,000 the others were getting. With staggering disregard for how the outside world worked, the South African authorities imagined they had smoothed over any worries Richards might have had over the country's inherent social inequality by promising to make him "an honorary white". His response was unequivocal: "I would rather die than lay down my dignity."

DENNIS RODMAN

Apparently, he's really very shy

Dennis Rodman dated Madonna; married Carmen Electra; posed naked for a PETA advert; wrestled professionally with the likes of Randy Savage and Hulk Hogan; had his own MTV show; was once in charge of the Lingerie Football League; was half of a Golden Raspberry Worst Screen Couple award for his first foray into acting – Jean-Claude Van Damme was the other half; is a staple of US reality TV; failed to contest charges of misdemeanour spousal abuse; once posed wearing a wedding dress to claim he was bisexual and married himself; and has so many piercings he must send airport security machines into meltdown. With a private life that is anything but, and very little apparently off limits, it seems remarkable that former basketball star Dennis Rodman has only written four volumes of autobiography so far. Mind you, they have titles like *I Should Be Dead By Now* and *Bad As I Wanna Be*.

He started his playing career as a small forward, a versatile, high-scoring position that involves backing up the bigger, stronger power forwards and mopping up offensive rebounds. In basketball-speak, a "rebound" doesn't actually have to hit the backboard or the rim, it is a shot that has missed the basket and is caught or controlled by somebody else. Rodman turned rebounding into an art form and seemed to wriggle his way through the airborne congestion under the basket with such guile and agility he earned the nickname "The Worm". Where he really excelled, though, was on defensive rebounds – intercepting the ball around his own basket before opposition forwards could control it. This was made all the more remarkable because at, by professional standards, a dwarfish 1.98 metres, he was playing a position usually reserved for much bigger men. During a career at the Detroit Pistons, San Antonio Spurs, Chicago Bulls and Los Angeles Lakers, between 1986 and 2000, he was the league's top rebounder five times and remains top of the career rebounding average table, while winning five championships.

In spite of such impressive statistics, it was always Dennis Rodman the Soap Opera that garnered the column inches. This pierced, day glo-haired tattooed, self-styled bad boy made his debut in 1993, when, after contemplating suicide, the previously shy and retiring Rodman opted instead to "kill the impostor" that was leading his life for him and let the real man come through. Since retiring from the game, and now entering middle age with anything other than dignity, he's kept tabloid headline writers busy with an apparently ceaseless succession of bizarre behaviour. As well as the reality TV – *Celebrity Apprentice, Celebrity Championship Wrestling, Celebrity Big Brother, Celebrity Rehab* and *Love Island* – he's attracted attention of the authorities in connection with loud parties and drunk driving. At the time of writing, he has turned his hand to deejaying across the US and in Europe.

BABE RUTH

They didn't name a candy bar after him. Allegedly.

Babe Ruth is the man largely credited with pulling baseball out of the doldrums to install it as the US's number two spectator sport (after American football), all the while transforming himself into both the game's greatest ever player, and an icon that went beyond sport to represent American culture itself. Remarkably, though, when the man, who was for so long the most potent hitter in baseball history, joined his first Major League club, it was as a pitcher.

From 1914, when the nineteen-year-old Ruth joined the Boston Red Sox, he had a couple of very successful seasons as a pitcher, before it was noticed that the brawny youngster might be even better in the batter's box. They weren't wrong. After one transitionary season he settled into the role, and in 1919 set a league home-run record by scoring 29 of them in the same year. Remarkably, and apparently due to a combination of his ill discipline and the Sox's theatre impresario owner being strapped for cash, at the end of that season Ruth was sold to the New York Yankees for $125,000, more than double the previous transfer record. Yet the

Red Sox still seemed to come off worst out of the deal. During Ruth's four years there, they had won the World Series three times; after he left they wouldn't win another that century. The previously ineffectual Yankees, however, dominated the game until the mid-1930s, when Babe Ruth left the club. They won four World Series and topped the American League seven times, while Babe himself broke his own home-run record three times with his best figure, sixty in a season, not being bettered until 1961, when the season was eight games longer. His career total of 714 regular season home runs stood until 1974, and by 1930 he was being paid more than the president of the US, Herbert Hoover.

It was everybody's good fortune that Babe Ruth's electrifying powerplay batting – he once hit a pitch five hundred feet into the stands at Wrigley Field in Chicago – coincided with rule changes in 1920 designed to favour the slugger and therefore making the sport more exciting for spectators. The most significant was that the ball would now be changed at the first signs of wear, meaning it was easier for the batter to see and its movement through the air would be less erratic. Ruth embraced this situation by almost doubling his home-run record, hitting 54 in that season to become baseball's first superstar and trigger the national interest in the game. With him in the team, the Yankees became the first baseball side ever to bring one million customers through its turnstiles, allowing them to leave the Polo Grounds, shared with American football team the New York Giants, and build their own Yankee Stadium. Upon opening in 1923, the arena immediately became known as "The House That Ruth Built".

Babe Ruth retired from the game in 1935 after a season with the Boston Braves. Following a period of ill health he passed away in 1948. One hundred thousand people attended his memorial service at Yankee Stadium.

The truth behind the Baby Ruth

The iconic candy bar wasn't named after the baseball player; in fact it didn't even have the same name – it was the *Baby* Ruth. When it first went on sale in 1921 it appeared to be an embryonic example of celebrity merchandising, however, the company responsible, Curtiss Candy, had no agreement with the player whatsoever. They always claimed it was named after the daughter of former US president Grover Cleveland, a somewhat questionable claim considering the girl in question had died in 1904. The saga took an even more ludicrous turn when the baseball player attempted to launch his own brand of confectionary, the *Babe* Ruth, but Curtiss took him and the company manufacturing it to court, claiming that their product was too similar in name to their own. And Curtiss Candy won, so the Babe Ruth candy bar was no more.

KELLY SLATER
The streets have his name

As probably the greatest surfer the world has ever seen, Kelly Slater not only blew away the competition on the Association of Professional Surfers (APS) Men's World Championship Tour, but redefined the sport to a large degree. He began surfing in his home town of Cocoa Beach, Florida, at the age of five – his dad owned a fishing tackle and bait shop just off the beach, so that was where Kelly and his two brothers spent all their spare time. By age eight, he was showing enough promise to merit his first custom-made board; the precocious youngster requested a menacing open shark's mouth be painted on the board's underside. An entirely appropriate design, as it turned out. Within the vibrant local surfing community Slater quickly picked up tricks and moves from the older guys, and from poring over surf videos, then he simply ate up the opposition in junior competitions up and down the Florida coast. As he travelled further afield, he became so successful as a junior that he turned professional in 1990, before he'd even graduated from high school.

Poised for perfection – Kelly Slater is possibly the best surfer ever.

As a pro, Slater stormed through the APS Tour, becoming both the youngest ever champion when he won it in 1992 at age twenty, and the oldest when he won it in 2010 aged 38. In between those two titles, he won it another eight times, setting a new record for championship wins, and holding it from 1994 to 1998, he set a new standard for consecutive wins. One of the reasons Slater dominated the competition to this degree was a very different approach – as a radical young surfer, he took almost a skateboarder's attitude to the water, performing aerial stunts and jumps off big waves instead of merely riding the long breakers with poise and balance, which, of course, he could do as well. So impressed were judges at a contest in Tahiti in 2005, he became the first surfer to be awarded a 20–20 perfect score: that is, the full amount possible for each of his two waves.

Kelly Slater's life away from the waves is no less spectacular. He has been "linked" with Cameron Diaz, Gisele Bündchen and Pamela Anderson, and had a long relationship with the latter after meeting her on the set of *Baywatch*, in which he had a recurring role. He has appeared in minor roles in some two dozen films and TV shows; as a golfer he plays off a handicap of two; his rock band the Surfers – a Nirvana-ish sound with a penchant for Slater-composed ballads – sold over a hundred thousand copies of their first album *Music from the Pipe*. Large numbers of those sales came from Japan and France, not obviously surf-crazy nations, but countries where Slater has to employ bodyguards as he's unable to go anywhere without being mobbed. However, it's back home in Cocoa Beach, where he still lives, that he is most appreciated: in 1999, the town renamed Third Avenue, Kelly Slater Way, and in 2010 unveiled a life-size bronze statue of him on his board.

JIM THORPE

Was there nothing he couldn't do?

The term "all-round sportsman" takes on new meaning when applied to Jim Thorpe, possibly the most multitalented athlete ever to grace the track and the field and the basketball court and the baseball diamond and the gridiron football pitch *and* the dancefloor. These achievements were made all the more remarkable given that Thorpe was Native American, at a time when Native Americans were still called Indians – he was born in 1888 – and were not even granted US citizenship.

Something of a late starter, he was in his twenties before he settled at the Carlisle Indian Industrial School where, with no background in athletics or any previous training, after watching the college high jump team practice, he fancied having a go. He cleared 1.75 metres while wearing regular clothes and shoes to beat all of them. This set something of a precedent and other sports he tried his hand at included the 100 yards (he could run it in 10 seconds flat), the mile (4 minutes 35 seconds), long jump (7.16 metres), javelin (49.68 metres), shot put (14.5 metres)… you get the general idea. The college would frequently win athletic events with

Thorpe as the sole member of their team, while he also represented them at baseball and lacrosse, then in 1912 won a national college ballroom dancing competition. Indeed the only problems he had were with American football, as the athletics coaches didn't want their star performer knocked about in that sort of action. They needn't have worried as so few opposing defenders ever got near him: although he rarely showed up for practice, Carlisle won collegiate championships in 1911 and 1912, thanks entirely to Thorpe's phenomenal scoring record.

His athletics prowess earned him a place in the US team for the 1912 Olympics in Stockholm, where he easily won gold in both the decathlon and the pentathlon, while coming fourth in the long jump and seventh in the high jump, and he was also a part of the baseball team that was demonstrating the sport. Thorpe was given a hero's welcome on his return, but it wasn't to last as the following year he was stripped of his medals under the rules of amateur participation – during a college vacation he had been paid a few dollars for playing baseball, thus was deemed to be a professional athlete. This came about, in the face of widespread public support for the athlete, after several resentful right-wing newspapers established a racist campaign against him.

> "Sir, you are the greatest athlete in the world."
> **King Gustav V of Sweden, at the 1912 Stockholm Olympics.**
>
> "Thanks, King."
> **Jim Thorpe**

Unable to take part in further Olympics, he turned his attentions to professional sport, playing baseball for the New York Giants, Milwaukee Brewers and Cincinnati Reds, while enjoying a parallel football career. In 1915 he became one of the highest paid players in the country when he joined the Canton Bulldogs, taking them to American Professional Football Association (the NFL's forerunner) championships in 1916, 1917 and 1919. He stayed with them into the 1920s, and continued playing football into the 1930s. By which time he had taken up pro basketball, in the high-earning, incredibly popular Harlem Globetrotters-type touring team Jim Thorpe & His World Famous Indians.

On retirement from sports, during the Depression and in the pre-Civil Rights US, Jim Thorpe had huge difficulties finding regular work. He died in 1953 as a penniless chronic alcoholic. In 1982, following a long campaign, his Olympic medals and titles were reinstated.

SHANE WARNE

The spin doctor

If ever anybody needed an argument in favour of in-stump microphones, they need look – or listen – no further than TV coverage of Test matches involving Australia when Shane Warne was bowling. As delivery after delivery would bamboozle opposing batsmen, you'd hear whoever was keeping wicket smacking his

Shane Warne gives yet another batsman the finger.

big gloves together and uttering, in broadest Aussie and with varying degrees of disbelief, exclamations such as "Bowled Warnie", "Bowling Shane" and, when particularly overcome, an almost breathless *Shane Warne*". Warne's ability to alter the pace of his deliveries and the angle of his wrist at release to manipulate trajectory, and to subtly change his grip to vary the spin, meant batsmen could never relax when facing Warne, as they had no idea how the next ball was going to behave. The bowler himself played this up, and would give press conferences before Test series to announce he had developed yet another new ball and would have given it some sort of ridiculous name – Toppie... Zinger... Back Slider... Big Leg Break and so on. He seemed to save his most devastating form for England, when his team weren't above some truly imaginative mind games: in 2005 before (and during) a Test series, a seven-metre high statue of "Big Warnie", finger raised and celebrating another dismissal was strapped to the back of an open truck and paraded through the streets of London.

> "The first thing is to be patient, which is probably the hardest thing to do. Don't worry if blokes are whacking you out of the park because you still have the opportunity to get him out next ball, even if it's not the same ball."
>
> How Shane Warne did it.

At a time when pace bowling was dominating international cricket Warne led the way back to spin, and because the stresses are relatively less – although he did have to undergo shoulder surgery – he could bowl more and for longer. When he retired from Test cricket in 2007 he had taken a then record 708 wickets in 145 matches, for an average of 25.41 runs. He was pretty useful with the bat too, scoring over 3000 Test runs, and as his highest score was 99, that is the highest total not to include a century.

He's been able to apply a good deal of spin to his life away from cricket as well. Nowadays better known for infidelities more than anything else, his indiscretions invariably come to light thanks to ill-advised text messages. So he signed a huge deal to promote a phone messaging service. In the late 1990s it was revealed in the

Bring back Warnie

Nothing Shane Warne could do could reduce the Australian public's love for and appreciation of him. He is such a dyed-in-the-wool Aussie hero that after he retired and the Australians played a couple of disastrous Ashes series, some enterprising types set up a website with the pretty straightforward URL of bringbackshanewarne.com, and has established a fighting fund to pay for exactly that. Donations, at the time of writing, stood at just over A\$4000 (£2504).

press that he had been embroiled in a scheme to sell information about match day conditions – state of the pitch, weather and so on – to a shady Indian bookmaker known as John the Bookie. Warne is the face of Internet gambling operation 888 Poker. He even got a nicotine patch company to sponsor his giving up smoking.

JOHN WOODEN

Basketball? It's a way of life.

When John Wooden joined UCLA (University of California Los Angeles) as head basketball coach in 1948 it was through a mistake, as the West Coast university wasn't his first choice. The former college basketball Hall of Famer and three times All American was in demand, and as a Midwesterner wanted to stay close to his roots so had his eye on a post with the University of Minnesota, who he believed were poised to make him an offer. But he heard nothing from them, so went with the next best thing, head coach at UCLA, and so began the greatest, and longest, dynasty in the history of American sport. Wooden coached there for an incredible 27 years, culminating in a twelve-year period in which the Bruins (UCLA's basketball team) were NCAA (National College Athletic Association) champions an incredible ten times, with seven in a row between 1966 and 1973. This period also included four unbeaten seasons during which the team went on to a then record of 88 consecutive victories. It won Wooden Coach of the Year an unprecedented six times, and saw him inducted into the Hall of Fame once more, as a coach, the first man to be included for playing and coaching.

Wooden's run of success with UCLA was made all the more remarkable by the fact college teams turn over players with great frequency – far quicker than an NBA team – because players are there for a limited amount of time. Indeed, the most outstanding college players usually get snapped up by the professional teams after one or two years on campus. The secret to his success was treating every team he had essentially the same and applying a series of Principles for Life, that were given to him by his father, to both their playing and their everyday lives. He believed that basic basketball skills were second to how his team carried themselves as men, and the only way they would get the absolute best out of the game – a team game – was if they mastered those traits first. He fashioned the Pyramid of Success, building blocks of different attributes to life that fostered character in supporting layers and he made sure his players developed and adhered to these habits as the pyramid presented them. The base layer was Industriousness, Friendship, Loyalty, Cooperaton and Enthusiasm; the second Self-Control, Initiative, Alertness and Intentness; the third Condition, Skill and Team Spirit; the fourth Poise and Confidence; with Competitive Greatness on top. It built teams that were constantly in control and played for each other, and turned out players like Kareem Abdul-Jabbar, Jamaal Wilkes, Keith Erickson and Marques Johnson. And after he left, it was twenty years before the Bruins won another title.

The Games

Epic contests of heroism, heartache and horsepower

◀◀ Previous pages: Ali vs Foreman in Zaïre (see p.196) didn't disappoint anybody. Except maybe George Foreman, seen here as he takes the count.

The Games

"Sports don't build character, they reveal it."

John Wooden (see p 191)

It could be a steeplechase track in Liverpool, a boxing ring in Africa or a Turkish football ground, but classic sporting contests can happen just about anywhere. It's not always the battles for the biggest prizes that cause the most excitement either; sometimes these historic matches aren't even to win a race – Gilles Villeneuve's epic Formula 1 duel with René Arnoux was for second place, and hardly anybody can remember who actually won. And while the level of intensity that goes into one of these matches sometimes comes as something of a surprise – Borg vs McEnroe, 1974 – when there's a build-up like the there was ahead of Mary Decker vs Zola Budd or the Rumble in the Jungle, it pumps up the sense of event to cult proportions. In this chapter we look at some of the most memorable sporting clashes in history and discover it's not always action on the pitch or the track that gives them their cult status.

MUHAMMAD ALI VS GEORGE FOREMAN

World Heavyweight Championship; Kinshasa, Zaïre; 30 October 1974

When Muhammad Ali set out to regain the world heavyweight crown in 1974, not many gave him a chance, but by the time the Rumble in the Jungle was over, few would doubt he really was The Greatest.

Ali had attempted to win back the title before, three years earlier, when Joe Frazier had inflicted on him his first professional defeat. Then, in 1973, he lost to Ken Norton, suffering a broken jaw in the process. The reality was, he was ten years older than when he first won the title, was noticeably slower, and the new champ, George Foreman, was a beast. Bigger, taller, stronger and six years younger, Foreman was a devastatingly powerful puncher and had knocked out each of Ali's conquerors inside of two rounds. When Ali announced to the world he was going to dance around the giant and box him into submission, that same world feared for the challenger's life. But that was to underestimate the unstoppable force that was his personality and his career-long maxim that boxing was as much about the brain as anything else.

Ali's first advantage came in the choice of location. Formerly, and currently, known as the Democratic Republic of the Congo, Zaïre was ruled over by the corrupt, human rights trampling Lieutenant General Joseph-Désiré Mobutu, who seized power in 1965 and self-effacingly renamed himself Mobutu Sese Seko Nkuku Ngbendu Wa Za Banga, which, loosely translated means Great Unstoppable Warrior Who Goes from Victory to Victory Trailing Fire in His Wake. Clearly, a man the boxing promoter Don King could do business with. Both fighters wanted $5 million, the richest purse ever and King had no money, Mobutu craved recognition from the world, and the door to Kinshasa was ajar as it was an open secret the US backed his anti-Communist regime. With most of his country in dire poverty, Mobutu rustled up the $10 million, got his global event and played host to both entourages in his sumptuous palaces.

> "It's a divine fight. This Foreman – he represents Christianity, America, the flag. I can't let him win ... He represents pork chops."
>
> Muhammad Ali on his opponent.

With a huge two-day soul music festival – James Brown, B.B. King, Miriam Makeba, The Spinners – to kick things off, the event was unofficially promoted as a black cultural milestone: African America meets African Africa. This was something that Ali revelled in, experiencing the country's culture, running with local children and generally making himself available. It was reciprocated, too. The chant "Ali, Bomaye!" (Ali, kill him!) echoed first across Kinshasa, then the country and soon the entire continent seemed to be noisily supporting him. Foreman, however, was the grumpy American abroad – unsettled, unwilling to accept the unfamiliar and virtually a recluse. The six-week delay after a sparring partner's elbow cut his eye only increased his discomfort, while his opponent made more friends.

With the pre-fight mind games in the bag, when the opening bell sounded at four o'clock in the morning (for the convenience of US television) Ali stunned those watching by rushing at the champion and landing several unconventional right hand leading punches. Tactically provocative, they were to goad Foreman into action, and Ali backed up on to the ropes under the Foreman onslaught. Then, to the bewilderment of his corner, he stayed there for the next seven rounds as a virtually static target for the strongest puncher the sport had ever seen. And it worked a treat, as by round eight Foreman was physically exhausted and psychologically battered.

> "I'm so mean, I make medicine sick."
> Muhammad Ali, prior to The Rumble in the Jungle.

In the last three years, Foreman had only had one fight go beyond two rounds, and now he was punching a marathon as he gulped in hot, humid, equatorial air, while a man, who was rolling back into the slackening ropes to absorb the impact of the blows, taunted, "My Grandma hits harder than that!" With no Plan B, by round eight Foreman was noticeably tiring, and couldn't stop the momentum of a misdirected powerhouse pulling him off balance. And the challenger struck. Three quick right hands, followed by a crisp left hook, set up the perfect straight right on a defenceless champion's jaw. He was unable to get past his knees before the count reached ten and Muhammad Ali was once again heavyweight champion of the world

ZOLA BUDD VS MARY DECKER

Women's 3000 metre final, Olympics, 1984

This was always going to be more than a contest between two of the greatest female athletes of that era, and it turned into one of the defining moments of the Los Angeles Games. Mary Decker was The US's current Golden Girl, a superb natural athlete who, as a teenager in the early-1970s, had dominated middle distance running. Yet injuries had kept her out of competition between 1974 and 1980. However, she had spectacularly come back into contention in 1980, by shattering the women's mile record with a time of 4 minutes 17.55 seconds, the first sub-4 minutes 20 seconds time. These Games, on US soil, were seen as a kind of Homecoming Coronation, and she was a clear favourite among both bookmakers and the crowd to take gold in this event.

Zola Budd arrived at the starting line equally headline worthy, but support for her by the nation she represented was much less than unequivocal. The eighteen-year-old Budd had run the fastest time ever for the women's 5000 metres (15 minutes 1.83 seconds), but the record was not ratified by the International Association of Athletics Federations as Budd was South African and it was run in that country, which was excluded from international athletics as a protest against the pre-Mandela apartheid regime, conditions that excluded that athlete from the

Olympics. Yet she lined up representing Great Britain, having gained UK citizenship with apparently indecent haste, courtesy of an English grandfather and a fervent campaign by British tabloid newspaper the *Daily Mail*. This seemingly backdoor naturalization sparked a media furore and anti-apartheid demonstrations outside parliament and race meetings where the newly-Anglicised Budd was due to compete – which had to be cancelled.

Budd vs Decker was further played up in sections of the British media as some sort of David and Goliath-type affair with the tiny waif-like former, who ran barefoot, up against the seemingly Amazonian latter. And on the day, the race itself more than lived up to the hype.

Although it was Budd's usual racing style to start fast, open a big lead and try and stay in front, it was Decker who went ahead from the gun, with Budd hovering just behind. It pretty much stayed that way, until just over halfway through, when Budd ran wide to overtake and moved across to take the lead by about half a metre. Given the length of Decker's strides, this would seem to have been too close a cut-in, and there was a minor coming together of legs around fifty metres after the manoeuvre. Budd maintained position though, and the distance between them was such that at 1700 metres Decker's thigh bumped Budd's ankle and the leading runner wobbled noticeably. Almost immediately after one of Decker's shoes nicked Budd's calf, both runners lost balance and, as Budd pushed out her straightened leg to right herself, Decker took a tumble over it into the infield.

Decker landed heavily on her hip, and, unable to continue, was in tears as she was helped from the track. Budd continued in the lead but seemed to be affected by the resounding boos coming from the crowd as she entered the final straight – after all, she had just appeared to knock over the home-town idol – and faded back into the pack to finish seventh.

Perhaps the most remarkable thing about this race is that, some 25 years later, hardly anybody remembers who won it (Romanian Maricica Puica) or that Great Britain picked up an unexpected silver with the unfancied Wendy Smith-Sly's second place.

Why did Zola Budd run barefoot?

"Coming from a farming background, I saw nothing out of the ordinary in running barefoot, although it seemed to startle the rest of the athletics world. I have always enjoyed going barefoot and when I was growing up I seldom wore shoes even when I went into town. I tried running with shoes but I found them uncomfortable and decided to continue running barefoot – I felt more in touch with what was happening, I could actually feel the track."

Zola Budd (left) and Mary Decker, just before the collision.

Six somewhat fortuitous results

Maricica Puica wasn't the only one helped by another's misfortune.

ESB, the Grand National, 1956

Fewer than fifty metres from the finish line, Devon Loch had a five-length lead on his nearest rival, when for reasons never explained, the horse leaped into the air and landed in a legs-splayed belly flop allowing the then second-placed ESB to win.

Steve Bradbury speedskating, 2002 Winter Olympics

Unfancied Bradbury won his semi-final after avoiding the pile-up that took out everybody else. The same thing happened in the final, when he was so far back he was able to skate around the collision on the final bend and glide over the line for Australia's first ever Winter Olympics gold.

England vs Australia, 2005 Ashes series

In the first match Australian bowler Glenn McGrath was virtually unplayable, finishing with figures of 5 for 53 and 4 for 29. But the bowler tore ankle ligaments when he trod on a cricket ball in training, missing the second and fourth Tests, which England won, and was nursed through the third and fifth, which were drawn. Thus England took the series 2–1.

Tanja Frieden, snowboard cross, 2006 Winter Olympics

Favourite Lindsey Jacobellis had a three-second lead, and on the second-to-last jump opted for a flashy "method grab" – turning ninety degrees in the air and grabbing the end of the board. She landed on the edge of her board and momentarily lost control, allowing Frieden to streak past.

Arsenal clinch Champions League place, 2006

In the final match of the season, fourth-placed Tottenham Hotspur, only needed to win to gain Champions League qualification at the expense of Arsenal. The night before, ten of Spurs' first team were struck down with food poisoning, and although some were passed fit enough to play, they lost 2–1, while Arsenal's win carried them into fourth place.

Lewis Hamilton, Brazilian Grand Prix, 2008

Filipe Massa needed to win the season's last race, and for Hamilton to finish lower than fifth, to take the Formula 1 title. He won, but as Hamilton went into the final lap in sixth it began to rain heavily and cars started to lose traction. Hamilton's team had opted to save time earlier by leaving his car fitted with wet weather tyres. The superior grip these afforded allowed him to pass the car in front and take the Championship by one point.

BJÖRN BORG VS JOHN MCENROE

Men's final, Wimbledon, 5 July 1980

By this time, John McEnroe's fourth Wimbledon, the fiery, relatively young player's ability on grass courts was getting him noticed, but he was also well on his way to establishing the reputation that led to the Superbrat nickname in years to come. Indeed, he was greeted by a chorus of boos from the Centre Court crowd thanks to outbursts during his semi-final with Jimmy Connors a couple of days earlier, which had earned him an official warning. Björn Borg, on the other hand, turned up at this match with a formidable status. Ranked world number one, he virtually owned Wimbledon's men's tournament, having won it every year since 1976, and he was on his way to a 41-match winning streak on grass courts. The Swede also had a very different temperament to his opponent, and his unemotional approach to his game meant the press were setting this up as Borg's ice-cold control against McEnroe's latently explosive histrionics.

In spite of the reigning champion being an overwhelming favourite, McEnroe seemed to be spurred on by the tangible hostility around the court and stormed through the first set, winning 6–1. In fact a potentially unpopular upset looked on the cards – Borg was the current male tennis pin-up, with a huge and vocal support among the young women watching – until the twelfth game, in which he broke McEnroe's serve for the first time in the match and used that as a springboard to win the second set 7–5. Borg's ascension continued into the third set, which he took 6–3, with perhaps a greater degree of comfort than the score line might suggest. Although the fourth set seemed much tighter, Borg made steady progress, broke McEnroe to lead 5–4 and serving two match points in the next game looked certain to hoist his fifth consecutive Wimbledon title sooner rather than later. But his opponent was far from finished and with an unplayable backhand down the line, then an audacious volley, McEnroe took both of them.

> "McEnroe had been booed on to the court. At the end he was given an echoing ovation – because he had played like a man and behaved like a man. He had lost a tennis match but in terms of public acclaim he had won Wimbledon."
>
> *The Times*, 7 July 1980

Björn Borg vs John McEnroe

They played each other fourteen times between 1978 and 1981, winning seven matches each. In 1981 at Wimbledon, McEnroe took revenge on Borg winning the 1981 men's final 4–6, 7–6. 7–6. 6–4. And the American won the two US Open finals they met in, in 1980 and 1981.

He then won six points in a row, eventually forcing a tie break (thanks to a rule change the previous year, tie breaks now took place at 6–6 instead of 8–8). And what a tie break it was. They contested a then record of 34 points, with Borg reaching match point at 6–5 and 7–6 and McEnroe blowing set points at 7–8 and 8–9. Before McEnroe took the set 6-7 he would miss four more set points, while his opponent would blow three more chances to win the match. This riveting spell of tennis, with two seemingly inseparable players at the height of their games trading the lead for 22 minutes, is routinely referred to as one of the greatest moments in the history of the game.

The match was three hours old when the players went into the deciding fifth set, during which the more experienced and more composed Borg took his tennis up a notch with a deadly serve. Although the scoreboard said 8–6, the champion pretty much blew McEnroe away at this last ditch, as he was successful with eighty percent of his first services and only lost three service points in the whole set. However, it was a superiority that wasn't to last. To restore the balance this epic match deserved, McEnroe would take the title from Borg in the next year's final.

CARL LEWIS

Los Angeles Olympics, August 1984

This phenomenally talented athlete was determined to equal Jesse Owens' 48-year-old Olympic triumph of four golds at the same Games (Berlin, 1936) in both track and field events. Lewis was constantly being compared to Owens, as they excelled in the same events: 100 metres, 200 metres, 4 x 100 metres relay and long jump. Lewis arrived at the 1984 Olympics as the fastest man on the planet over 100 metres and holder of the low altitude long jump and 200 metres world records and as anchorman (last leg runner) of the world record-holding 4 x 100 metres relay team. That he should achieve such a goal during Olympics held in the US should have been an ideal situation for Lewis to clean up on future sponsorship and media deals. Yet, astonishingly, although Lewis equalled Owens' haul of medals, his commercial value actually *went down* following the Los Angeles Games.

> "They started looking for ways to get rid of me. Everyone was so scared and cynical, they didn't know what to do."
>
> Carl Lewis, on the aftermath of his triple gold medal win.

Winning at his events was almost a formality. He blitzed the 100 metres in 9.99 seconds, 0.2 of a second ahead of second place; his time of 19.8 seconds in the 200 metres was a new Olympic record; as anchorman for the relay team he was part of a new world record for the 4 x 100 metres of 37.83 seconds; in the long jump he took the minimum amount of jumps – two – because he didn't want to tire himself out for the sprint events he had coming up. As it was,

After match point in that epic game, Borg's icy demeanour evaporates.

he didn't even need both of them as his winning jump of 8.54 metres was his first. It was during the long jump that indications Lewis might not be the people's favourite became apparent. He was booed by the crowd for only taking the two jumps, as they were hoping to see him try to beat Bob Beamon's 1968 Olympic leap of 8.9 metres.

This was merely the beginning. In the wake of his quadruple success, fellow athletes began to openly condemn his boasts over his success – sarcastically referring to him as "King Carl" – and his media exposure was limited as magazines and TV were keen to avoid giving him another platform to show off on. Then rumours began to circulate that Lewis was gay and decathlon winner Daley Thompson appeared at an Olympic press conference sporting a T-shirt inscribed with, "Is the World's Second Greatest Athlete Gay?" Lewis's manager inadvertently fed the rumour by proclaiming his client to be the "Michael Jackson of athletics". When Lewis dressed in a manner best described as "flamboyant" posing for a Pirelli Tyres calendar wearing red high-heeled shoes, he gave further support to the claim.

And although he strenuously denied he was gay, in the mega-buck world of sports sponsorship perception is everything. While Carl Lewis should have been raking it in with both hands, post-Olympics, his two main sponsors, Nike and Coca Cola, dropped him. His fellow athlete, high jumper Dwight Stone, neatly summed up the whole affair when he said: "It doesn't matter what Carl Lewis's sexuality is, Madison Avenue perceives him as homosexual."

Carl Lewis the athlete

In the aftermath of the 1984 Olympics and the brouhaha surrounding Carl Lewis as a personality, it's sometimes forgotten that in his prime he was a truly phenomenal athlete. Between 1984 and 1996, he won nine gold medals at four different Olympics – including four consecutive long jump triumphs – eight World Championship golds at three meetings, and two Pan American Games gold medals. He went undefeated in long jump throughout the 1980s – 65 contests, the longest unbeaten run in athletics – and he jumped further than Bob Beamon's 8.90 metre (29 feet 2.5 inches) but astonishingly never held the long jump world record. He was a record holder in the 4 x 100 metres and 4 x 200 metres relays and broke his own 100 metres world record twice to run a fastest time of 9.86 seconds in 1991. In 1999 he was voted Olympian of the Decade by *Sports Illustrated* magazine.

RED RUM VS CRISP

The Grand National, Aintree, Liverpool, 31 March 1973

Although 38 horses started the 1973 Grand National, very few people have ever been able to remember more than two of them – the joint favourites, Red Rum and Crisp. Although their starting prices might have been the same, they were about as different as it's possible for two horses to be, and it made for a contest that promoted in the press, prior to the race, became the equine equivalent of "Class War".

Crisp was a huge, aristocratic Australian thoroughbred, that had such success over the jumps down under, shattering course records as he won race after race, that he was nicknamed the Black Kangaroo. Word was he was sent to the UK because he had no real competition left in Australia. When, in 1971, he took up residence in Fred Winter's sumptuously appointed yard in Lambourn, Berkshire, it was assumed the former National Hunt champion jockey turned champion

Six Sensational Fixtures

Wilt Chamberlain becomes the NBA's first 100-point player, 1962

As the Philadelphia Warriors went on to a home court victory of 169–147 over the New York Knicks, the crowd chanted "Give it to Wilt" as their giant centre had racked up scores of 23, 18 and 28 in the first three quarters. With 46 seconds to go Chamberlain grabbed his final basket of the game to bring up the magical 100 and the court was mobbed.

Nadia Comaneci, perfect ten, Montreal Olympics, 1976

The fourteen-year-old Romanian gymnast won three gold medals and her performance on the uneven bars was the first perfect score of ten points at an Olympics. So unexpected an event, the scoreboard was not equipped to display it and had to show her faultless tally as one.

England vs West Indies, 1984

This was the first time in Test cricket a touring side had defeated its hosts 5–0. The series became known as "Blackwash", and was seen as the peak of the greatest ever West Indies side that included Viv Richards, Clive Lloyd, Michael Holding and Gordon Greenidge.

Baseball World Series finals, 1989

These finals between the San Francisco Giants and the Oakland Athletics are not simply memorable for the As sweeping the Giants 4–0 in the best of seven series, but also for the fifteen-second, 6.9 on-the-Richter-Scale earthquake that rocked the Giants' stadium as the teams warmed up for game three, causing a ten-day postponement.

Tiger Woods at the US Masters, Augusta, 1997

After a slow start, Tiger took the lead on Friday, then announced himself to the world. Not only the youngest to wear the winner's green jacket (at 21), Tiger also was the player to win by the biggest margin (12) and with the lowest 4-round total of 270 (18 under par).

John Isner vs Nicolas Mahut, Wimbledon, 2010

As the fifth set of this match carried on to a second day, the most accurate description of it was "unremarkable". Then when darkness fell on it once again, that set's score stood at 59–59. With neither player yielding, it was only fatigue that halted Mahut, giving Isner a 70–68 game victory. The match had lasted eleven hours and five minutes, over three days.

National Hunt trainer would work wonders with him. Red Rum, however, was billed as some backstreet scrapper, who lived in a cobbled yard in Southport, just outside Liverpool, at the back of his trainer's used car showroom. For exercise, Red Rum had a gallop on the local beach, finished off with a swim in the Irish Sea. Come race day, though, this didn't seem to trouble the punting public. Such was Red Rum's popular support – he'd become the tabloids' darling – the two were both offered at 9/1.

While the odds might have been even, the handicapper's weights were a different matter: such was Crisp's success story since arriving in the UK, he was carrying the maximum of weight, twelve stone (76.2 kilos), a full 23 pounds (10.4 kilos) more than Red Rum. Over the four miles and 856 yards (7.242 kilometres) of two

Sebastian Coe vs Steve Ovett
Late 1970s to mid-1980s

When Great Britain produced these two great middle-distance runners at the same time, their rivalry became the stuff of newspaper legend. It was a clash of class – Ovett was painted as the working-class 'ero, Coe as something of a toff; a conflict of styles – Ovett a slightly showy natural runner with a devastating finishing kick, Coe a hard-training, calculating tactician of the track; and a personality clash with Ovett, an abrasive plain speaker and Coe smoother and media-savvy. The truth was they were far closer in background than was promoted – different ends of middle class – and Coe could be every bit as short with the press and officials as his opponent. But it did seem they didn't particularly like each other, which added a considerable frisson to their meetings on the track. Which, remarkably, weren't that many.

Coe and Ovett raced against each other in the Schools Cross Country Championship of 1972 – both finished way back in the field – then only three times in senior international competition. In the 1978 European Championships, Ovett beat Coe to take gold in the 800 metres; two years later at the Moscow Olympics, Ovett triumphed in the 800 metres, while Coe took gold over his rival in the 1500. Where the competition between them really took place was among the world records they traded for over half a decade. In 1979 Coe broke the world mile record; in 1980 Ovett took that from him; in 1981 Coe regained it; a week later Ovett snatched it back; then in 1985 Coe set a faster time. Likewise with the 1500 metres: in 1980 Ovett broke Coe's record, which he lost to American Sydney Maree in 1983, then won back off him less than a week later. The European 1500 metres record that Coe broke in 1979, Ovett took from him in 1980. They even chased each other for the BBC Sports Personality of the Year award – Steve Ovett won it in 1978, only to hand it over to Sebastian Coe the following December.

circuits of the Aintree track, this was a massive advantage, as among the Grand National course's sixteen fences are some of the most challenging jumps in National Hunt racing – in recent years animal welfare organizations have forced modification of some of them, citing potential cruelty.

Up until the sixth fence, the infamous Becher's Brook, Crisp had been easing his way up through the pack, and, as they jumped the seventh, took the lead from Grey Sombrero and was looking every inch the champion. Of Red Rum at this point, the most positive thing you could say was that he hadn't fallen over. By the time they hit the fifteenth fence – the Chair, the most notorious jump on the course – Crisp was pulling away from the field, with his co-favourite back in twelfth place. Although Red Rum was moving rapidly up through the pack, and by the time they came in for the second circuit he was placed second, it was as if Crisp was turbocharged and he was over twenty lengths in front.

> "I watch it occasionally on video, and it was only bang on the line he got there. One day I'll be watching and Crisp will beat him."
>
> **Ginger McCain, Red Rum's trainer.**

With two fences to go – just under half a mile (0.8 kilometres) – Crisp was still way out in front, but Red Rum was noticeably gaining ground. Not that that should have been cause for concern, as with four hundred metres of finishing straight to go he was still fifteen lengths to the good. But that extra weight was taking its toll, and Crisp's jockey Richard Pitman resorted to the whip to urge his mount on, but it had the adverse effect of sending his mount veering to the left and losing even more precious ground. The horse was slowing with every stride as Red Rum relentlessly reeled his opponent in to take the lead about two paces from the line and cross it a mere three quarters of a length in front.

Both horses had wiped nearly twenty seconds off a 39-year-old course record. Crisp would beat Red Rum the next year when the two raced at level weights, but Red Rum went on to win two more Grand Nationals and a place in our Legends chapter (see p.180).

AC MILAN VS LIVERPOOL

UEFA Champions League Final, Ataturk Olympic Stadium, Istanbul, 25 May 2005

There was a moment, probably around half-time, when even the most dyed-red Scouser might have felt his faith waiver, and be tempted to turn the television off or leave whatever pub he happened to be in. While for the twenty-odd thousand in the ground and about half as many again in its immediate vicinity, the interval represented a particular form of torture. As the teams disappeared down the tunnel, Liverpool were 3–0 down and being outplayed in a manner suggesting the club's fifth European Champions' trophy was no longer a realistic expectation.

Indeed the surprises had started before the ball had been kicked thanks to Liverpool manager Rafael Benitez's decision to do without the reliable, ball-winning defensive midfield services of either Dietmar Hamann or Igor Biscan. Although it left the Reds' centre backs needlessly exposed, it was believed that, as the move put the attack-minded Harry Kewell on the pitch, attack would become the best form of defence. Which was made to look pretty much academic during the first minute, when midfielders Steven Gerrard and Xabi Alonso were spectators as Paolo Maldini advanced on a free kick from Andrea Pirlo and, on the volley, swept the ball past Jerzy Dudek. Kewell went off injured in the 22nd minute, but still Benitez ignored the need for a central holding player, bringing on attacking midfielder Vladimir Smicer. And he paid the price as AC Milan began to pile on the pressure, achieving shooting positions apparently at will. With six minutes to go in the half Andriy Shevchenko took the ball down the right wing and crossed for Hernán Crespo to slot home; then two minutes later Crespo bagged another when Ricardo Kaka strolled through the Liverpool defence to feed the striker who coolly chipped the advancing keeper. Game over. Or at least it might have been if they hadn't forgotten to tell Steven Gerrard it was.

Right from the second half kick-off, the skipper was urging his team forward, something that was much less risky since the introduction after the break of Hamann, who got busy breaking up Milan's attacks before they had time and space to really get going. Then, with the half barely started, came a miraculous six minutes: in the 53rd minute Gerrard headed in a cross from John Arne Riise; three minutes later, Smicer's long range shot added another; then on the hour Gerrard was pulled down by Gennaro Gattuso in the area, and Alonso stepped up to take the spot kick. Nelson Dida saved, but the Spaniard beat him to the rebound and suddenly it was 3–3. The fight had gone from Milan although they rallied briefly in extra time. Neither side could score, meaning the penalty shoot-out beckoned.

Each side had been here before, as both had won their previous Champions League finals in this manner. But that didn't stop the first spot kicker, Milan's Serginho, from hoofing one over the bar. Hamann stepped up and scored. Pirlo had one saved. Djibril Cisse scored for Liverpool. Jon Dahl Tomasson was successful for Milan. Riise's kick was saved. Kaka scored, making it 2–2. Smicer netted to put Liverpool 3–2 up, meaning as Shevchenko lined up Milan's final attempt he had to score to keep the shoot out alive. He didn't. Dudek stopped it and all hell broke loose in Istanbul and on Merseyside.

> "The English club proved that miracles really do exist. I've now made Liverpool my English team. They showed that football is the most beautiful sport of all."
> Diego Maradona, after watching the game.

GILLES VILLENEUVE VS RENÉ ARNOUX
French Grand Prix, Dijon, 1 July 1979

The most remarkable thing about this spectacular example of determined, devil-may-care motor racing is that it was for second place; by the time Gilles Villeneuve and René Arnoux started their high speed duelling the actual race was effectively done and dusted, with the winner, Jean-Pierre Jabouille, maintaining a fifteen-second lead.

It all began in earnest late in the race when Arnoux, confident his Renault team-mate Jabouille was going to win, became determined to come second, thus making this French Grand Prix a total French triumph – two French drivers first across the line, driving French cars, using French fuel and oil (Elf) and running on French tyres (Michelin). He went around Villeneuve as he went into the third to last lap, taking the lead, only to have the Canadian pass him to regain it on the next. Arnoux displayed brilliant driving as he made a valiant charge, trying time and time again to squeeze past his rival on either side, only to be held off – quite literally – with some breathtaking positioning by Villeneuve. At the start of the final circuit, the two were neck and neck, with sparks flying from their wheels as they

Gilles Villeneuve (right) and René Arnoux were the best of friends off the track.

nudged each other trying to gain advantage on the bends. Arnoux managed to get his whole car in front, so at the next corner Villeneuve swung out wide to try and pass. Arnoux blocked him off, as the cars bumped jarringly. Villeneuve went into a brief skid, yet stayed in control and on a hairpin bend, approximately halfway around, moved over and audaciously slipped through on the inside. Again the cars collided as the Frenchman attempted to keep his advantage, but Villeneuve pushed through and held his position to take second place by 0.24 seconds.

As a display of driving this battle has gone down in Formula One history as one of the most exciting ever seen, and Villeneuve's performance was fittingly lionized because his Ferrari 312T4 was slower and altogether inferior to Arnoux's Renault.

> "I knew I'd been beaten by the best driver in the world"
> René Arnoux after that epic last lap battle.

It's also a testament to the approach of racing drivers and the racing Establishment in those days that they were willing to engage in such risky driving and neither was penalized for it. When cars are bumping wheels at those sorts of speeds, it's incredibly easy for their wheels to get locked together or for the car coming in from behind to end up "climbing" over the other, and in either case one vehicle ends up being thrown into the air. All Gilles Villeneuve had to say after the race was, "That was really fun!"

STEVE PREFONTAINE VS LASSE VIRÉN
Men's 5000 metre final, Munich Olympics, 10 September 1972

This duel was a clash of personalities and appearances as much as running styles, with the 21-year-old University of Oregon student Steve Prefontaine very much US athletics' rock star, with his shoulder length-hair and a droopy soup strainer moustache. College crowds loved him, meaning sold out stadiums wherever he competed and the chants "Pre, Pre, Pre, Pre…" starting up as he took to the track. Lasse Virén was only a couple of years older, but as a police officer in his native Finland, he was an altogether less colourful character. Prefontaine was stocky and muscular, while Virén was built much more in the traditional distance runner mode of slim and wiry. Although both were very successful, their approach to the event couldn't have been more different. The Finn ran tactically, taking it easy for the first few laps then delivering an explosive kick as races reached their climaxes; Prefontaine got out in front immediately and usually outlasted his rivals as he maintained a flat out pace. Prefontaine arrived at this race as the US 5000 metre record holder, while a week previously Virén had taken gold in the 10,000 metres, after falling over and losing around 25 metres, then still winning in a world record-setting time.

In the 5000 metre final, true to form, Prefontaine set off at a blistering pace almost daring a field that included Virén, Tunisian Mohammed Gammoudi (the

Six incredible winning streaks

Camarero, flat racing
The Puerto Rican thoroughbred set the consecutive wins record when, between April 1953 and August 1955 he finished first 56 times on the, er, trot.

Julio César Chávez, light welterweight boxing
Between the very first fight of his professional career in February 1980 and September 1993, when his match against Pernell Whitaker ended in a draw, Julio César Chávez had won 87 consecutive fights. This fantastic sequence included 24 defences of the World Championships he held at three different weights.

Chicago Bulls
When the Bulls won the NBA (National Basketball Association) Championship three years in row, 1990–1993, it was called the "three-peat" and sports commentators said it would never happen again. As it was they didn't have to wait too long – the Bulls repeated the feat two years later, when they won the title from 1995 to 1997. Coincidentally, Michael Jordan was away playing professional baseball for the two years in between the team's winning runs.

Byron Nelson, PGA tournaments
Although never a superstar in the world of professional golf, the American won a record eleven PGA Tour events in a row in 1945. During one of those wins he carded a then record-breaking low score of 62 for 18 holes and a 72-hole score of 259.

Johnny Weissmuller, swimming
The man later known for playing Tarzan in a series of 1940s movies was perhaps the greatest swimmer ever: as an amateur competitor he was unbeaten between 1921 and 1929, during which time he set 67 world records and won five Olympic golds.

West Indies cricket team
Between 1975 and 1990 the West Indies, initially led by Clive Lloyd, completely dominated world cricket: they didn't lose a Test series in those fifteen years; and during that time they set a still standing record of 27 consecutive matches won.

Six memorable local soccer derbies

Celtic vs Rangers; Glasgow, Scottish League Cup Final; 1957
Celtic more than simply lifted the trophy when they redefined the term "bragging rights" to win this derby 7–1, which remains the biggest margin of victory in any British major final.

Flamengo vs Fluminense; Rio, State Championship; 1963
Played at the Maracanã Stadium in downtown Rio, this "Fla–Flu" derby holds the world record for the largest attendance at a football match, with a crowd of 194,603. The game itself was a goalless draw.

Manchester United vs Manchester City; First Division; 1974
Manchester United went into this end of season game staring into the jaws of relegation, and needed to win. It was goalless for eighty minutes, until Denis Law, a former Old Trafford legend, now ending his days at City, scored against his old club with a cheeky back heel. He left the pitch immediately, and United went down.

Galatasaray vs Fenerbahçe; Istanbul, Turkish Cup Final; 1996
The Istanbul derby usually sparks local passions, and never more so than when, to celebrate his Galatasaray side winning the cup, manager Graeme Souness personally planted a huge club flag in the Fenerbahçe pitch. Rioting followed immediately, Souness's dismissal not long after that.

Al Ahly vs Zamalek; Cairo, Egyptian League; 1999
This game is taken so seriously in Egypt that a foreign referee is brought in as it is assumed any local man will be biased, and it is played on a neutral ground. In 1999 French referee Mark Batta sent off a Zamalek player in the second minute, and the rest of his team walked off and refused to come back. It was the fourth time in the fixture's history that the game had to be abandoned.

Internazionale vs AC Milan; Champions League Quarter Final; 2005
Chaos descended when, with Milan 3–0 up, the referee disallowed an Inter goal and bottles, flares and general debris rained down on to the pitch. The teams were withdrawn when Milan's keeper was hit by a flare and the fire brigade were called upon to put out brush fires on the pitch. A later attempt to restart the game was similarly disrupted and the match was abandoned after 75 minutes with the result standing.

favourite) and Great Britain's Ian Stewart to keep up. For about the first four thousand metres they did just that, the foursome pulling away from the pack, with the lead constantly shifting between Virén, Gammoudi and Prefontaine until the American's methods looked to be paying off. With around a thousand metres to go, he established a constant lead as the others seemed to be tiring from the relentless pace. But he hadn't counted on the finishing power of both Virén and Gammoudi. At six hundred metres out, the more experienced duo were slowly speeding up and had edged in front, with Prefontaine finding reserves of energy from somewhere to try and regain his lead. The trio came round the final bend apparently locked together with Gammoudi slightly in front. As they came into the finishing straight Virén made his move, with an acceleration so smooth it made it look as if the others were going backwards. This final burst was too much for Prefontaine, who slipped back to fourth place as the Finn finished a second ahead of Gammoudi, who took silver, with Ian Stewart in third.

It is reckoned that Prefontaine's failure in the event was down to inexperience at this level, as while he was a legend on the US college circuit, Virén and Gammoudi were regular competitors on the world circuit. It was assumed at the time that Prefontaine had a long career in front of him and the 1976 Olympics would provide a rematch in which he would have a much better chance. Sadly that never happened as the runner was killed in a car crash in 1975, and while Virén once again took gold in Montreal in both the 5000 and 10,000 metres, it sparked an ongoing middle distance debate about who would have been the greatest.

TOTTENHAM HOTSPUR VS ARSENAL

English First Division, White Hart Lane, London, 3 May 1971

Arsenal were lying second in the table on 63 points, with Leeds United above them on 64, but the league leaders had played all their games and Arsenal had this one left. Back then in English football it was two points for a win and one for a draw, with goal *average* rather than goal difference used to separate teams with the same number of points – goal average divided the number of goals conceded into the number of goals scored. To win the title Arsenal had to win or draw goalless – anything else and they'd be stuck in second place. More than that, however, Arsenal were playing in the FA Cup Final the following weekend, so this was their chance for a league and cup double, a feat only previously achieved by Spurs. There was a great deal more at stake than just local pride. And the locals turned out in force.

It was a 7.30pm kick-off, but if you arrived much later than 2.30pm you weren't going to get in, as in the days before all-seater stadiums you just turned up and joined the queues. Just past lunchtime the "queues" had completely swamped the surrounding streets and, in consultation with the police to ease the crush, the club opened the turnstiles at about 3.30pm. Before 5pm they had closed them again as the ground was quite literally bulging at the seams – the official attendance was

51,992 (the ground capacity was 60,000) but it was obvious there were a lot more people than that in there. This was before health and safety had been invented, so walkways, staircases, gangways… any square foot of concrete had at least two people on it.

The game itself more than lived up to expectations. Arsenal didn't attempt to play for the goalless draw, but went all out to win, just as their rivals were equally intent on spoiling any party they might be planning. But in spite of the intensity and fierce attack and counter attack football, it looked like ending nil-nil, until the 87th minute, when the Spurs keeper could only punch away a strike from Arsenal centre forward John Radford. The ball rolled out to the Gunners' winger George Armstrong who chipped it back into the penalty area, where striker Ray Kennedy sent a thumping header into the Tottenham net. Refusing to lie down, Spurs blitzed the Arsenal goal for the longest three minutes, until the final whistle blew releasing about half of the packed crowd onto the pitch, where they remained for over an hour until Arsenal manager Bertie Mee came out to take the adulation. Five days later Arsenal beat Liverpool at Wembley to win the FA Cup and clinch that first Double.

DALEY THOMPSON VS JÜRGEN HINGSEN

Men's decathlon, Los Angeles Olympics, 8 and 9 August 1984

In the world of track and field, the decathlon's ten punishing events over two con-secutive days are acknowledged as the true test of the all-round athlete, requiring a singular blend of skill, stamina and dedication. Truly great decathletes are a rare species, yet during the first half of the 1980s we were privileged enough to have two at the same time: Great Britain's Daley Thompson and Jürgen Hingsen of what was then West Germany. The two swapped the world record back and forth between them from 1982 until 1992, with the points total being raised six times during that spell. As evenly matched as they appeared, though, when they met in competition it was invariably Thompson who triumphed over his bigger, stronger rival – Hingsen stood at two metres tall and was known as the German Hercules. It was thought that Thompson possessed much greater determination, and was able to raise his game when under the pressure of intense competition, and the twosome's competitions didn't come much more intense than during the 1984 Olympic Games.

> "It's tough out there. It's not as easy as I make it look."
> **Daley Thompson, when asked about Hingsen's throwing up on the track.**

Daley Thompson went into the com-petition as European, world and Olympic champion, while it had been Hingsen's turn with the world record since May of that year, and this was a particu-larly acute showdown. Due to West Germany's boycott of the 1980 Olympics in

Hingsen (left) and Thompson; these days they send each other cards at Christmas.

Moscow, Hingsen had been unable to compete when Thompson took gold, so he was determined to prove a point this time around. Thompson, likewise, was desperate to win, as there was always a sense that because so many nations had opted out of the competition in Moscow, those medals weren't quite the genuine article. In true Thompson fashion, he ramped up the rivalry before the event by declaring, "There are only two ways he [Hingsen] is going to bring a gold medal home – he'll have to steal mine or enter another event."

Thompson started the competition well, with a time of 10.44 seconds in the 100 metres, with Hingsen finishing back in third. Although Thompson took event number two, the long jump – with a leap of 8.01 metres that would have achieved fifth place in that Games' long jump event – the big German narrowed the gap by finishing a close second. Hingsen was strongly fancied in the next event, the shot put, but Thompson produced a personal best of 15.72 metres to maintain his lead. Hingsen then won the high jump, but hurt his knee, and Thompson took the fifth event, the 400 metres, to close the first day with 4633 points (then the highest first day total ever recorded) to Hingsen's 4579.

Hingsen was favourite for the first two events of the second day, the 110 metres hurdles and the discus, approaching them with a renewed vigour to win both – his discus throw of 50.82 metres was a personal best. It reduced Thompson's lead to a mere 32 points. Which seemed to give the British athlete added impetus. Thompson won the pole vault with relative ease, as Hingsen, hit by bad luck, was physically sick during the event, and as a result underperformed in the javelin, giving Thompson another victory. In the final contest, the 1500 metres, all Thompson needed to do was finish to take gold, and if he managed a time of 3 minutes 34.8 seconds or less, his points total would mean he took the world record back from Hingsen. Way out in front and on course to beat that time, the show-boating side of Daley Thompson took over, and he pulled up to saunter across the finish line as if on a Sunday stroll. His time was 3 minutes 35 seconds, meaning he had equalled the record points total and he and his arch rival, who took silver – yet again – now shared that honour.

But this is a story with a happy ending, as two years later Thompson's 110 metres hurdles performance from that day was retimed and found to be one second quicker than recorded, giving him the single point needed to belatedly take the record. And as for him and Hingsen, these days they are very good friends, exchanging Christmas cards and meeting up at least once a year.

SOUTH AFRICA VS AUSTRALIA

One Day International, New Wanderers Stadium, Johannesburg, 12 March 2006

In this fifth cricket One Day International of that winter's series, Australia scored an astonishing 434 for 4, only to be overhauled after lunch when South Africa used their fifty overs to rack up figures of 438 for 9. The game has since been hailed as cricket's greatest ever one day event, and it certainly was for batsmen, with a remarkable number of new records being set, several of which were still standing at the time of writing, five years later. At the time it was the highest aggregate total in a One Day International, almost two hundred ahead of the previous best set by India and Pakistan in 2004 (this record still stands); each side's score beat the previous best (this has since been beaten, but they remain in second and third place); and South Africa's total remains the highest successful run chase in ODI cricket. The 28 sixes hit during both innings was a record, but has since been passed, but the 88 fours it produced has yet to be bettered.

As far as individual achievements went, the only record set wasn't one to be bragged about – Australian Mike Lewis's figures of 0 for 113 made him not only the most expensive bowler in ODI history, but the only one to have more than 100 runs hit off his 10 overs. Sadly for him, both of those records still stand. Elsewhere, and rather more successfully, South Africa's Herschelle Gibbs hit 150 off 100 deliv-

Six longstanding rivalries

The America's Cup
So named after the schooner *America*, that came from, er, America in 1851 to beat England's Royal Yacht Squadron (all fifteen of them) in a race around the Isle of Wight, winning a silver claret jug. The yacht club that holds the trophy can be challenged at any time by any other club, which usually means the US vs the Rest of the World. It is the oldest sports trophy still currently active.

The Ashes
Dates back to 1882, when following a mock obituary for English cricket in *The Times* after Australia won at the Oval for the first time – "English cricket has been cremated and the ashes will be taken to Australia" – the next tour down under was dubbed the Quest to Regain the Ashes.

The Babcock Trophy
An annual fixture since 1909, the British army take on the navy at rugby. Now played at Twickenham, it's a highlight of the amateur rugby season.

The Boat Race
Oxford and Cambridge universities have been racing against each other on the Thames since 1829 and ten years later the race became an annual event.

The Jewelled Shillelagh
The University of Southern California Trojans and the University of Notre Dame Fighting Irish, from Indiana, compete annually for exactly that – a polished oak shillelagh, engraved "From the Emerald Isle".

The Ryder Cup
Named after Samuel Ryder, who donated the trophy, this team competition pits the US's top golfers against those from Europe, on a biannual basis.

eries on his way to 175 off 111 balls, while Australia's Ricky Ponting smashed 150 off 99 balls, finishing up with 164 from 105.

Australia won the toss and Ponting put his side in to the crease, where it became immediately obvious that there were big scores to be had. Openers Adam Gilchrist and Simon Katich made 50 each and shared an opening partnership of 97, then Ponting came in with a lightning century – 73 balls, a personal best for the skipper

– hitting 9 sixes and 13 fours as he roared to 164. Michael Hussey put on 81 in a mere 51 balls, and there was even a twist in what ought to be called the tail: Andrew Symonds and Brett Lee were the last batsmen, and by that point the South African attack was so dispirited they scored 40 runs off the final 2 overs, including 4 no balls in the 49th.

South Africa came to the crease facing a mammoth, never-been-done-before task, which got considerably harder when opening batsman Boeta Dippenaar went for one in the second over. That brought to the crease Gibbs whose heroics inspired those around him, and the other batsmen were able to build an innings on his score of 175, which included 21 fours and 7 sixes. But although the middle order was laying solidly – wicket keeper Mark Boucher got 50 and Johannes van der Wath 35 – the wickets were steadily falling. While it first looked as if South Africa didn't have a chance, they had played themselves back into contention, but now things were getting tight.

> "Everbody out there had one of the greatest days of their lives, and we got an unbelievably big total, but Herschelle and the boys have just been too good. You couldn't ask for more"
>
> **Ricky Ponting sums up the epic encounter**

As the match went into the last over, Boucher and Andrew Hall were batting. South Africa needed seven runs off six balls and the usually reliable Brett Lee had the ball. Boucher hit a single – they now needed six off five. Hall hit a big four, to leave two off four. He tried it again next ball, but was caught. Last man, fast bowler Makhaya Ntini, came in, and the crowd held their collective breath as he edged Lee for a single. One run was needed; there were two balls to do it in. Boucher brought up his fifty in style with a four. Game to South Africa, by three runs with one delivery to spare.

Big-scoring batsmen Ponting and Gibbs were presented with a joint Man of the Match award, but in the spirit of this epic contest, Ponting handed it over to the South African.

Sporting Scandals

When the regulations and the rules are set aside
and when sport is not the only story…

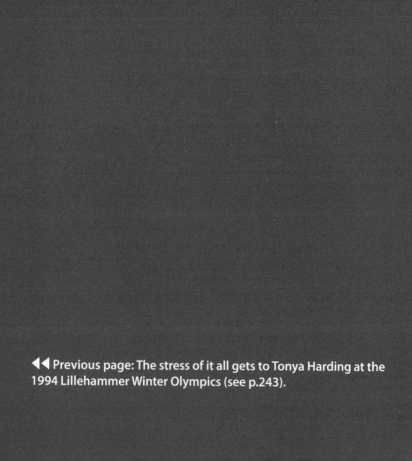

◀◀ Previous page: The stress of it all gets to Tonya Harding at the 1994 Lillehammer Winter Olympics (see p.243).

Sporting Scandals

"I just have to remember that one thing… that restaurants are for eating in and nothing else. "

Boris Becker

The belief in victory at all costs – which frequently prevails in sport as well as war – is sometimes hard to reconcile with the spirit of the game. The idea of fair play is also easily and regularly undermined by the involvement of politics or business. Just how sportsmen create unfair advantages for themselves (aka cheat) takes many forms: there's having a quiet word with match officials; trying to take out an opponent through violence or rule violations, and, perhaps most commonly, the use of performance enhancers on the edge of legality.

Some sportsmen and sportswomen don't even want to win – hence the blight of match fixing – whereas others find their careers hampered by events in their private lives that are mercilessly pored over by the press. "It's only a game" the saying goes: if only that were so…

BALCO

Artificial advantages

Founded by Victor Conte in 1984 as a vitamin supplement company, the Bay Area Laboratory Co-Operative (BALCO) was at the centre of one of the biggest of all doping scandals, involving Major League Baseball (MLB), Olympic track and field, professional cycling and the National Football League, to name just the most high profile sports involved. Among the products developed by the company were various performance enhancing substances, including testosterone cream (known to athletes as "the cream") and the steroid THG (known as "the clear"), which were largely undetectable in blood and urine tests. These "designer drugs"were distributed by BALCO throughout the 1990s. The scandal was uncovered when Jeff Novitsky, an agent with the Internal Revenue Service, began investigating the company in 2002 after a tip-off. The following year a grand jury was convened and many leading sportsmen and women, including several BALCO clients, were called on to testify. The evidence gathered led to the indictemnt of Conte, fellow BALCO executive James Valente, sports coach Remi Korchemny and trainer Greg Anderson.

> The steroid THG was known as "the clear", because it was largely undetectable in blood and urine tests.

One athlete whose career now came under intense scrutiny was baseball star Barry Bonds, whose personal trainer happened to be Greg Anderson. Bonds' account of his connections with BALCO, which amounted to an admission of taking prohibited substances unknowingly, failed to discourage the interest of the authorities and he was eventually indicted on charges of perjury and the obstruction of justice. After a further four years of pre-trial wrangling, the case came to court in March 2011. At the time of writing, Bonds had been found guilty on one count of obstruction of justice but not on three counts of perjury, pending a likely appeal. Anderson again refused to testify against his friend (in relation to the perjury trial) a stance that has already led to a jail term for contempt of court in 2006.

But Bonds isn't the only superstar athlete to draw heat. Marion Jones, the US Olympic sprinter, once touted as "the fastest woman in the world", was found to have been taking a BALCO concoction well before her three gold and two bronze medals at the 2000 Sydney Olympics. Her perjury in front of the grand jury led to a six-month jail stint and she was stripped of her Olympic medals. British sprinter Dwain Chambers was another athlete to get caught out when he tested positive for THG in 2003. He was subsequently banned from competitive athletics for two years and stripped of the medals he'd won between mid-2002 and November 2003. Many of the athletes embroiled in the scandal still insist – like Bonds – that they took the drugs unknowingly, believing they were legitimate vitamins. Boxer Sugar Shane Mosley attempted to sue BALCO founder Victor Conte for disputing that assertion but the case was subsequently dropped.

The full scope of BALCO's operations may never emerge. It seems clear that the company's clients were particularly numerous in baseball, but the ensuing climate of suspicion has impacted on many sports. Of the four people indicted in 2004, Valente and Korchemny were given probationary sentences after pleading guilty to distributing banned substances. In a plea agreement with the authorities, Conte and Anderson admitted to steroid distribution and money laundering. Anderson subsequently served three months in prison and three months of home detention, while Conte received just a four-month prison sentence followed by four months of house arrest – surprisingly modest penalties for helping so many professional athletes bring their sports into disrepute.

THE BODYLINE SERIES
Short but not sweet

The Ashes, a series of five cricket matches between England and Australia held around every two years, is one of the most fiercely contested of all sporting encounters. The 1930 series – played in England but won by Australia – was dominated by the visitors' finest batsman, the phenomenal Donald Bradman, who managed to amass a staggering 974 runs at an average of 139.14. For England's 1932–33 tour of Australia, skipper Douglas Jardine was determined to prevent "the Don" from repeating such a performance. His plan was to employ the newly devised tactic of "fast leg theory", which entailed the bowler pitching the ball short so that it rose towards the body of the batsman on his leg-side, forcing him to take defensive action that would facilitate being caught by a leg-side fielder. Jardine had picked fast bowlers Harold Larwood, Bill Voce and Bill Bowes to spearhead the attack, priming the trio to think of Australians as uneducated and unruly, and branding Bradman "the little bastard". As it happened, the Don missed the first Test match in Sydney and England won convincingly with Jardine only resorting to leg theory to break a stubborn last wicket partnership.

However, the Australian press had taken exception to what a *Sun* journalist termed "bodyline" bowling, although any bad feeling temporarily evaporated when the Aussies won the second Test in Melbourne; Bradman hitting an undefeated second innings of 103. But, with the series now level at 1–1, the gathering storm finally broke at Adelaide. After the visitors had notched a first innings total of 341, the sparks began to fly during Australia's reply. In Larwood's second over, Aussie captain Bill Woodfull took a blow over the heart that sent him reeling from the crease. It took him several minutes to recover. As play resumed, Jardine ruthlessly set his fielders close and the lowering mood intensi-

> "There are two teams out there, one is playing cricket. The other is making no attempt to do so."
> **Bill Woodfull, Australian captain.**

Harold Larwood digs it in short.

fied when Bert Oldfield was hit on the head by a Larwood delivery which fractured his skull. Oldfield later blamed himself for mistiming the shot, but Woodfull was heard to complain, "This isn't cricket, it's war." He was equally forthright when England manager Pelham Warner came to the Australian dressing room: "I don't want to see you, Mr Warner. There are two teams out there. One is playing cricket. The other is making no attempt to do so." As the hosts slumped towards a 338-run defeat, the Australian Board of Control sent a brusque communiqué to the game's parent body, the MCC, in London claiming: "Bodyline bowling has assumed such proportions as to menace the best interests of the game … In our opinion it is unsportsmanlike. Unless stopped at once it is likely to upset the friendly relations existing between Australia and England."

Stung by these allegations, the MCC not only defended its team, but also offered

Underarm and underhand: Australia vs New Zealand, Melbourne, 1981

Many sports lay claim to the mantle of fair play. Cricket likes to think it tops the list for sportsmanship with a long amateur tradition nourishing the idea of gentlemanly behaviour. Even in February 2010, when leading stars were facing accusations of match-fixing and dubious antics such as "sledging" (onfield insults) were routine, the BBC still found time (without irony) to run a story on a cricket team from the crime-ridden Compton district of South Central Los Angeles planning to tour Australia. The point of the piece was to show how cricket's unique sporting spirit had managed to tame the gangland habits of some residents in one of the US's most challenging urban districts. Some one should have reminded Greg and Trevor Chappell of this unique heritage in 1981. In a close limited-over fixture, New Zealand needed an over-the-boundary hit ("a six") off the last ball to beat Australia. Rolling an underarm delivery along the ground to ensure the ball could not be hit for a six was not illegal; it was just completely unthinkable – except to Greg Chappell the Australian captain who gave the order to his younger brother Trevor to do just that. Hostile reaction from the crowd was swift and the batsmen walked off in dismay. A storm of criticism followed from cricketing luminaries that included the players' brother Ian Chappell and both countries' premiers. Robert Muldoon, prime minister of New Zealand, spoke for many when he dubbed it the "most disgusting incident" in the entire history of the game. Such gamesmanship was never permitted again and underarm deliveries were forever banned in limited overs competitions. For Trevor Chappell (in any case overshadowed by the sporting exploits of both his brothers) it ensured a unique place in cricket's hall of infamy though to be fair he was, as the expression has it, only "following orders".

to cancel the remainder of the tour. However, the British secretary of state for dominion affairs and the Australian prime minister intervened and suggested that it wasn't worth jeopardizing vital trade links over a game of cricket. The fourth Test at Brisbane partially restored the tourists' reputation when the tonsilitis-stricken Eddie Paynter left hospital to hit an unbeaten 83 for England in their first innings. He also struck the winning six that secured the series. For the fifth Test at Sydney the slow pitch mitigated against bodyline tactics, but the Australians were still soundly defeated and England's 4–1 triumph was complete. Larwood took 33 wickets in the series. However, his refusal to sign a letter of apology for his part in the bodyline crisis cost him his Test career, as the MCC passed a new law stating "any form of bowling which is obviously a direct attack by the bowler upon the batsman would be an offence against the spirit of the game".

KOBE BRYANT
Off court, out of bounds

Kobe Bryant was seventeen years old when he signed to play basketball for the Los Angeles Lakers. It was and remains extremely uncommon for a player to skip college and become a pro directly from high school, not just because players aren't fully developed physically but because they're unlikely to have enough life experience to handle the pressures of professional athletics. With a National Basketball Association (NBA) contract and a nationally televised platform comes immediate fame, and the spoils of celebrity – parties, drugs, women – are readily available.

> With a National Basketball Association (NBA) contract and a nationally televised platform comes immediate fame, and the spoils of celebrity – parties, drugs, women – are readily available.

Bryant was raw and arrogant when he came out of Lower Marion High School, but that's to be expected from a newly minted teenage millionaire. For the most part he kept his head down and focused on the game (with the occasional foray into the music studio to record a number of unreleased rap tracks), quickly evolving into a player who was frequently compared to his hero, the phenomenal Michael Jordan. He won his first three consecutive NBA championships starting in 1999, the same year he met his future wife, then seventeen year-old high school senior Vanessa Lane. The two married in 2001, but that wasn't the last diamond ring Vanessa would receive. Two years later her husband stood accused of raping a nineteen year-old in a Colorado hotel, and the only way he could think to get out of hot water with his wife was to buy her a massive diamond (it worked). Now known as the "Kobe Special", it was most recently referenced in connection with Tiger Woods during his recent marital troubles.

With his wife firmly by his side, Bryant denied any significant wrongdoing. It was a classic case of he-said she-said, with his accuser alleging rape, and him insisting it was consensual. The woman in question, Katelyn Faber, was working at the hotel when Bryant arrived. He requested a tour of the premises, which she provided, following it up with a hug and kiss. Both agree the hug and kiss were consensual but then their stories split: Bryant admitted to having sex with the woman but insisted that both parties knew and agreed about what they were doing. She, on the other hand, had her own version of events, telling local law enforcement officers that Bryant had forced her after an unexpected kiss, and that her pleas to stop fell on deaf ears. And just to be clear, it's highly unusual for the public to know such details of a rape investigation, but due to a leak at the sheriff's department a number of classified documents became publicly distributed. In addition, Bryant's high-powered legal team attempted to reverse the implementation of Colorado's rape shield law, which prohibits a woman's sexual history to be used against her credibility in rape cases. On the evidence of the rape kit used when Faber was examined at hospital, it was alleged by the defence that she had engaged in sexual activity with another man around the same time as the encounter with Bryant, a claim which the defence used to question the legitimacy of her account. The case never made it to court, with the parties settling in a civil suit.

Kobe Bryant (with ball) doing what he does best, in action for the Los Angeles Lakers.

Six sex scandals

Kobe Bryant isn't only sportsman to have had troubles unrelated to their performance…on the pitch that is.

All in a day's work? Jackie Gallagher-Smith and Gary Robinson
In a 2005 lawsuit, caddy Gary Robinson claimed that he was an "unwitting sperm-donor" for his progolfer (and devout Christian) employer who, he said, had seduced him after failing to conceive with her husband. Robinson withdrew the lawsuit when it transpired that, under Florida state law, he was unable to demand a paternity test.

"Boom Boom" Boris Becker
Sport's most notorious "quickie" took place in 1999. Having just played in his last Wimbledon tournament, and after arguing with his pregnant wife Barbara, the German tennis ace headed for the fashionable London restaurant Nobu and a necessarily brief encounter with Russian beauty Angela Ermakowa on the stairs. The result was love child Anna but also the end of the Beckers' five-year marriage.

Caught out: Denny Neagle
In 2004, following $40's worth of oral sex from a Denver hooker, Colorado Rockies pitcher Neagle discovered that he was the one who had bitten off more than he could chew. Pulled over and charged by the police, Neagle's $51 million contract was immediately terminated, with the Rockies citing his behaviour as not "consistent with what our organization represents".

The dog days of Stan Collymore
Having sex with strangers in public places and encouraging people to watch or join in is known as "dogging". It was a pastime of former English soccer star, Stan Collymore, until *The Sun* newspaper caught him at a notorious site and revealed his "addiction" in 2005. Despite the media fallout, Collymore managed to maintain a career as a respected sports pundit.

Trading "lives not wives": Fritz Peterson and Mike Kekich
In 1973 the baseball story on everyone's lips was the antics of two New York Yankees colleagues. Like characters in an Updike novel, old friends Peterson and Kekich decided to swap wives and homes. While it worked out well for Fritz Peterson and Susanne Kekich – who are still together – Mike Kekich and Marilyn Peterson split soon after. A Matt Damon and Ben Affleck movie of the story, provisionally entitled *The Trade*, is in the pipeline.

CALCIOPOLI

Italian football corruption: no winners

The history of Italian soccer is so mired in scandal that on two occasions the season has ended with no team being awarded the *scudetto* – the championship title. The first time was in 1927 when, in the run-up to a key game, a Juventus defender, Luigi Allemandi, was promised payment if he gifted the game to Torino. As it happened, Allemandi played well and the official offering the bribe refused to pay up despite Torino winning the game. When the story hit the press Torino were subsequently stripped of the title and Allemandi banned for life (he was pardoned after a year).

The 1980–81 season saw the exposing of an even larger match-fixing scandal. This time the scam, labelled *totonero* ("black betting"), was run by two small-time fixers, Massimo Cruciani and Alvaro Trinca, who had good contacts (several Lazio players ate at Trinca's restaurant). When the pair came clean about their activities, which were designed to swindle money from illegal bookmakers, a network of associations with players, referees and club officials was uncovered. The scope of the subsequent inquiry even touched Italy's star striker Paolo Rossi, then playing for Perugia, who was banned from the game for two years. Rossi always denied any involvement in the scandal and the ban was reduced to allow him a memorable role in Italy's 1982 World Cup win.

Further match fixing took place between 1984 and 1986, but the biggest of all Italian footballing scandals was uncovered in 2006. Once again it involved Juventus but this time the man at the centre of the controversy was their general director, Luciano Moggi. Known as *moggiopoli*, or more commonly as *calciopoli* (a name that can be roughly translated as "Soccergate"), the corruption went well beyond the narrow agenda of promoting the interests of Juventus. Moggi was one of a "triad" of Juve officials who, it was alleged, dominated and controlled the whole league via a vast network of associates, bribed match officials and club administrators. Other clubs were also keen to secure refereeing favours, and the subsequent investigation, masterminded by lawyer Guido Rossi, unearthed evidence to suggest that it was almost impossible for a club to prosper without playing by the triad's rules. Fiorentina were a case in point: having suffered from a sequence of highly dodgy refereeing decisions, results began to pick up after the team's boss got in touch with the man in charge of allocating referees, Paolo Bergamo. As the scandal dragged on, it became blindingly clear that the level of contact between referees and club officials, such as Moggi, was excessive and extremely dubious. Retribution followed but, as is the way in Italian football, the initial punishments were reduced after appeals. Moggi was banned from football for five years; AC Milan, Fiorentina, Lazio and Reggina had points docked for the start of the next season. But it was Juventus who were made to suffer the most. Relegated from Serie A (the Italian league's top division) to Serie B and stripped of two championships, most of their leading players left on transfers before the team regained promotion. The 2005–06 champions trophy was then awarded to Juve's arch-rivals, Inter Milan; the 2004–05 season (as in 1926–27) ended up as another blank page in the record books. You wouldn't bet against it being the last.

CRASHGATE

Something rotten at the heart of Formula One?

In Formula One do you drive for yourself or for your team? The answer, of course, is that you are supposed to do both. This apparent driver's dilemma was highlighted by Nelson Picquet Jr's notorious outing for the struggling Renault team at the 2008 Singapore Grand Prix, in which he crashed into the wall at Turn 17. As journalist Joe Saward put it: "one likes to believe that no team would ever be so desperate as to have a driver throw his car at a wall", but when Picquet later claimed that his Renault team, led by boss Flavio Briatore and chief engineer Pat Symonds, had planned for him to crash, the wheels started to come off the idea that this was just an unfortunate accident that happened to have gifted the race to Picquet's co-driver, Fernando Alonso. In Picquet's version of events, not only had the two drivers not been competing with each other, but he was acting under instructions to

> As the FIA pursued the case, the media pondered whether it was one of the worst cases of cheating in sporting history, or simply business as usual for Formula One?

defer to the senior driver – in the most spectacular way possible. The crash caused the deployment of the safety car that under new rules also led to closure of the pit lane. The net effect was to eliminate the advantage of the front runners and cause delays for cars needing to refuel. Alonso had already refuelled, which meant that from a position some way behind the pace he suddenly had a brilliant opportunity to win the race – which he promptly did. Neither Picquet nor anybody else suffered harm from the incident, though the FIA, the sport's governing body, claimed that it was a reckless action by a team determined to win at all costs and that injuries could well have occurred. As the FIA pursued the case, the media pondered whether "Crashgate", as the incident became known, was one of the worst cases of cheating in sporting history, or simply business as usual for Formula One?

Several of the principal characters involved were hardly strangers to controversy. The flamboyant Briatore – who has dated supermodels Naomi Campbell and Heidi Klum – had once skipped a prison sentence for fraud by fleeing to the Virgin Islands, before making his name in the 1980s as a shrewd if ruthless business operator with the Benetton clothes chain. In 1990 he became manager of Benetton's Formula One team and twice struck gold with drivers: discovering the young Michael Schumacher and later Fernando Alonso. Trouble surfaced in the

Drugs in cycling: Choppy Warburton and his bottle

One sport still stands out above all others for close connections with drug taking. That sport is cycling. In 2007 the Tour de France was rocked by four positive tests and two team withdrawals. One wearer of the yellow jersey, Michael Rasmussen, was retired by his team due to his unavailability for drug tests prior to the race. He suffered a two-year ban. In 2010 there were over twenty reported cases of positive tests. Prior to drug testing's introduction in 1966, there were decades before doping was prohibited in any way. The likes of cocaine, strychnine and amphetamines were so widespread that the 1930 rulebook for the Tour de France even had to remind riders that drugs were not actually provided. One assessment, by French team manager Marcel Bidot in the 1950s, was that three quarters of cyclists in the Tour de France were doped. Tales of wasted cyclists are legion, with a favourite alibi for suspicious symptoms being dodgy fish suppers. Sports historian Tim Harris probably calls it correctly when he says that what is "unnatural" is not so much the drug-taking but the extreme punishment cyclists endure for the sake of money and glory. Others suggest that we should not worry about a level playing field: the key distinction is not between riders who took drugs and those who did not, but between the few who got caught and the others that evaded a net with some very big holes.

Competitive cycling's relationship with drugs goes back at least as far as the 1890s, a time when strychnine, laudanum and arsenic were available at chemists, and caffeine or cocaine solutions were regularly used to pep up cyclists. Enter James "Choppy" Warburton, a flashy character from the north of England, once a talented runner , then a leading trainer. Among the cyclists he coached were the Welsh prodigies, Thomas and Arthur Linton, and the pugnacious "mighty midget", Jimmy Michael. Warburton's habit of giving his cyclists a quick swig from a little bottle had been noted, but since doping wasn't officially illegal, it's difficult to imagine what charges would have stuck, had it not been for an oddly lacklustre Michael accusing his trainer of "poisoning" him when competing in the 1896 Chain races at Catford in London. Warburton was subsequently banned by the National Cyclists' Union, one of two key events that effectively halted his career. The second was Arthur Linton's death, aged just 28, following the 1896 Bordeaux–Paris race, during which a reporter observed him on the brink of collapse ("with glassy eyes and tottering limbs") just before staging a remarkable recovery and crossing the line in first place. Rumours attributed the amazing success to the bottle. Linton died a couple of months later in Wales, probably of typhoid fever. Was Warburton in some way to blame? To this day no one knows what was in the famous bottle, but Gerry Moore and Andrew Ritchie, authors of *The Little Black Bottle* (2011), argue that Michael actually got Warburton into trouble in order to get out of his contract. Choppy Warburton died in penury in 1897 while attempting to clear his name.

1994 season when Benetton were accused of using unauthorized traction control (though it was never proven), and the team were also involved in several questionable incidents involving the notoriously competitive Schumacher.

Although cleared of any involvement with Crashgate, Alonso has also rarely been far from the headlines. Revealed to be an innocent party when the scandal broke Alonso drove for McClaren during the 2007 "Spygate" controversy, when the team was censured after Ferrari technical secrets found their way into their rival's possession. However three years later, at the German Grand Prix, he was deemed to have overtaken his Ferrari teammate Felipe Massa (who was leading the race with a few laps to go) just a little too easily. Both drivers were subsequently found to have been following "team orders" and Ferrari were fined $100,000. As for Picquet he was fully exonerated of accusations that the Singapore crash was his idea, when his bid to clear his conscience emerged months later after Renault had shown him the door. The fallout from the scandal seems to have been limited and certainly not the collapse of Formula One some were predicting. After attempts to sue Picquet for false allegations collapsed, Renault declined to dispute the FIA charges and the implicated duo of Briatore and Symonds left the team. Briatore, who always claimed innocence of any wrongdoing, received an unlimited ban from involvement in Formula One; Symonds, who accepted he "took part in the conspiracy", a five-year ban. These were later overturned by a French court in a case brought by both men against the FIA. Matters were finally resolved in an out-of-court settlement which would allow Briatore and Symonds to be back on the Formula One grid by 2013. Apart from the hard-pressed fans and the Renault team, the real loser in the saga may well turn out to be Picquet. Despite various rumours, there is still no sign of him returning to Formula One after his sacking; nor is there likely to be for a driver with a record of whistleblowing on his employers and only one podium place to his name.

THE CHICAGO "BLACK SOX"

Say it wasn't so, Joe

Back from a tour of duty in World War I and raring to resume his career as one of the best power-hitting baseball stars of the era, "Shoeless" Joe Jackson helped lead the Chicago White Sox to the American League Pennant in 1919. Next stop, the World Series, where the White Sox would face the Cincinnati Reds, a team with solid pitching but not much in the way of hitting, and almost no experience of playing in the post-season championship. As it turned out, the Reds would take the nine-game series 5–3 while the Sox only succeeded in covering themselves in shame.

> To indicate that the fix was in, Cicotte planned to hit the Reds' first batter and duly nailed Morrie Rath square in the back with his second pitch.

Rose Ruiz's short cut

Being first across the line in a marathon usually means you're the winner: the snag occurs when you don't actually complete the course. At the Boston marathon of 1980, Rose Ruiz appeared to have clocked the third fastest time in women's marathon history and set a new record for the city of 2:31:56. Ruiz had taken part in the New York marathon some months earlier, but as suspicions mounted concerning the Boston result, a witness reported meeting her on the Manhattan subway during the earlier race. At the close of the Boston course Ruiz seemed to bystanders curiously energetic and none of the footage of the race shows her anywhere on camera except near the finish. Doubt was also raised over how she could have bettered her time so dramatically from New York – an improvement of 25 minutes. Twenty years after the race a reporter for *The Eagle Tribune* spoke to Ruiz who still insisted she ran all of the race, and would even be competing in another marathon soon. To this day her motivation is unclear: some have speculated that she never intended to win the race outright but just wanted to impress work colleagues by finishing with a good time. Yet as commentators have stated, Ruiz's real feat was to end the event's "age of innocence" once and for all.

The series seemed like a dead cert for the Chicago side, and despite Sox owner Charlie Comiskey's legendary stinginess, his players would all stand to earn an extra $5000 (double most of their salaries) for winning the league title. For first baseman "Chick" Gandil it wasn't enough, so when he was approached by bookies seeking an inside edge, he was happy to comply, asking for $80,000 to throw the series. Of course, he would need some teammates on board to make the plan work. He began with ace pitcher Eddie Cicotte who, with an expensive home, and a wife and kids to support, signed up to the plan after some initial reluctance. Outfielder Hap Felsch was easier to convince, and with those two in pocket Gandil was able to turn the shortstop Swede Risberg, second baseman Buck Weaver, infielder Fred McMullin and pitcher Lefty Williams. To round out the side, Gandil still needed outfielder Shoeless Joe, eventually securing his trust for $20,000.

The first game of the series took place in St Louis with Cicotte on the pitcher's mound. To indicate that the fix was happening, Cicotte planned to hit the Reds' first batter and duly nailed Morrie Rath square in the back with his second pitch. With the Sox's ace finishing his outing throwing softballs, Chicago went on to lose the first game 9–1. Game two was more of the same, this time with Lefty Williams pitching for the Sox who lost 4–2. With rumours already flying that the series was fixed tensions were running high, and after the game Chicago's catcher Ray Schalk complained to his manager about the quality of the pitching. There was a lot of money promised to the players, but the bookmakers weren't always reliable about paying up, so for the third game Gandil and his fellow conspirators played hard and won. The same situation provoked winning play in game five, but the other games all went to the Reds, who went on to win the series in eight games.

The scam finally came to light about a year later, as Chicago prosecutors were investigating an unrelated instance of game fixing. Cicotte cracked under questioning and brought down all those involved. The eight conspirators were banned from baseball for life, and as the popular Jackson was leaving the courthouse a disenchanted young fan is supposed to have called out: "Say it ain't so, Joe". Sadly, it was.

DONALD CROWHURST

Around the world single-handed, almost

In 1968, one giant sporting feat remained unaccomplished. No one had ever sailed around the world, single-handed, without stopping. Still less had anyone done it as part of a race. But over the course of that year, nine sailors took up the challenge, posed by *The Sunday Times* newspaper, which offered the Golden Globe Trophy.

The going was almost unimaginably tough. Five sailors were forced to retire from the race. One, Bernard Moitessier, completed his circuit, but decided on the way around to withdraw from the actual race – and went wandering off into the Pacific Ocean a second time. A British sailor, Nigel Tetley, hit a storm in the Azores, just 1300 miles short of the finish line; he lost his boat and was eventually rescued from his liferaft. Only one competitor, Robin Knox-Johnston, actually finished the race, after enduring ten months of solitary marine punishment.

Knox-Johnston's remarkable achievement was quickly overshadowed, however, by the scandal which engulfed the ninth competitor. Donald Crowhurst was a weekend sailor who made navigational equipment for yachts. His boat, the *Teignmouth Electron*, was an experimental, plywood-hulled trimaran, and ill-suited to the demands of the race. As he struggled to meet the 31 October deadline for inclusion in the race, most of the other competitors having long since set sail, Crowhurst suffered from increasing exhaustion and stress. His business began to fail and he entered into an ill-advised contract which meant that withdrawing would likely ruin him.

Crowhurst finally sailed from Devon's Teignmouth harbour on the last allowable day and, still, his boat wasn't ready. As he headed south into the Atlantic, he quickly realized that the *Teignmouth Electron* could never survive a southern storm. Yet still he continued, making painfully slow progress – his children remember charting his position, as he reported it by radio, on a map in their playroom. Then, on 10 December, surprising news arrived over the airwaves. In one 24-hour run, Crowhurst reported having made 280 miles – a new record. On

Six strange sporting fines

Team Ferrari for driving too slowly

In 2010's German Grand Prix, the Ferrari Formula One team was fined $100,000 (£68,000) for appearing to give race leader Felipe Massa instructions to slow down and allow teammate Fernando Alonso to pass him and win the race. It contravened regulation 39.1, which states, "Team orders which interfere with a race result are prohibited."

Robbie Fowler for political gesturing

After scoring his second goal in a 1997 Champions League game against Brann Bergen, the Liverpool striker lifted his shirt to reveal a T-shirt bearing a message supporting Liverpool's striking dockworkers – in the form of a send-up of the Calvin Klein logo. For this gesture of solidarity, he was fined £900 by the Union of European Football Associations (UEFA).

David Gower and John Morris for Australian aviation

On the third day of an Australian tour match against Queensland, in 1991, England cricketers Gower and Morris were both out before lunch. Rather than hang about the pavilion, they headed to a nearby airfield, rented a Tiger Moth biplane and buzzed the match while Robin Smith and Allan Lamb were at the crease. The flight cost them £2027 – £27 for the plane and £1000 each in MCC fines.

Dave Kingman for rodent remittance

Oakland As' baseball star Dave Kingman was made to pay a $3500 fine in 1986 for having a live rat in a pink box delivered to sports reporter Sue Fornoff during a game. The animal had a note tied to its tail reading, "My name is Sue."

Lionel Messi for wishing Mrs Messi a happy birthday

Argentine soccer wizard Lionel Messi had to cough up €2500 when he scored for Barcelona against Racing Santander in 2011, and revealed a T-shirt on which he'd printed "Feliz Cumple Mami" or happy birthday, mum.

Chad Ochocinco for wad waving

When the Cincinnati Bengals wide receiver caught a fifteen-yard pass in a game against the Baltimore Ravens in 2009, officials stopped play to view a CCTV replay for a possible infringement. Ochocinco produced a dollar bill from somewhere in his kit and held it out towards the referee, as a joke. The ref ignored him and the player was subsequently fined $20,000.

Christmas Eve, he told his wife he was lying off Cape Town, indicating that his boat had made still more incredible speed.

The speed was incredible indeed: it wasn't real. On 6 December, Crowhurst had begun to keep two nautical logs, a true one and an elaborate phoney version concocted with the aid of global weather reports and some extravagantly complex navigational calculations. He even began tape-recording himself describing what he pretended to see, and sailed as far south as the Falklands in order to film the view he would have seen, coming north after his circumnavigation. Crowhurst's plan, it seems, was to rejoin the race as the boats returned home again through the Atlantic. His logbook would "prove" his achievement. On 10 April, Crowhurst broke eleven weeks' radio silence to report that he was approaching Cape Horn, at the southernmost tip of South America. Soon after, however, he discovered that he was the last person left in the race, and would, if he continued at the same spanking pace, probably win the £5000 prize for the fastest time. This appalling prospect, what with the inevitable publicity and scrutiny, seems to have caused his deteriorating mental condition to worsen, catastrophically. He began making

Sumo wrestlers assembling at the Tokyo Grand Sumo tournament, January 2009, Tokyo, Japan.

rambling metaphysical jottings, and largely left his boat to look after herself – yacht and master drifting, together, towards disaster. On 1 July, he wrote his last words: "It is finished, it is finished. It is the mercy. It is the end of my game. The truth has been revealed." The *Teignmouth Electron* was discovered, ten days later, six hundred miles west of the Azores. She had never left the Atlantic.

Sumo corruption scandal

Japanese sumo wrestling is as much bound by longstanding traditions of honour and strict codes of behaviour as it is by modern rules and regulations (see p.116), yet it's a sport that's been rocked by more than its giant participants stamping down on the ring before a bout. In the summer of 2010, sumo found itself embroiled in a match fixing scandal so serious that sponsors withdrew their support and the Japanese national TV channel NHK withdrew from live coverage of tournaments.

There's been a whiff of fight-rigging surrounding the top levels of sumo for over fifty years, ever since television and big money became part of something that hadn't really changed since feudal times. Yakuza involvement had long been assumed, even though many were reluctant to believe it. This time, however, the allegations were so well founded that the Japan Sumo Association (the sport's governing body) was forced to openly acknowledge the situation and make an apology. The current scandal first came to light when the police began investigating illegal betting on baseball games (Japan's other major sport) and discovered that sumo wrestlers were placing bets using gangsters as middlemen. When the police seized a number of phones, they were found to contain text messages, from sumo to sumo, discussing how they would throw fights and the money involved. This was usually less than 150,000 yen ($2000), but sumo is notoriously poorly paid, hence the wrestlers' susceptibility to bribing. It was also revealed that a number of ringside tickets, which are usually reserved for VIPs and corporate sponsors, had found their way into the possession of Japan's most powerful crime syndicate.

While match-fixing is not a crime in Japan, illegal betting obviously is, and in February 2011 the police sought prosecutions against two serving wrestlers – a virtually unprecedented action in the history of sumo though at the time of writing no formal charges had been made against any party. The JSA is also taking drastic measures to try to restore the sport's reputation among sponsors, the media and sumo's many fans, going as far as cancelling a major tournament in Osaka – the first such cancellation since 1946. Several top level wrestlers and one coach have also been dismissed, while yakuza members have been banned from tournaments. It remains to be seen if this is enough to regain the respect of the Japanese people, for whom sumo and its Shinto tradition is an important part of the national character.

DECKER VS BUDD: THE AFTERMATH CONTROVERSY
Los Angeles Olympics; 1984

At the Los Angeles Olympics, the women's 3000 metres always promised to be a sensational race: the blonde, all-American pin-up Mary Decker against the elfin, barefoot waif from the South African veld. It didn't disappoint (see p. 197). When Budd overtook and crowded the then-leading Decker, the American fell and was unable to continue. Distraught and suffering an injured hip she was carried from the infield, in tears, by her visibly shaken boyfriend, British athlete Richard Slaney. The crowd responded by applauding their fallen heroine and loudly booing Budd as she completed the race. Budd finished seventh but was immediately disqualified by official track observers for obstruction. She sought out Decker to apologize, but the American was having none of it and theatrically declined to shake hands. While Budd kept her counsel, Decker made no secret of the fact that she believed Budd had robbed her of a medal, stating at a press conference that it was Budd's fault as she had "cut in without being far enough ahead." Unsurprisingly, this sparked something of a transatlantic tabloid war, with the British press siding with Budd and their American counterparts backing the Decker version of events. The Olympic officials, though, quickly sided with Budd, cancelling her disqualification after just one hour, having used that time to study a film of the incident. The officials were following the track running convention that maintains the runner to the rear of a potential contact situation has the responsibility to let the runner in front know that he or she is being impeded, either by a shout or a light touch on the shoulder. While Decker acknowledged the convention, she maintained it was not a licence for an overtaker to move anywhere on the track. After the Games, she continued to talk up the event and in the following year refused to apologize for her attitude towards Budd, telling an interviewer: "I have no reason to apologize. I was wronged." The two met again on the track in July 1985 at London's Crystal Palace, where Decker won and Budd finished fourth, although the main event of the meeting was what would happen next. They shook hands, hugged and appeared to have made up, a sentiment endorsed by Decker who, years later, admitted "the reason I fell was because I was inexperienced at running in a pack."

ENGLISH FOOTBALL'S BETTING SCANDAL
The first fix

On 12 April 1964, the *Sunday People* ran an article accusing two England internationals, Tony Kay and Peter Swan, of betting on a fixed match. The story had come from the match-fixer himself: well-travelled Scottish striker Jimmy Gauld had sold the scoop to reporter Mike Gabbett for a very substantial £7000 and his taped interviews with his co-conspirators were the first to be used to secure a conviction in British legal history. Gauld's Mansfield Town colleagues Brian Phillips and

Sammy Chapman, and four other journeyman players were all implicated in the scandal, but the players who had furthest to fall were the big-name trio from Sheffield Wednesday: Tony Kay, Peter Swan and David "Bronco" Layne.

Layne had broached the subject of betting in November 1962 after bumping into ex-Swindon Town teammate Gauld, who had formed a syndicate after breaking his leg. Kay and Swan reasoned that Wednesday always lost to Ipswich Town and, having bet £50 at 2-1, the players won £100 each after a 2–0 defeat that didn't even need rigging. No one thought any more about the transaction until Gauld squealed and ruined the careers of Swan and Kay, who had become the country's most expensive player following a £65,000 transfer to Everton.

Despite being in Alf Ramsey's England plans in the run-up to the 1966 World Cup, Kay never played professionally again after receiving a lifetime ban and a four month jail term. On his release, he was summoned by the Kray twins to advise them on taped evidence and later spent twelve years in Spain after being accused of selling a fake diamond. After having his ban overturned, Swan returned to the Wednesday ranks in 1972 and later helped Bury to promotion and managed Matlock Town to FA Trophy glory in 1975. However, he and Layne fell out with Kay after he collaborated with Paul Greengrass on the somewhat slanted BBC drama, *The Fix* (1997).

Dressing for effect

When American tennis star Gussie Moran was refused permission by the Wimbledon authorities to depart from traditional white attire in 1949, she came up with another idea. A daringly short skirt with patterned lace knickers was her way round the dress code – knickers had never before been visible – and they received so much media attention that there was even discussion in the British parliament. Thereafter she was always "Gorgeous Gussie". Since then barely a season goes by without some further attempt to push sartorial boundaries, such as Venus Williams' flesh coloured undergarments at the 2011 Australian Open, which gave the unprepared viewer the mistaken impression that she was, as the phrase has it, "going commando".

When it's not the players making the running it can sometimes be the authorities themselves. Female squash does not usually hog the headlines, but when British player Vicky Botwright indicated in 2004 that she would take to the squash court in black bikini bra and thong-style briefs the media took notice, encouraged by the notion that a concerned Women's International Professional Squash Association (WIPSA) opposed the move. It was true they didn't exactly sanction the idea, but then again they knew all about it since the whole thing had been dreamt up as a PR stunt for the sport, fronted by the very capable Botwright, now dubbed the "Lancashire hot bot" and suddenly a very popular search topic on Google. She ended up regretting the prank but it is not likely to be the last stunt of its kind.

Six random acts of violence

Tonya Harding was more the exception than the rule. Most violence in the world of sport takes place on the field of play, or in Eric Cantona's case just on the outside edge.

Blood in the water: Melbourne Olympics (1956)
A few weeks after the Hungarian uprising was ended by Soviet tanks, at the Olympic water polo semi between – you guessed it – the USSR and Hungary, hostilities were renewed. Incensed at their loss of liberty, the Hungarians opted for verbal provocation and aggressive defence. The game was a real scrap with blows from both sides below the water line; when a frenzied crowd saw Ervin Zádor emerge bleeding from the pool the referee ended it early. Victory went to Hungary who were 4–0 up.

Eric Cantona's "kung-fu kick": Crystal Palace vs Manchester Utd
The French striker's kick aimed at an abusive Crystal Palace fan launched a huge media storm in 1995. Even now – and this despite torrents of ter-race vitriol raining down on pressured soccer players every single week – Cantona's dive into the crowd and follow-up punches have remained a one-off. The incident was hailed in some quarters as further testimony to the player's unique genius.

A kick in the stumps: New Zealand vs West Indies (1980)
The moment when the polite façade of cricket was irrevocably shattered. Angered at the umpiring, West Indies' paceman Michael Holding kicked two stumps skywards, his foot ending up as high as his head. For those unused to cricket's genteel customs it is an action comparable in shock value (say) to throwing a racquet at the scoreboard at Wimbledon or snapping the pin on the sixteenth green at the Augusta Masters.

The malice at the Palace: Detroit Pistons vs Indiana Pacers (2004)
Basketball's brawl to end all brawls started with an on-pitch confronta-tion, before a Diet Coke missile (why Diet?) from the crowd hit Pacer Ron Artest who then launched a counter offensive. Colleagues waded in after him to join the rapidly developing melée. Artest got hardest punishment losing close to $5 million salary and receiving a ban for the rest of the sea-son. Five spectators and five players faced charges for assault and battery, but it wasn't the players who came out worst. Several of the crowd were taken to hospital with injuries and those involved in the incident were banned for life from Pistons games.

Marty McSorley and Donald Brashear; Boston Bruins vs Vancouver Canucks (2000)

Over the course of a typical National Hockey League season roughly forty percent of the league (a whopping three hundred players) drop their gloves and turn the ice into a boxing ring. McSorley, a classic hard man with more than three thousand penalty minutes to his career, decided to turn the usual violence up a notch, and with three seconds left in the Bruins' game against Vancouver he wound back his stick and sent a slashing blow to the side of Brashear's head. Brashear toppled to the ice immediately concussed, blood pouring from his ear and mouth. No penalty box would suffice for this level of brutality. McSorley was duly charged and convicted of assault in a Canadian court, receiving eighteen months probation and a year's ban from the sport he had played professionally for twenty years.

Zinedine Zidane's headbutt: Italy vs France (World Cup Final, 2006)

Zidane's headbutt to Italian defender Marco Materazzi's chest was winessed by hundreds of millions. Initial speculation had it that Materazzi had called Zidane a terrorist or insulted his ailing mother. The shirt-tugging

defender eventually revealed that Zidane had said "If you want my shirt that badly, I'll give it to you at the end of the match", to which he retorted: "I'd prefer your whore of a sister". The instantly iconic event inspired numerous online virals, a video game, some Austrian bookmaking commercials and the hit French pop song, "Coup de Boule". The French star apologized for setting a famously bad example to children, but remained unrepentant. In such bizarre ways was Zidane's immortal fame further secured, but it was the Italians who got the result on the pitch.

All about the headbutt: during a 2006 French TV interview Zidane explains all.

THE FOOTBALL WAR
Deadly rivalry

Despite its name, The Football War owed less to the beautiful game than to years of tension between Honduras and El Salvador. Some three hundred thousand Salvadorans had migrated to its larger neighbour and, by 1969, they numbered twenty percent of the peasant population. However, the Honduran farmers' union had long been lobbying President Lopez Arellano to reclaim lands it insisted were held illegally by foreigners and, just as the effect of these repossessions began to bite, the two countries drew each other in a play-off for the 1970 World Cup finals.

Bloodgate

Faux blood capsules are usually the stock in trade of magicians and amateur dramatics not professional sportsmen. This all changed when London rugby union side Harlequins – oddly their name is a reference to the stock clown figure of traditional Italian comedy – decided to try fooling the referee into permitting additional substitutions by the strategic use of counterfeit blood. The injured players would have to leave the pitch; fresh and more tactically useful team-mates would then come on. This seemed a particularly good idea in a 2009 game against Irish team Leinster in the Heineken Cup. The bleeding Tom Williams came off the field to be replaced by a specialist goal kicker. Unfortunately for Williams, a camera had caught him winking at colleagues, which only deepened the suspicions of one of the officials. The subsequent investigation led to the Quins' director of rugby, Dean Richards (a former England international), facing a three-year ban from coaching – the harshest individual punishment – and Harlequins being fined £258,000. The club's physio, Steph Brennan, who admitted faking blood injuries on five separate occasions, was given a two-year ban from rugby and struck off by the Health Professions Council – although he later won his legal appeal against the latter judgement. The image of the sport was even further tarnished, however, when it was discovered that club medic Wendy Chapman had, under great pressure, attempted to cover up the subterfuge by cutting Williams's lip, as a result of which she had to face a General Medical Council hearing. Though temporarily suspended by the GMC, its disciplinary panel eventually decided that her action, though "not in the best interests of her patient", had not impaired her fitness to practise, and she was allowed to continue her career as a doctor. Williams himself had a twelve-month ban reduced to four on appeal. Denounced at the time as a grotesque example of cheating that threatened to tip the manly sport of rugby union into a moral abyss, the torrent of indignation seems rather swiftly to have died away.

The first leg was played in the Honduran capital, Tegucigalpa, on 8 June and the home team's 1–0 victory would have gone unnoticed had a despairing eighteen-year-old Salvadoran, Amelia Bolaños, not shot herself after watching the game on TV. Back in El Salvador, she was hailed as a martyr and the night before the return leg in San Salvador the visitor team's hotel was besieged, with rotten eggs and dead rats hurled through the broken windows.

A further insult occurred when the Honduran flag was burned before the kick-off and a dishcloth run up the flagpole in its place. Unsurprisingly, crowd trouble followed the match, which ended 3–0. Because the two teams were now level on points, a play-off between them took place on a neutral ground, Mexico City's Aztec Stadium, on 26 June. Played in torrential rain, El Salvador won 3–2 with a late goal. However, rather than accept defeat gracefully, Honduras broke off diplomatic relations and El Salvador retaliated with air raids and military incursions on 14 July.

The war lasted just 100 hours, yet managed to claim over 2000 lives. An armistice was signed on 20 June, but world attention was by then almost solely fixed on Neil Armstrong's moon walk. As for the football, El Salvador went on to beat Haiti in a two-leg decider to reach the World Cup finals for the first time in their history. That was as good as it got. Drawn in Group 1 alongside Belgium, the Soviet Union and the host team Mexico, they lost all three games conceding nine goals and scoring none.

TONYA HARDING
Passing the baton

Tonya Harding did not fit the idealized image of the female figure skater. She was no graceful ballerina type floating effortlessly across the ice; she was a compact ball of explosive energy with great leaping ability. She approached the sport with a bluntness telling of her blue collar upbringing, and she certainly wasn't afraid to get her hands dirty. Even in the good times she was never the public favourite: that distinction was first held by Olympic gold medallist Kristi Yamaguchi before passing Harding over for the lanky Nancy Kerrigan.

It's the relationship with Kerrigan that made Harding notorious, and without which her 1994 sex-tape could never be classified as "celebrity". Other notable events of that year included the Winter Olympic Games in Norway, and as prelude, the US Figure Championships. Harding was particularly busy leading up to the US trials, what with double practice sessions every day on top of planning a hit on her biggest domestic rival.

Harding sent her husband Jeff Gillooly to break Kerrigan's knee before the trials. Gillooly subcontracted the task out to the muscle, one Shane Stant, who sneaked up on Kerrigan as she finished a training session only days before she was due to compete. Though possessing a massive height and weight advantage over Kerrigan, Stant's aim was terrible, and he only managed to bruise her thigh with his aluminium baton. Still, she was unable to compete and Harding easily took the title, earning a spot on the Olympic roster in the process.

Harding condemned the attack, but the trail quickly led to her husband and public opinion turned against her. To her horror, Kerrigan became even more adored, and thanks to Stant's incompetence was perfectly fine to compete in the Olympics. Harding on the other hand was nearly removed from the team by the US Olympic Committee, and only maintained her place after threatening to sue (she hadn't at the time been successfully linked to the actions of her husband). She was perhaps the most hated woman in Norway upon her arrival, and was forced to take up residence outside the Olympic village, shunned by athletes and fans alike. Her performance suffered as well, and though she'd placed as high as fourth in the previous Olympics, this time she landed in eighth, while Kerrigan won silver.

After the Games came the lawsuits. Gillooly copped to a plea where he named all of his associates in the affair, including implicating Harding. The disgraced skater eventually pleaded guilty to a charge of obstruction, and slipped away from the public eye before returning four years later to offer an apology to Kerrigan during a televised reconciliation special. Kerrigan, looking uncomfortable next to the stocky bull of a woman, nervously accepted. Tonya Harding's later exploits included a stab at a professional boxing career; she had to quit after three victories because of asthma attacks.

BEN JOHNSON
Too good to be true

The year was 1984, the Olympics were being held in Los Angeles and the Soviet Union had boycotted the Games as part of a Cold War standoff between the nuclear superpowers. The missing Soviets may have influenced results in gymnastics and weightlifting, but they had no one who could come anywhere near the 100 metres time posted by US sprinter Carl Lewis. That challenge fell to Lewis's neighbour to the north, Canadian Ben Johnson.

In the lead-up to the Games there was playful but aggressive bantering between the two, and Johnson, who hadn't beaten Lewis in their previous six races, failed again to secure gold. Lewis had no small ego, which made his win that much harder to stomach for the heavily muscled sprinter from Ontario. But except for one extremely close race that Lewis won heading into the 1988 Seoul Olympics, Los Angeles marked the last time Johnson would lose to the American.

After the disappointment of Los Angeles, Big Ben went on an unbeatable streak, winning every event he entered, and in 1987 he appeared to have solidified his legacy as sprinting royalty by crushing both the 60 metre and 100 metre world records. He was adored in Canada, and was inducted into the Order of Canada for bringing honour upon himself and his home country.

At the Seoul Olympics Johnson was electric. He'd just lost (finally) in a warm-up event to Lewis, sparking another round of chest pounding from both sides. But for the 100 metre final Johnson was flawless, powering down the track to gold and breaking his old world record in the process. Canadian newswires exploded with joy. Johnson was a true hero of the nation, for all of two days. He failed the urine test immediately following his race, testing positive for anabolic steroids, and was quickly stripped of the Olympic gold medal he'd worked his whole life to earn.

Denial by the athlete, and the nation, was the first reaction. Johnson made a statement to the press saying that he'd "never, ever knowingly taken illegal drugs".

SONNY LISTON'S DEATH

When Sonny Liston was at the top of his game he had a bad boy reputation and a notorious criminal past that made him the biggest anti-hero among heavyweight boxing champions the world had yet seen. Feared for his long reach and huge fists, one writer at *Sports Illustrated* evocatively summed him up while commenting on the famous photo of Liston dressed as Father Christmas on the cover of the December 1963 issue of *Esquire* magazine: "there was Liston glowering out from under a tasselled red-and-white Santa Claus hat looking like the last man on Earth America wanted to see coming down its chimney."

In his youth he had been a small-time stick-up man known locally as the "Yellow Shirt Bandit", for the same piece of apparel he'd wear in all his robberies. His boxing career was no less dubious: he was managed by men with known mob connections, and rumours persist as to whether he took dives in his two fights against Muhammad Ali. However, it's his death in January 1971 that has posed the most unanswered questions. Liston's dead body was found by his wife at their home in Las Vegas, slumped by their bed with a broken footstool on the floor nearby. Talk immediately surfaced that the former champ had died of a heroin overdose – that bags of the drug and a syringe were found in the room, and that "track marks" on his arm confirmed his addiction. The coroner's report, however, gave the cause of death as heart failure and lung congestion, and offered no evidence of heroin in his system; no drug paraphernalia was found at the apartment, and the needle marks were explained as the result of a recent hospital stay following a car accident. Indeed Liston was known to have an aversion to needles, to the extent that he baulked at getting the jabs required for travelling abroad, at one point scuppering a lucrative European tour. But the rumours of underworld involvement and drug-related misadventure continue to have currency some forty years later. One acquaintance of Liston suggested he may have been involved in a loans racket, and was murdered – in a way that looked like an overdose – for demanding a larger stake in the operation. As fewer and fewer people are still alive who might know what really happened, it means that the sad, sorry end of Sonny Liston will forever be a mystery.

Conspiracy abounded, especially regarding a certain mystery figure seen talking with Johnson just before his post-race test – Johnson supporters were certain that this person had tampered with the sample, and a very real manhunt to identify him began (one Canadian going so far as to offer $10,000 for information). Johnson eventually admitted he had taken drugs in his career but in his 2010 autobiography remained adamant that immediately prior to the Olympic final it was the mystery man who was to blame for him failing the doping test.

He was given a two-year ban from the sport, and in the meantime faced a government inquiry into athletics and drug use. Shoving aside the shame, Johnson returned to sprinting but never reached the same heights, and was again caught doping in 1993 and once more in 1999. As if we needed any other proof of his poor decision-making, he subsequently took jobs as trainer for Colonel Gaddafi's footballer son, Saadi (who later tested positive for a banned substance while at Italian club Perugia) and for Diego Maradona at Boca Juniors.

ANDREAS AND HEIDI KRIEGER
Love, drugs and lies

When East Germany, a country of sixteen million people, achieved a haul of forty gold medals and second place in the medal table in the 1976 Montreal Olympics, not even their biggest critics could have suspected the scale of their massive state-sponsored, performance-enhancing drug programme. Of all the victims of the initiative none has such a poignant tale as the shot-putter formerly known as Heidi Krieger. From the time she turned sixteen, the sporting authorities had prescribed her massive doses of the potent steroid Oral-Turinabol ("vitamin pills" they told her) alongside birth control pills. The programme had been administered by East German national athletics medical team

> Measures such as forbidding deep-voiced female competitors to give interviews, papered over the abuses being inflicted on the athletes.

duo Manfred Ewald and Manfred Höppner with doses given not just to Heidi but to an estimated ten thousand or so athletes over a period of twenty years. It was precisely the same drug as taken by disgraced Canadian sprinter Ben Johnson, except in Heidi's case the doses were significantly larger.

East Germany's success in Montreal and rise in the rankings had been powered by the performance of female contestants like Heidi. The deception was not perpetrated just on the athletics community or the public. Heidi and her colleagues were totally unaware of the true nature of the supplements they were taking, trusting as many East Germans did at the time, that their masters had their best interests at heart. Problems did arise. Heidi's growing mannishness did not go unnoticed. There were violent mood swings and other pains no doubt all contributing to her sense of not being comfortable in her body. As she later reported to a journalist: "I didn't have control. I couldn't find out for myself which sex I wanted to be." Her solace was sport but after peaking in 1986 with a gold in the European Championships Heidi's body began to recoil from her immense and artificially propelled training load. By 1991, as suspicions over East German drug doping grew, Heidi dropped out of athletics. By 1994 she had become suicidal and a year later contemplated a sex change operation which was completed a couple of years later – after which she emerged as Andreas.

In retrospect what seems surprising is how successful Ewald and Höppner were, and how they managed to get away with it. But in the 1970s and 1980s athletics drug testing was still getting its act together. East German athletes were often accompanied at tests by "minders" of the same sex. Contestants were skilfully weaned off the drugs in the run-up to events to avoid detection, while other measures, such as forbidding deep-voiced female athletes to give interviews, papered over the abuses inflicted on the athletes. Some of the long-term ailments female athletes suffered from include liver abuse, increased susceptibility to cancer, skin and reproductive disorders, increased body hair and enlarged clitorises. In 1977, when fellow shot-putter Ilona Slupianek was disqualified after a doping test, team management just tightened the controls, increased pre-race testing and prevented athletes from travelling who were at risk of failing tests.

When Höppner and Ewald were finally called to account and convicted of being "accessory to the intentional bodily harm" of athletes in 2000, the prosecution team were not short of witnesses. One of these was swimmer Ute Krause who started receiving the same blue pills in 1977. Near the start of her drugs programme she had put on "fifteen kilos in weeks" before becoming bulimic and suicidal. Despite the convictions neither medic ever spent time in jail and it wasn't until 2007 that a fund of $4.1 million was paid out to 157 former athletes in an out-of-court settlement. Hundreds, possibly thousands, of others affected will never be compensated. After the trial a happy Krause and Krieger got together and later married, though long after the sex change Krieger still has to receive injections to lock down his masculinity. His one gold medal is now encased within a trophy named after him given every year in Germany for persons fighting against drug-taking in sport.

THE "NAZI OLYMPICS"

1936 and all that

The scandal of the 1936 Berlin Olympics was that it took place at all. Many nations debated a boycott, chiefly on the grounds of Nazi anti-Semitism, but few came through. The British dithered for over a year before accepting the German invitation. The French kept changing their minds, but finally decided to send a team. In the end, 49 nations took part – twelve more than in 1932 – and the Soviet Union was one of the few to refuse an invitation. (Though the Russian stand, it should be said, was not exactly heroically anti-Nazi: they had boycotted every previous Games as well.)

The debate in the US was particularly noisy, perhaps because newspapers and Jewish organizations there were less blind to the racist nature of the Nazi regime. The anti-boycott voices proved more powerful, however. Avery Brundage, president of the US Olympic Committee, raged against "treason for political reasons in some quarters at home". His true colours, arguably, were revealed when he claimed that there was actually a Jewish, Communist conspiracy to keep the US out of the Games.

> After visiting Germany, the US Olympic Committee's secretary, Frederic W. Rubien, managed to persuade himself that there was "absolutely no discrimination" against Jews, even though he must have seen signs saying "No Jews Allowed"

After visiting Germany, the US Olympic Committee's secretary, Frederic W. Rubien, managed to persuade himself that there was "absolutely no discrimination" against Jews, even though he must have seen signs saying "No Jews Allowed" all over the country, and despite the fact that Jewish athletes had been almost universally dropped (Rubien used the unfortunate word "eliminated") from the German team. This was because "they are not good enough as athletes", said Rubien. "Why", he added, "there are not a dozen Jews in the world of Olympic calibre". Yet the US team alone had included several Jewish athletes – before a number were dropped ahead of Berlin for "political" reasons. Two Jewish sprinters in the US 4 x 100 metres relay team, in fact, lost their places on the actual day of competition.

In Olympic history, the race scandal has centred not on Jewish athletes, however (nor even on Berlin's eight hundred German Roma people who were rounded up and interned immediately before the Games). The controversy is all about the

> Hitler told the Nazi aristocrat Baldur von Schirach that "the Americans ought to be ashamed of themselves for letting their medals be won by Negroes"

black American athlete Jesse Owens, who won four gold medals at Berlin, but was supposedly "snubbed by Hitler". Some say the dictator refused to shake Owens' hand, others that he turned his back on him. Perhaps, but the writer Paul Gallico, who was there, described how Hitler gave Owens "a friendly little Nazi salute – the sitting down one with the arm bent", and Hitler gave no other athlete better treatment. The dictator, in fact, was acutely conscious of the need to put on a show. Half the point of the Games – alongside demonstrating German racial superiority, of course – was to prove what a peacable, tolerant nation Germany was.

The truth, of course, was very different. Hitler told his friend Albert Speer, in private, that Owens' victories annoyed him, and argued that "primitive peoples" should be excluded from the Games. Hitler told the Nazi aristocrat Baldur von Schirach that "the Americans ought to be ashamed of themselves for letting their medals be won by Negroes", and added "I myself would never shake hands with one of them". Jesse Owens' side of the story is more complex. He later told the legendary journalist William L. Shirer that Hitler had seemed "a good sport", for saluting him. "I like his smile", he'd thought. If anyone had snubbed him, he reckoned, it was US president Franklin Roosevelt, who had failed to send him a congratulatory telegram. Owens may have shown a disappointing lack of solidarity with his Jewish colleagues, but as a black man in 1936 he had a point. In Germany, he could use the bus and the rest room alongside white competitors. At home, the US practised a system of racist segregation that was arguably almost as vicious as Nazi anti-Semitism, and which would remain in place until long after the end of World War II.

OLYMPICS BLACK POWER SALUTE

Fists of pride

Following the assassination of civil rights leader Martin Luther King, Harry Edwards, the founder of the Olympic Project for Human Rights (OPHR), urged African-American athletes to boycott the 1968 Mexico Games in protest at continued racial discrimination. However, sprinters Tommie Smith and John Carlos found a much more powerful way to protest on 16 October 1968, when they gave a black power salute on the winners' rostrum after taking gold and bronze in the 200 metres.

Standing between them was Australian Peter Norman, who had trailed Smith's world-record time by just 0.03 seconds. While preparing for the medal ceremony in the athletes' lounge, he had heard the Americans discussing how Smith would sport a black scarf to symbolize black pride, while Carlos would open his tracksuit to reveal a bead necklace commemorating victims of racial violence. They were also planning to step on to the podium in black socks to denote the poverty of most African-Americans. However, Carlos had forgotten the black gloves he was supposed to wear for a head-bowed, clenched-fist salute during the playing of "The Star-Spangled Banner" and it was Norman who suggested that Smith wore his right-hand glove and give Carlos the left and, thus, ensured that their pose became one of the most iconic images in sporting history.

The athletes were booed as they left the stadium and US Olympic Committee chief Avery Brundage (who raised no objection to the Nazi salute when he led the US team at the 1936 Berlin Games) ordered Smith and Carlos to be suspended from the track squad and ejected from the Olympic village. He even persuaded sprint legend Jesse Owens to plead with the other athletes not to replicate their actions (Owens was later reduced to tears by accusations of Uncle Tomism). Yet, even though Brundage succeeded in having Smith and Carlos sent home, he couldn't prevent the all-white members of the rowing eight from following

Norman's example of wearing an OPHR badge or the 400 metre trio of Lee Evans, Lawrence James and Ronald Freeman from wearing Black Panther berets during their medal ceremony.

Ultimately, Smith and Carlos paid a heavy price for their gesture. After *Time* magazine produced a cover grotesquely parodying the Olympic motto "Faster, Higher, Stronger" with the words "Angrier, Nastier, Uglier", they received death threats and hate mail. Each struggled to sustain a National Football League career, with the Cincinnati Bengals and the Philadelphia Eagles respectively, and Carlos's wife eventually committed suicide under the strain. Eventually, both athletes went into education, with Carlos serving as a community liaison during the 1984 Los Angeles Olympics and Smith coaching the US track team at the 1995 World Indoor Championships before being named the California Black Sportsman of the Millennium in 1999.

As for Norman, he was ostracized by the Australian sporting establishment and excluded from the 1972 Olympics. Having narrowly avoided amputation after a serious leg injury, he succumbed to depression and alcoholism. Yet, he retained close links with Carlos and Smith until his death in 2006.

PETE ROSE
Gambling with a reputation

Pete Rose is without question one of the greatest baseball players in the history of the game. He holds the Major League Baseball record for most hits in a career (4256), won three World Series with two different teams, a couple of Golden Gloves and was selected as a league all-star seventeen times. For all but half a season spent in Montreal, he played for the Cincinnati Reds, then the Philadelphia Phillies before moving back to Cincinnati to take on the role of player-manager. It was in this final stage of his career that the man lovingly known as Charlie Hustle was caught gambling on baseball, and as punishment was banned from the game for life.

To be clear, Pete Rose liked to gamble, and it's believed that for one long stretch in the 1980s he was risking upwards of $15,000 per day. When first approached by investigators he readily admitted placing wagers on basketball and football games, as well as on horse and dog races, though people weren't so interested in those perfectly honest acts. One of Rose's bookies, in an attempt to lessen his own punishment for a drugs charge, revealed that the ballplayer's bets extended beyond sports unrelated to his own, and to the very games he himself was managing.

A former federal prosecutor by the name of John Dowd was brought in to study the allegations. He uncovered a paper trail of phone and bank records that corroborated the information provided by Rose's former bookie, and discovered the sad fact that when Rose didn't have cash to cover his line, he'd put up baseball memorabilia instead (including the bat he used to break Ty Cobb's career hits

John Carlos, Tommie Smith and Peter Norman (right to left) in one of sport's defining historical images.

record). The Dowd inquiry revealed that Rose had a serious gambling problem, and definitively determined that while manager for the Cincinnati Reds he'd placed bets on his own team.

Rose maintained his innocence for some fifteen years before admitting his guilt in the pages of his 2004 autobiography *My Prison Without Bars*. Three years later, in a televised interview, he stated that he'd bet on his team every night, because he loved his team, he believed in them, and he wanted them to win. While there's no evidence to suggest he ever bet against his own players, Dowd's records suggested that Rose conspicuously held off betting on the Reds when Bill Gullickson was pitching, hardly a vote of confidence in a team member.

Though there's an odd tinge of nobility in betting on your own team, doing so brings up too many potential issues for comfort. Rose could have brought back an injured player before he'd fully recovered in order to earn a win, or put in someone from the bullpen on too little rest. If he found himself in a hole, he could have fed inside information to bookies in exchange for their tearing up his markers. There is no evidence to suggest he did any of these things, but the door was theoretically open, and for these reasons such gambling is countered by severe penalties. Rose's disgraced removal from baseball includes any possible induction into the Hall of Fame and a lifetime ban on any level of involvement with Major League Baseball. Though some have sympathy with a self-confessed gambling addict, there is no sign yet that the ban will be reversed.

CASTER SEMENYA
Drawing the gender line

In 2009 and 2010, the South African middle-distance runner Caster Semenya was winning women's 800 metres events with an effortlessness which outraged some of her rivals. They complained of unfair advantage: "she", they said, was actually a "he". One unattributed rival claimed to be "literally running against a man", while the Canadian runner Diane Cummins protested that Semenya was "on the very fringe of the normal female athlete biological composition".

Many wondered how Semenya's rivals could know such details, and the comments sounded suspiciously like the complaints of poor losers – a cruel and opportunistic response to the fact that Semenya's features aren't especially feminine. Semenya's own feelings aren't reported but many South Africans were outraged. This wasn't just sour grapes, they urged: this was racism. The point, some said, was that Semenya didn't conform to a white conception of femininity: all those rich, pale northerners just couldn't deal with being outrun by a black girl from a poor part of Africa.

The International Association of Athletics Federations (IAAF) was left with a problem. What if the complaint was justified? Gender infringements weren't unknown. Dora Ratjen, who came fourth in the women's high jump in the 1936

Berlin Olympics, was later revealed to be a man called Heinrich. In the 1960s, hundreds of female athletes from East Germany were so overdosed with anabolic steroids that they became, in effect, hormonally male. Some went on to live as men, including shot-putter Heidi Krieger (see earlier in this section).

Cummins had a point. A line has to be drawn somewhere, otherwise men could simply compete alongside women – or rather they'd compete on their own, as female athletes would instantly all but vanish from competition. Drawing that gender line, however, is a nightmare for sports authorities, as it is now understood that approximately one in one hundred babies born do not conveniently and perfectly fit into one biological sex or the other. It can be a question of anatomy, chromosomes or hormonal development, and the variations may be inconsequential or transformative, but in a world of blurred boundaries, where should maleness end and femaleness begin?

Testing of chromosomes (men have a Y – on the standard model, women don't) was considered the answer, for a time, but by the Beijing Olympics of 2008, such crude measures had been replaced by an official Gender Verification Lab, which looked at multiple factors, including hormone levels, and attempted to come to more nuanced decisions. The aim was to establish not what sex a female or intersex athlete was, but whether s/he benefited from any athletic advantage from her chromosomal or hormonal uniqueness.

It's not an unreasonable position, but privacy remains a major headache for sports authorities – and for any athlete unfortunate enough to be accused of a lack of femininity. Having your gender identity questioned, and your medical records combed over, all in the glare of international publicity, makes being accused of taking performance-enhancing drugs look like a breeze. After she was stripped of a silver medal won at the 2006 Asian Games, for failing a "gender verification test", Indian athlete Santhi Soundarajan was reported to have attempted suicide. In July 2010, Caster Semenya was cleared to return to competition. At the time of writing, her gender status, as is proper, remained officially private.

SHERGAR'S KIDNAPPING

"A clue? That is something we haven't got" – Chief Superintendant James "Spud" Murphy

Back in 1983, it didn't strike anyone as lax to protect one particular kind of multi-million-dollar investment with just a latched wooden gate. After the theft of Shergar, a record-breaking racehorse, from the studfarm in Ireland that was his home, no horse-breeder would ever make that mistake again.

Shergar had retired at the age of three. His six major wins, in the early 1980s, had grossed £436,000 in prize money. At Epsom, Shergar was so far ahead that the runner-up jockey, John Matthias (riding Glint of Gold), thought he had won. Shergar's 1981 Derby win was by a margin of ten lengths, a record distance that century. His seemingly effortless wins, coupled with the white marking on his face, and four white "socks", made him a quirky "celebrity" of sorts. Owned by Prince Karim Al Husseini (better known as the Aga Khan), Shergar was not sent to the US, as expected, but put out to stud in Newbridge, County Kildare. The horse had been "syndicated" – investors could buy a stake in him – and forty shares were sold at £250,000 each. Shergar fathered 35 foals in his first year and breeders paid up to £80,000 to have one of his offspring, but his stud career came to a very sad end. On the evening of 8 February 1983, Bernard Fitzgerald, son of the head groom, James, answered the door to a man dressed as a member of the Gardaí (the Irish police). He was knocked to the ground and three other men marched in, armed with pistols and a sub-machinegun. "We have come for Shergar", one of them said.

Two gunmen guarded Fitzgerald's family while James was marched off and ordered to help load Shergar into a horsebox. James was then driven away by three of the men before being dropped off seven miles away. Then he was told a password, "King Neptune", which the thieves would use to identify themselves with, and ordered to keep walking, not to turn around and not to call the police. He did as he was told, and walked to the nearest village where he phoned his brother. Neither James nor his family were harmed. Fitzgerald contacted the stud manager, who then phoned Shergar's vet, who contacted Captain Sean Berry (chairman of the Irish Thoroughbred Breeders' Association), who then called the Irish finance minister. Quite why nobody phoned the police immediately is a mystery, but the crime wasn't reported to the Gardaí for hours. The thieves had cleverly chosen the night before a major racehorse sale, so there were plenty of horseboxes on the roads.

The trilby-sporting James "Spud" Murphy was the senior police officer in charge of the case. His gumshoe hat was not the only thing that endeared him to journalists. He sought the aid of clairvoyants and famously reponded to one question with the telling words: "A clue? That is something we haven't got". Meanwhile, the kidnappers opened negotiations with the Aga Khan, using the password they had given James Fitzgerald. Not only were the thieves under the mistaken impression that the Aga Khan was the sole owner of the horse, but they also seriously underestimated the syndicate's *sang froid*. Shergar's owners concluded that making a deal with kidnappers would set a bad precedent and decided they would not capitulate.

> "To be honest, anyone could have ridden Shergar. As we came round Tattenham Corner, I had to pinch myself. We were going that well. To me, it was like a fairytale. Eighteen and winning the Derby. It doesn't normally happen like that."
>
> Walter Swinburn, who rode Shergar to victory at the Epsom Derby in 1981.

The IRA were the chief suspects, and in the ensuing clampdown all known Republican bases were raided. Many arms caches were discovered but no clues as to the horse's whereabouts. The conspiracy theorists had a field day, with wild speculation fingering everyone from Colonel Gaddafi to the Italian Mafia. An IRA supergrass, Sean O'Callaghan, later claimed that the affair was indeed the work of the

IRA. O'Callaghan wrote that an IRA associate had implied Shergar had been shot within hours of his abduction, after the horse panicked. He also stated that the ransom demand was £5 million. However, an investigation by the *Sunday Telegraph* told a different story. Its unnamed source, a former IRA member, claimed that Shergar was shot four days after his theft, on the IRA chief's orders. According to him, they would have freed Shergar if they had not been under such tight surveillance. Rumour has it that Shergar's remains are buried on a farm on the outskirts of Ballinamore.

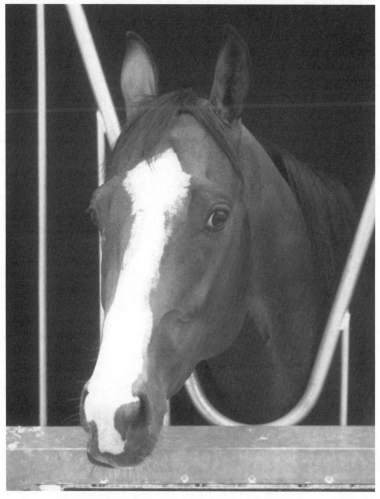

The unlucky Shergar at his stables in Newmarket, England (1980).

Esha Ness: the 1993 Grand National winner that never was

First out of a field of thirty and, at the time, the second fastest finish in Grand National history: you would think that John White's ride on the 50–1 Esha Ness would have been enough for a famous victory. Instead, the 1993 race, at England's renowned Aintree course, became the "race that never was". It was estimated that bookmakers had to repay over £70 million on bets with no outcome and even larger numbers of viewers on television (upwards of two hundred million worldwide) found themselves bemused by a race that seemed to take place but didn't. The biggest event in steeplechase racing in the UK had calamitously stumbled before the first hurdle.

The problems began at the start, with anti-race protestors holding up proceedings which then got more confused because of the damp and blustery conditions. The limp starting tape got mixed up with horses and riders not once but twice (the second time wrapping around jockey Richard Dunwoody), and though a false start was announced, the cue for riders to stop – the recall flag – didn't get displayed. Off went thirty of the thirty-nine horses including Esha Ness who was probably never on better form. Years later White revealed why he didn't stop: "There had been a couple of false starts but you're in behind a lot of horses and looking straight in front of you and then bang, you're off and the sole thing in your mind is trying to win." Chaotic scenes followed Esha Ness's finish and that of the other horses but thankfully the debacle never became the subject of conspiracy theories. It was a fiasco and a farce but still just an accident. The race was declared void. In future Grand Nationals the tape was raised at a forty five degree angle to reduce the risks of such a problem ever happening again.

THE SPANISH PARALYMPIC SCANDAL
Disabling dishonesty

In order to qualify as a member of an intellectual disability basketball team, it must be determined by medical test that you have an IQ under seventy, a score that would technically define you as "feeble-minded". This minor detail didn't stop Spain from sending a fully capable squad of roundballers to the Australian-held Paralympic Games in 2000.

The category for lesser intellects was still in its infancy, having only been introduced at the Atlanta Games in 1996. Plenty of time, though, for the Spanish Paralympic Committee (SPC) and their ex-vice president Fernando Martín Vicente to be accused of a shocking fraud. Vicente's involvement was particularly surprising, considering he had a disabled son and was president of the country's national association for mentally handicapped athletes. Vicente denied suggestions from *El Mundo* newspaper – that were never in any way proved – that he profited personally from state support but later he still resigned from his post in the face of a media storm surrounding the team's composition.

Perhaps the scandal wouldn't have come to light if Spain hadn't so completely dominated all competition on their way to securing the basketball gold medal (winning in the finals by thirty points, and beating Japan by sixty in the group stage). Or maybe it was the fact that they'd invited Carlos Ribagorda to join the team, a young journalist looking to make a name for himself. Ribagorda played with the squad for two years before he and the rest of the twelve men representing Spain flew to Australia to compete. Eyebrows were raised as they progressed through to the finals, and even papers back home began questioning the validity of the win.

Newspapers abuzz over a possible conspiracy, Ribagorda came forward, telling the press that ten of the twelve men on his team were at least of average intelligence, and that neither he nor his teammates were ever subjected to tests that may have proved their ineligibility. He also suggested that two Spanish swimmers, a sprinter and a table tennis player were more capable than suggested, though the focus of public disgust fell mainly on the basketball team.

As a result of Ribagorda's revelation his team was stripped of its gold medal, and the Paralympics have dissolved the intellectual disability category for all sports at future Games. Vicente took the fall for the SPC, insisting that he had no personal oversight of the original tests for the competitors – tests everyone could agree were flawed. The whole affair also appears to have inspired the Johnny Knoxville vehicle, *The Ringer* (2005), which extracted a little humour from a famously embarrassing incident for the Paralympic Games.

MICHAEL VICK

Fighting dogs and the media pack

Michael Vick was at one point the fullest expression of the modern National Football League quarterback. Selected as the first pick by the Atlanta Falcons in the 2001 draft, he had a powerful arm, could read the rush and escape the pocket with a sprinter's pace, and was a respected leader. At six feet tall he is slightly on the short side (his height making it tough to see over his linemen), but he more than made up for that with his athletic ability.

2004 was a stellar season for Vick, taking his team to an 11–5 record and reaching the National Football Conference divisional championship game. Though they lost, Vick had secured hero status in Atlanta, and though the next two seasons were average at best, Falcons fans knew they had a quarterback to build the franchise around. Apparently no one told Vick, who squandered his chance at a long and

BALL TAMPERING

When you're facing a cricket ball travelling at up to 100 mph, any unpredictable movement it makes in the air is problematic. Cricket's fast bowlers routinely shine one side of the ball with spit and a quick buff against the trouser leg, hoping to manipulate the ball's aerodynamics. This "swing" bowling can be devastating, so cricket tries to limit the amount of polish any ball can receive. However, cricketers are adept in finding ways to gain advantage, and while there is no rule prohibiting shining the ball using sweat or saliva, the use of manufactured substances is illegal. The most notorious shine aids are hair gel and lip balm combined with sweat, but recently sugar has hit the headlines. In 2004 Indian batsman Rahul Dravid was fined for rubbing a wet lollipop across one side of the ball, and in 2008 English batsman Marcus Trescothick admitted that he'd been sucking Murray Mints during the 2005 Ashes series to give his spit that little extra shining power.

Picking at the seam in order to raise it is another ball-tampering tactic, although it's difficult to distinguish the effects from normal wear and tear. In 2001, on tour in South Africa, Indian batsman Sachin Tendulkar was fined and given a suspended ban after the match referee saw TV close-ups of him apparently scratching at the ball's seam. More dramatically, in 2010 Pakistani captain Shahid Afridi was filmed apparently biting the ball; his claim he was smelling it was judged unconvincing, and he eventually made a (rare) confession. Roughening one side has the same effect as polishing the other, and in 1994 England captain Mike Atherton was pulled up for apparently rubbing dirt from his pocket on to one side of the ball. He denied any wrongdoing, but was fined £2000 by England boss Ray Illingworth anyway. In 2010 in South Africa, English bowlers Stuart Broad and James Anderson faced allegations of deliberately treading on the ball with their spikes to scuff the surface, but no charges were brought.

The most famous ball tampering incident, known as "Ovalgate", happened at the Fourth Test between England and Pakistan at the Oval in London in 2006. On the fourth day, as England were playing themselves back into the game, Alastair Cook was caught on the toe by a remarkable swinging ball from Umar Gul. It could have been the turning point for Pakistan, turning a draw into a win, but umpires Darrell Hair and Billy Doctrove stopped play and inspected the ball in the middle of the pitch. After a tense pause, TV cameras bearing down on all sides, they decided that the ball had been tampered with and awarded England five penalty runs. Pakistan played on for a time, but after the tea break the entire team seemingly refused to return to the field. At least, they stayed off for so long the umpires abandoned the match. Pakistan then declared themselves ready to play on, but it was too late and, in a cloud of confusion and accusations, England were awarded the game. It was the first time a Test match had ever been forfeited in such a controversial fashion.

stable career with his involvement in a dog fighting ring he operated out of his ranch in Virginia.

There are men acquitted of murder playing in the NFL. There are players who have been busted for drug use, for public fights, for carrying concealed weapons, for sexual assault, but none of these acts raised the hackles of the viewing public more than Vick killing dogs. Truth be told dog fighting is a brutal business. Dogs are trained to fight to the death, their owners often using smaller, weaker dogs as practice for the main events, and if a dog doesn't look like it will achieve the desired potential, it is unceremoniously put down. While on the mend from a broken leg, Vick reportedly focused all his attention on the fighting ring, both hosting events and culling his kennel by such means as hanging and drowning.

When federal prosecutors raided his ranch in 2007 they found plenty of evidence to convict Vick and his partners. Dog fighting is a crime in all fifty states of the union, and taking the animals across state lines to fight in Maryland and the Carolinas upped the level of impropriety to federal offence. Vick was able to arrange a suspended sentence for the state charges, but the federal judge sent him away for just shy of two years. While incarcerated his finances collapsed, leaving him next to nothing in the bank alongside a ruined reputation and few prospects for the future.

Vick was released from prison just prior to the start of the 2009 NFL season. There were rumours that a few teams were interested in signing him on a trial basis, but it appeared that the public backlash might simply be too great to overcome. Eventually the Philadelphia Eagles took the chance, and as predicted the public went crazy. There were protests and threats of boycotting the season. Advertisers were poised to pull their endorsements, and animal rights groups attacked both the Eagles and Vick relentlessly. Vick took the criticism with a surprising amount of grace. He publicly admitted his guilt and promised to make amends by speaking for and participating in animal rights activities. Eventually the public cooled, and Vick slowly regained his superstar form, taking over the reins at starting quarterback for the Eagles' 2010 season. There was even talk of him receiving the NFL's Most Valued Player Award, but after a dismal post-season performance in which he killed any chance of victory by throwing an interception in the last drive of the game, some spectators are still sure to be less kind than the parole board.

THE WINTER OLYMPICS SKATING SCANDAL

Judges on thin ice

The Russians – both Soviet and post-Soviet – had dominated figure skating from the 1960s, winning Olympic gold in the pairs a staggering ten out of eleven times. At the 2002 Winter Olympics in Salt Lake City they were represented by the sparkling duo of Elena Berezhnaya and Anton Sikharulidze whose main rivals were the popular Canadians, Jamie Salé and David Pelletier. In championship skating, competitors get to perform twice – a short programme and a long one. By the halfway stage Berezhnaya and Sikharulidze were clearly in the lead, but with the Canadians hot on their heels. For the decisive long programme, the Russians chose a routine that emphasized their classical refinement, while Salé and Pelletier – skating to the music from *Love Story* – opted for something more cutesy and crowd-pleasing. From the response of the spectators and the US television commentators it was no contest: the gold medal must go to the Canadians. It didn't seem so obvious to the nine judges, who had to assess both the technical merit of the routines and the more subjective issue of presentation. True, Sikharulidze had made a small but conspicuous error near the start, but the Russian routine was, arguably, more demanding and their presentation more sophisticated. In the end, five of the judges (Russia, Ukraine, Poland, China and France) plumped for Berezhnaya and Sikharulidze, while the other four (US, Canada, Germany and Japan) preferred their rivals. Yet again Russia had triumphed.

> From the response of the spectators and the US television commentators it was no contest: the gold medal must go to the Canadians. It didn't seem so obvious to the nine judges.

If a disappointed Salé and Pelletier accepted the result with a good grace, the US and Canadian media did not. But the ensuing brouhaha may well have died down soon enough if the French judge, Marie-Reine Le Gougne, had not been confronted by Sally Stapleford, chair of the technical committee of the International Skating Union (ISU). The day after the event, Le Gougne admitted that she had voted for the Russians under pressure from Didier Gailhaguet, the head of the French skating federation. It was apparently all part of a deal in which the Russian judge would vote for the French pair in the forthcoming ice dance competition – an accusation that Gailhaguet vehemently denied. To add to the confusion, Le Gougne then retracted her original statement, claiming that she had in fact voted according to her conscience and that the Russians deserved to win. In a desperate attempt to stop the scandal getting further out of hand, the president of the International Olympic Committee (IOC), Jacques Rogge, and the ISU president, Ottavio Cinquanta, took the unprecedented step of awarding a second set of gold medals to Salé and Pelletier, while allowing Berezhnaya and Sikharulidze to keep theirs. The result was now officially a draw.

Although Le Gougne and Gailhaguet were suspended for three years, the ISU decided not to investigate the possibility of Russian collusion in the incident. However, a few months later a Russian "businessman" – who denied any involvement – was detained in Italy in the wake of an FBI investigation that suggested he had set up the deal in the hope of securing a French visa. The case fizzled out when the US authorities failed in their attempt to get him extradited. Since 2004 the ISU has introduced a more transparent judging process that is less vulnerable to corruption.

The Shocks

Always expect the unexpected

◀◀ Previous page: US net minder Jim Craig fends off another Soviet attack on the way to the Miracle on Ice (see p. 280).

The Shocks

"First they ignore you, then they laugh at you,
then they fight you, then you win."

Mahatma Gandhi

Sporting shocks are what make sporting lives so entertaining. The whole purpose of playing or following a sport is that you're never ever one hundred percent sure what's going to happen at any given event. But that's not always the simple matter of an unexpected result or an underdog succeeding when nobody gave them a chance, although such occurrences are usually worth the price of admission – Mike Tyson against Buster Douglas, or Dennis Taylor taking on Steve Davis at snooker or Italy seeing off Scotland at Murrayfield in rugby's Six Nations.

Sometimes sporting shocks aren't nearly as straightforward as that: witness Bob Beamon's amazing leap, or Jean Van de Velde's astonishing eighteenth hole meltdown, or the so-called Immaculate Reception. When sportsmen and women take to the field of play, literally anything can happen, and here we look back on, and occasionally snigger at, some of the most memorable.

ERIC BRISTOW VS KEITH DELLER: THE DELLER CHECKOUT
Embassy World Darts Championship, Jollees Cabaret Club, Stoke-on-Trent, 1983

Keith Deller, the 23-year-old from deepest Suffolk, didn't even look like a professional darts player, or at least not in the accepted sense of it. He was young, slim, didn't smoke, hardly ever imbibed and seemed to worry about what he looked like: indeed, one pundit likened him to a member of The Osmonds. He had got into the finals via the interminable local darts club qualifying rounds, rather than being invited as one of the elite players, and the man he was up against was two times world champion and three times World Masters winner Eric Bristow, ranked number one in the sport. At one point during this match, commentator Sid Waddell remarked Deller wasn't so much the underdog as "the underpuppy".

But the lad from the Fens had got to this final the hard way, defeating John Lowe and Jocky Wilson, world numbers three and two respectively, in the quarter- and semi-finals. In fact not only had he earned his right to be there, but he was making a real game of it as he took the best-of-eleven tournament to 5–5, so it all hung on the final set.

Bristow stepped up first and scored a clinical 140; Deller replied with 123, having narrowly missed the second treble top to land that dart in the treble one. Next throw Bristow managed 100, Deller 140 to move into the lead at 261–238. Bristow threw 140 next, with Deller stumbling with 100, meaning either side could now wrap the match up with their next three darts. Bristow, needing 121, threw a single 17, followed by a triple 18. He now required 50 – a bull's-eye – to take the championship, yet was aware that Deller was on 138. The Crafty Cockney went for what the commentator referred to as the "percentage shot" and scored a single eighteen, to take it to the next round of darts when he'd need a double sixteen. That was much less risky than shooting for the bull's-eye. Deller stepped up to the oche looking very young and proceeded to land a treble 20, leaving 78, then a treble 18, leaving 24, then checked out on double 12.

To this day that particular 138 finish is known as "the Deller Checkout".

> "People at home were surprised by Keith, because he'd never been on telly, but all the players knew him. He already had the respect of the players because he'd been on tour to America with us and won the LA Open."
>
> Eric Bristow, on his 1983 opponent.

SCOTLAND VS ITALY: DREAM TO REALITY
Six Nations Championship, Murrayfield, Edinburgh, 2007

Italy were hardly the rugby superpower and went into this match without a single away win in their history in the tournament, and having never won twice in a Six Nations season. However, as many in the sixty thousand crowd were still taking their seats, the Italians had served notice this was about to change – these rank outsiders had scored and converted three tries in the space of six minutes to find themselves 21–0 ahead. And it wasn't so much that they had suddenly come good, more that Scotland were a total shambles. With nineteen seconds on the clock, Phil Goodman kicked straight into the grateful hands of Mauro Bergamasco who ran it in, then after four minutes Chris Cusiter misplaced two passes in as many minutes, and each was run in without a tackle attempted by, respectively, Andrea Scanavacca and Kaine Robertson, a relocated New Zealander.

Scotland managed to regroup and did make something of a comeback. After sixteen minutes Rob Dewey powered across the line for a try, then captain Chris Paterson added another, with each being successfully converted. But although this pulled the score back to a far more respectable 21–14, Scotland hadn't improved hugely and Italy seemed to have got a rush of blood to the head and their defence had gone missing. That score line was still standing as the match went into the final quarter of an hour. Which is when Italy got three penalties – all scored – in quick succession and managed to get through for another try, again successfully converted. Although Scotland did pull back three points courtesy of a late penalty, they were powerless to stop this astonishing defeat as the game finished up 37–17 to the Italians.

Andrea Scanavacca ignores the Scottish defence to run in Italy's second try.

After the final whistle, Pierre Berbizier, the Italian coach, summed up this almost surreal experience: "For the fans and the players something like this was always a dream. Now it is a reality." His opposite number Frank Hadden was more mundane but no less honest in his comment: "It went absolutely pear-shaped out there."

BOSTON RED SOX VS NEW YORK YANKEES

American Baseball League Championship Series, 2004

Enmity between the Red Sox and the Yankees is frequently referred to as the most intense rivalry in the US, in any sport, so an American League Championship Series was bound to be a highly charged affair. (This is a best-of-seven games play-off to see which AL team will meet the National League champions in the World Series.) Matters were ramped up by the fact that the two teams had met in these play-offs twice in the previous five years and, although the two teams had been evenly matched in the division, the Yankees had won on each occasion. The 2004 contest didn't look set to change that, either.

The Yankees had the home advantage given to the team with the best record in the regular league that season – they get to play four matches at home, which are the first and last two – and made it count, winning 10–7 and 3–1, with the Yankees' pitchers dominating both matches. And things didn't get much better when the contest moved to Boston's Fenway Park, as the Yankees dominated the batting to set a post-season run-scoring record and take that game 19–8. It looked all over for the Red Sox, as, in the history of the American League, no side had ever come back from three games to nil down to win a play-off series, and the fourth game started so badly that in the ninth innings they were three outs away from a third defeat to their dreaded rivals. But thanks to Dave Roberts' running, the Red Sox brought it back to four runs each to go into extra innings. The tenth and eleventh were both scoreless, but the Red Sox took two runs on the twelfth to stay in the series at 3–1.

> "All empires fall sooner or later."
> **Larry Lucchino, Boston Baseball Club president**

Game five was so tight it went to fourteen innings, with Boston eventually edging it 5–4, meaning they'd be heading back to Yankee Stadium with their confidence high, while their opponents would have been aware that a seemingly unassailable position was slipping away. The Red Sox took that game 4–2, and as the first team ever to come back from 0–3 to get to a seventh game (the series would be stopped as soon as one team won four), the momentum was with them. And it stayed with them for a resounding and historic 10–3 victory in that final game, giving the Boston Red Sox their first series win since 1986.

Six sporting embarrassments

Both US relay teams drop the baton
At the Beijing Olympics in 2008, the men's and the women's 4 x 100m relay teams dropped their batons during qualifying races, meaning for the first time since 1948, there was no US representation in either final.

Gary Kasparov outsmarted by a machine
In 1997, IBM's chess-playing super computer Deep Blue faced off against one of the greatest players the world has ever seen and came out on top in a six-game series, two wins to one with three matches drawn.

Lennox Lewis knocked out by Hasim Rahman
When Lewis defended his WBC and IBF heavyweight titles against journeyman Hasim Rahman in 2001, the champ had apparently been distracted by a bit part in *Ocean's Eleven* and hadn't taken the fight seriously. The 51/1 underdog had, and knocked Lewis out in the fifth round.

Munster Rugby defeat the All Blacks
When lowly Munster Rugby beat the All Blacks 12–0 in 1978, it was the New Zealanders' sole loss on that year's tour and their only defeat ever to an Irish side. The match has since been the subject of a book and play, respectively, *Stand Up and Fight* and *Alone It Stands*.

Netherlands beats England at cricket
In a preliminary match of the 2009 Twenty20 World Cup, the Dutch scored two runs off the final ball to score 163 for 6 and win by four wickets. A defeat made all the more shameful because it happened at Lords.

Newcastle United lose to Hereford United
Non-league Hereford had already held First Division Newcastle to a draw away, in the 1972 FA Cup; now thanks to a screaming thirty-yard shot and a scrambled late winner they could win in front of their own fans. The pitch invasion at the final whistle by thousands of youths in parkas has become classic BBC footage.

SONNY LISTON VS CASSIUS CLAY: BOXING LESSONS
World Heavyweight Championship, Miami, Florida, 1964

Muhammad Ali has for so long been the modern day-boxing icon it's often difficult to imagine a situation in which he was the underdog, but back when he was still Cassius Clay, a far more fearsome beast stalked the planet. Sonny Liston was possibly the most awe-inspiring boxer the world had ever seen. He was known for sheer brute power – he knocked men out with his left jab. A relatively modern analogy of Liston as a fighter would be Mike Tyson without the social skills and a wonkier moral compass, but with a greater natural proclivity for violence: Sonny Liston actually *liked* prison because he got fed fairly well and it gave his life a sense of order. He had acquired a reputation as being "unbeatable", written about in the boxing press as able to hold the title for as long as he wanted it or until old age took its toll. Such hyperbole was brought about by the manner in which he had won and held on to the title two years previously: two fights in which he had totally destroyed Floyd Patterson in under three minutes with barely controlled but sustained assaults. Now Clay admitted to being scared and went into the ring a 7/1 outsider.

Yet straight away he achieved something the previous champ hadn't: he survived the first round by staying close enough to encourage Liston's assaults but being sharp enough to keep out of their way. There was more of the same in the second, but by now the champion was starting to look frustrated and his challenger's relentless jab was beginning to bring his left eye up. During the third round the unthinkable happened – Sonny Liston got cut for the first time in his professional career. As round four progressed, the champ was starting to tire – he hadn't trained much for this fight because he'd never needed to in the past – and he was beginning to look demoralized. Then things took a bizarre turn and Clay returned to his corner at the end of that round with his eyes streaming, unable to see properly and wanting to quit because he was in so much discomfort. Substances used to treat Liston's cut had found their way on to Clay's face via the champion's gloves and were burning his eyes. Trainer Angelo Dundee washed out what he could, and pushed Clay off his stool back into the ring for the fifth, which he initially fought half blinded, but still managed to avoid what little fight Liston had left. Midway through the round his eyes cleared and he went to work in the style we came to know and love, hitting the near-defenceless champion at will and totally crushing his spirit. This clinical slaughter continued throughout the sixth round, as if Clay wanted to prove a point by utterly humiliating the man they'd called "unbeatable". When the bell went to start the seventh, Liston wisely opted to stay on his stool.

> "Sonny Liston is nothing. The man can't talk. The man can't fight. The man needs talking lessons. The man needs boxing lessons. And since he's gonna fight me, he needs falling lessons."
> **Cassius Clay during the pre-fight build-up.**

The world had a new heavyweight champion, who, the next day, renounced the name Cassius Clay. Within a few weeks he was reborn as Muhammad Ali.

DENNIS TAYLOR VS STEVE DAVIS

World Snooker Championship, Crucible Theatre, Sheffield, 1985

This marathon final went right down to the black ball on the last frame of the best-of-35 match, with BBC2 transmitting until the very end in the early hours of Monday morning, and, on that Sunday evening, watched by as many as 18.5 million viewers. These were record figures for an apparently minority sport, also for a post-midnight BBC programme and for anything on BBC2, a record which has yet to be surpassed. Part of the fascination – as well as the soothing click of the balls, obviously – was the emergence during the tournament of Dennis Taylor, the quietly spoken Ulsterman with the comedy glasses, who had never won a title in over a decade as a professional, and found himself up against the three times world champion and world number one Steve Davis. And although Taylor had made a strong showing in the tournament so far, beating Silvino Francisco, Cliff Thorburn and Tony Knowles, the final went very wrong, very quickly.

The match began at 2pm on Saturday, with Davis immediately showing why he was the defending champion as he put on a snooker exhibition that left Taylor mostly sitting on his chair, and 0–7 frames down at the close of that first afternoon session. The evening session didn't get off to a better start either: very soon the

The man with the upside-down glasses, Dennis Taylor, wins the World Championship.

seven had turned into an eight and, as Taylor admitted afterwards, "I wanted the ground to open up and swallow me." But midway through the ninth frame, Davis missed a pretty straightforward green and Taylor was in. By the end of that evening session there was a far more respectable 9–7 on the scoreboard. On Sunday afternoon, after sharing a bottle of champagne with his wife and a close friend the previous night, Taylor had his mojo working and pulled the tie back further to 11–11, and the twosome traded the lead until quite late in the evening session when Davis put on a bit of a spurt to arrive at 17-15. As the 33rd frame got under way, the organizers hadn't actually sent the trophy to the engravers, but they were certainly giving it a final polish in anticipation of an imminent presentation. Taylor, however, had other ideas.

With some inspired play he won the next two frames, meaning the tournament was going into its final frame at quarter past eleven. With so much at stake and each player aware of how fatigue could lead to errors, the frame was played at an agonizingly slow pace, with no large breaks and an unusual number of safety shots. After 45 minutes there were still plenty of balls on the table and Taylor was ahead 44–28. Then he missed a red and Davis went on something of a run to bring the score to 62–44. Taylor looked beaten and all Davis needed was to pot the brown. The champ took the shot, the ball bumped across the mouth of the pocket a couple of times and didn't go down. Each took a turn to miss before Taylor got it down, then sunk the pink and the blue. Davis leads by 62–59 and all that's left up is the black. After a series of misses by each man, Davis overcuts a seemingly simple shot gifting the ball to Taylor. He puts it down, Ulster goes wild and the rest of Britain can go to bed.

MIKE TYSON VS JAMES "BUSTER" DOUGLAS
WBC/IBF/WBA World Heavyweight Championship, Tokyo, Japan, 1990

One of the reasons this heavyweight championship fight was held in Tokyo instead of a more US prime time-friendly high rollin' location such as Las Vegas or Atlantic City was because Tyson's habit of finishing fights very quickly was hurting ticket sales in his native US. But that was part of what made "Iron Mike" the overwhelming fighter he was and meant Douglas was being offered at 40-1 or better. He was a competent fighter, but apparently no better than that, and the bout was being talked about as little more than part of Tyson's training programme for his desired showdown with Evander Holyfield. Tyson loved to fight as often as humanly possible, believing it to be the best way to keep in shape, and had fought nine times in the three years since winning the title. Such a frequency meant going down the rankings to find opponents – or should that be "fresh meat"?

By this point Mike Tyson was being touted as possibly the greatest heavyweight of all time – he was still only 23 – but the unfancied Douglas came at him from the opening bell peppering the champion with jabs, thus keeping him at bay. Unable to get under these blows and inside to work on Douglas's body before delivering a trademark uppercut – this was why the relatively short Tyson loved taller opponents – he didn't have too much of a Plan B, and soaked up punishment in the first five rounds. During this time Douglas landed a few solid right crosses that brought Tyson's left eye up and it's a mark of how little his corner expected him to be hit that they hadn't bothered to bring an endswell – what looks like a miniature iron, that's frozen and used to push down swelling.

> "He's just like Humpty Dumpty. They're not going to be able to put Tyson back together again."
>
> **Former heavyweight champion George Foreman in the aftermath of Douglas's victory.**

In the middle rounds, Tyson began to pull his way back into it, and, right at the end of the eighth, floored the challenger with a murderous uppercut. Clearly shaken, Douglas knew his best chance was to try and finish this as soon as possible and came out for the ninth round like a whirlwind, keeping Tyson pegged back, frequently on the ropes. Then in the tenth Tyson's legs looked as if they were gone and he was far less mobile. Douglas landed an uppercut of his own, followed by a four-punch combination. It did what had never been done before and dumped Mike Tyson on to the canvas. He did his best to get back into it, managing to climb to his feet ahead of the count, but when the referee saw he'd put his gum shield back in so badly that one end was sticking up out of his mouth like a tusk, he rightly called a close to proceedings.

BOB BEAMON'S LEAP

Olympic Games, Mexico City, 1968

If you're only ever going to win one major international competition in your entire career, then it's best it involves an Olympic gold, but if you also set a world record that will stand for over twenty years, then you don't really need to win anything else. When Bob Beamon won gold in the men's long jump at the Mexico City Olympics of 1968, his phenomenal leap of 8.9 metres even shocked himself – eventually. The jump was so long he sailed past the end of the measuring board at the side of the landing pit, so officials had to measure it with a tape. Then when they put the

> "Compared to this jump, we are as children."
>
> **Igor Ter-Ovanesyan, Soviet long jumper and competitor on that day.**

distance up on the board, the jumper was unable to convert from the metric units to the feet and inches he was familiar with. He knew he'd jumped a long way, because he'd felt himself get more height than usual and therefore was in the air for what seemed like an age, but he had no idea quite how long that way was. When a friend with mental arithmetic skills informed him, Beamon sank to his knees with his hand over his face, providing one of those Games' most-seen images.

Although the men's long jump world record had been steadily creeping up during the 1960s, eight new distances had only advanced it from 8.21 metres to 8.35. This jump had destroyed it and Beamon, who had set himself a goal of 8.53 metres, didn't really believe he'd ever get that. He had some very useful contributing factors, inasmuch as the Mexico City stadium was over two thousand metres above sea level so the thin air provided little resistance – there was a huge amount of jumping and sprinting records set at those Games – and he had wind assistance right on the maximum permitted of two metres/second. But that said, nobody else jumped near that distance, so it wasn't all down to circumstance.

Bob Beamon's record

It's a mark of how much modern athletes are constantly improving that, at the time, it was thought Beamon's jump was beyond the limits of regular human achievement and would never be beaten. Eventually though – and it took 23 years – Mike Powell bettered that jump with an astonishing sea level effort of 8.95 metres in 1991. However, as an Olympic record, Beamon's still stands and even Carl Lewis didn't get near it during his 1980s Olympic long jump reign.

APPALACHIAN STATE UNIVERSITY VS UNIVERSITY OF MICHIGAN: MIRACLE IN MICHIGAN

Michigan Stadium, Ann Arbor, Michigan, 2007

It was only a pre-season tune-up game for two college football teams, nothing too serious, but it ended up on the cover of *Sports Illustrated* and the front page of *The New York Times*, who described it as one of the greatest upsets in the *history of American sport*. In front of 109,000 stunned home fans, and live on television, comparative minnows Appalachian State edged a victory over the University of Michigan Wolverines, in a contest that is now routinely referred to as "the Miracle in Michigan".

A side from the Division 1 FCS (Football Championship Subdivision), the second tier of the NCAA (National Collegiate Athletic Association), had never beaten a team from the top flight Division 1 FBS (Football Bowl Subdivision). And not just any team, but the team that had finished the previous season in fifth place. Indeed, there were over 120 teams separating them. To give an idea of the difference in status, the University of Michigan had a stadium capacity of 110,000, had won the top tier title 38 times and had 286 of their players turn professional. Appalachian State seated 16,500, had won eight championships and sent 29 of

Bob Beamon, Mexico City, 1968 – about as close as man has got to flying.

their graduates into the National Football League. Las Vegas bookmakers wouldn't offer odds on a Michigan victory. But Appalachian State, aptly nicknamed the Mountaineers, were never going to let those sort of obstacles stand in their way.

As expected, the Wolverines went ahead almost straight from the kick-off, but that only appeared to be a wake-up call for Appalachian State, who didn't just score a touchdown by way of a quick reply, but wide receiver Dexter Jackson had the temerity to put a finger to his lips as he silenced the home crowd on his run in for his first of two touchdowns. From there, the game swung backwards and forwards. The Mountaineers went in after two quarters 28–17 in front, but they seemed to stall somewhat in the second half. They only scored three points in the third quarter and had gained none at all during the final period until they found themselves 31–32 down with 97 seconds to go. A 68-yard Appalachian State drive culminated in a 24-yard punt for the field goal that put them two points in front with 27 seconds to go. A final Michigan push forward took the ball to the Appalachian twenty-yard line, where the attempted field goal kick was smothered by a truly heroic block by safety Corey Lynch, who then ran the ball and the clock down the field.

Appalachian State Mountaineers 34, University of Michigan Wolverines 32. And rank outsiders across the US are able to say "Remember Michigan" every time their chances are written off.

BILLIE JEAN MOFFITT VS MARGARET SMITH
Second Round, Wimbledon, 1962

This was back before either of them had got married so were yet to become Billie Jean King and Margaret Court, and prior to Moffitt joining Smith at the top of the women's tennis tree for about ten years from 1963. At this Wimbledon, Smith was already ranked number nine in the world and had just won her third consecutive Australian Open. Also in 1962, she held both the French and the US Open titles. Previously a Wimbledon quarter-finalist, this year she was the top seed and was strongly fancied to win it as the fourth and final part of her Grand Slam – holding Wimbledon and the French, US and Australian Open titles at the same time. Moffitt, on the other hand, was eighteen-years-old, and although she had been half of the previous year's ladies doubles winners, had gone out of the singles in the second round, meaning her match against the best female player in the world was only her second individual effort at the All England Club.

Which seemed to get to the youngster early on, as Smith's superior skills and sheer power intimidated Moffitt into a 6–1 drubbing in the first set. This would, many assumed, be a walkover. Not quite. If anything, that first set humiliation drove Moffitt on and the notion of such an exalted opponent raised her game accordingly. During the second set the confidence and will to win, that would soon push her to the very top came through. She surprised Smith with an exhibition of net-rushing and aggressive, powerful tennis that showed no respect for her

Six other Wimbledon bombshells

Roger Taylor vs Rod Laver, 1970
Laver was on a run of 31 winning matches, was favourite to win the tournament and so fancied over this English journeyman that even sections of the UK press suggested Taylor needn't bother to turn up. However, after he narrowly lost the first set, the crowd got behind him and he overwhelmed Laver to win 4–6, 6–4, 6–2, 6–1.

Peter Doohan vs Boris Becker, 1987
The teenage tyro Boris Becker was expected to win his third Wimbledon, with this unseeded Australian as mere cannon fodder. Doohan more than stepped up to the occasion and played the game of his life to beat the defending champion 7–6, 4–6, 6–2, 6–4 before fading back into obscurity.

Jennifer Capriati vs Martina Navratilova, 1991
Although by age 34 Navratilova's best days were behind her, just about everybody assumed the wily old pro's experience would be more than enough to get her past a 15-year-old debutante. It wasn't. Capriati won in straight sets – 6–4, 7–5 – to become the youngest ever player to reach a semi-final.

Richard Krajicek vs Pete Sampras, 1996
Krajicek, the big-serving, giant (two metres) Dutchman not only battered three times winner "Pistol Pete" 7–5, 7–6, 6–4 in the quarter-final, he also went on to win the tournament.

Jelena Dokic vs Martina Hingis, 1999
Dokic was just sixteen years old, ranked 129th in the world, and had come through the qualifiers yet she blew the world Number One away in just 54 minutes, 6–2, 6–0.

Virginia Ruano Pascual vs Martina Hingis, 2001
Maybe memories of the Dokic debacle were still in Hingis's mind, but two years later she produced a similarly disastrous, error-strewn performance against the world's Number 83 to crash out 6–4, 6–2.

opponent's reputation, overwhelming her at times to take the second set 3–6. On a winning streak, she managed to push into the third set, but Smith's greater stamina started to show as the contest wore on. Yet from somewhere Moffitt dredged up the energy for a final rally to take the set 5–7, and with it the match.

Six spirited outsiders

Foinavon
A 100/1 donkey that won the 1967 Grand National simply because he was so far behind the field his jockey was able to steer him around the pile-up of over a dozen horses and riders at the 23rd fence. Foinavon was so awful that after clearing that fence he had a hundred length lead which was cut to twenty by the time he reached the winning post.

Goran Ivanisevic
When ranked outside the world's top one hundred, he became the only wild-card entry ever to win Wimbledon, when, in 2001, he beat Pat Rafter 6–3, 3–6, 6–3, 2–6 and 9–7. His exuberant celebrations and curious facial hair meant the crowd even forgave him for beating Tim Henman in the semi-final.

Greece's national football team
They beat the host nation and tournament favourites, Portugal, 1–0 in the 2004 European Championships final as 150/1 outsiders. Quite why the odds were this long is a bit of a mystery, as the Greeks had already turned Portugal over 2–1 in the opening match.

Ireland's cricket team
They have achieved legendary status in the one day game, their finest hours coming in the 2007 World Cup in the West Indies, during which they drew with Zimbabwe and beat Bangladesh and Pakistan, and the 2011 World Cup with a victory over England.

Jack Fleck
In 1955 US golf legend Ben Hogan was standing on the verge of a record-breaking fifth US Open title, when Fleck, who had only been playing full time for six months, forced him into and won an eighteen-hole play off. He prepared for the match by listening to Mario Lanza records on a portable phonogram and ate sugar lumps all the way round.

Wimbledon FC
The self-styled Crazy Gang used to lay claim to being, "everybody's second favourite team" and they had vast swathes of the country solidly behind them in 1988, when they beat the mighty Liverpool 1–0 in the FA Cup final, a game made even more memorable by their giant goalkeeper Dave Beasant, who became the first to save a penalty in an FA Cup final.

Never before had the women's top seed gone out in the second round, and Moffitt went all the way to the quarter-finals, where she was beaten 6–3, 6–1 by Anne Haydon-Jones.

JEAN VAN DE VELDE

British Open Golf Championship, Carnoustie, Scotland, 1999

The enduring image from this tournament is of Frenchman Jean Van de Velde, pitch wedge in hand, trousers rolled up to his knees, standing in the shin-deep water of the Barry Burn and looking rueful. As well he might. At this point, the eighteenth hole of the final day's play, he was midway between being poised to become the first French golfer to win the Open since 1907 and the most spectacular meltdown in the tournament's history.

Up until that last day, the initially unfancied Van de Velde had been making steady rather than showy progress up the leader board. His essentially error-free play had taken him from nowhere in sight at the end of the first day, to the top spot at one over par on Friday, a position he held on Saturday evening and although only at even par, he was by then five shots in front of the field. Continuing to err on the side of caution, he maintained that lead all through Sunday's play to stand on the eighteenth tee secure in the knowledge that anything up to six strokes on the 499-yard par four would mean he took the claret jug. If you didn't need to make up ground – as Van de Velde clearly didn't – this was a relatively straightforward hole requiring safe iron shots and a couple of lay-ups.

Maybe he was looking for some sort of grandstand finish, but the previously careful Frenchman stepped up with his driver and pushed the ball into the long grass to the right of the fairway. Still not a real problem: all he needed to do was pitch it out and lay up to go over the burn just in front of the green with the next shot. Instead, he took a number two iron to go for the green. The ball flew out of the rough, went to the right of the green, and hit a grandstand with such force it bounced back across the burn into some very deep heather. Pitching out of this only made things worse: the ball travelled just far enough to land in the water. In another moment of madness he actually considered trying to play it out of the 35cm deep water, but good sense seemed to prevail and he took the drop from behind the burn. Of course his pitch ended up in a green-side bunker. While he got out of that to leave a simple putt, that he sank, it added up to a triple bogey and the man who had been way out in front found himself in a three-way play-off.

No, he didn't win it. Scotsman Paul Lawrie came out on top, leaving Jean Van de Velde to share second place with Justin Leonard.

PITTSBURGH STEELERS VS OAKLAND RAIDERS: "THE IMMACULATE RECEPTION"

Three Rivers Stadium, Pittsburgh, Pennsylvania, 1972

The shock here was that such a dour, defensive, totally forgettable game produced a play so remarkable it was immediately given its own name and has gone down in NFL annals as "The Greatest Play of All Time". The match concerned was an American Football Conference post-season play-off game between the Pittsburgh Steelers and the Oakland Raiders, to determine who would meet the winner of the National Football Conference play-offs in the Super Bowl.

Pittsburgh hadn't even made the play-offs for 25 years but this season they had the best team they'd had for ages and looked as if they had an excellent chance of going all the way to the Super Bowl. They were ahead for most of the game, thanks to two Roy Gerela field goals, and seemed able to deal with everything Oakland had to offer. Then, with less than two minutes on the clock, the Raiders quarterback Ken Stabler carried the ball for thirty yards for a touchdown, which was duly kicked for the extra point. Suddenly the Steelers were 6–7 down, with one minute, thirteen seconds on the clock. It got worse. Following the kick-off, three passes went astray leaving them at fourth and ten on their own forty-yard line with 22

Steelers' running back Franco Harris displays the ball at the end of the game.

seconds on the clock. As Steelers' quarterback Terry Bradshaw took the ball he was coming under great pressure from the opposing linemen, was pushed right and had to abandon the agreed play to hurl the ball hopefully towards running back "Frenchy" Fuqua who had been making a decoy run. As Fuqua jumped for the ball, he collided with the Raiders' safety Jack Tatum. The ball looped away a dozen yards or so and was grabbed inches off the grass by Steelers' quick-thinking running back Franco Harris, who shrugged off a couple of tackles as he gratefully carried it into the endzone. Touchdown! 12–7 Pittsburgh! Or was it?

As the Steelers celebrated what they believed to be the game's deciding play, the Oakland bench were going berserk claiming the reception was illegal, as one official signalled for a touchdown and the others very carefully kept their arms by their sides. The dispute was over an NFL rule stating that the only offensive player allowed to catch a pass was the first on that team to touch the ball. Therefore, if the ball had bounced off Fuqua before Harris caught it, the touchdown wouldn't count, but if it had hit Tatum then it was good. For several agonizing minutes the officials conferred, before referee Fred Swearingen raised arms – the touchdown stood. Fans swarmed on the pitch, meaning it was impossible to try and convert the touchdown and the result stayed at 12–7. After the match, when Fuqua was asked if the ball had indeed touched him, he simply smirked and told reporters the whole thing was a deliberate play their coach had cooked up.

MEN'S 4 X 400 METRES RELAY
IAAF World Athletics Championships, Tokyo, Japan, 1991

Great Britain vs the US in the men's 4 x 400 metres relay always produced fireworks on the track, but all too often the honours ended up with the US as that nation seemed to produce top-class sprinters on a conveyor belt. The British team that lined up for this final was certainly one of the strongest in years, consisting of specialist 400-metre runners Roger Black and Derek Redmond, 200-metre sprinter John Regis and 400-metre hurdler Kriss Akabusi. It was the same four that had taken gold in this event at the European Championships the previous year, but the Americans – Andrew Valmon, Quincy Watts, Danny Everett and Antonio Pettigrew – were strongly fancied to maintain their domination of the event. The Jamaican team, too, were also expected to do well after showing strong in the heats.

As expected, Valmon got off to a storming start, but Roger Black kept up, with the two of them leaving the Jamaican runner behind to edge out in front. As they came around the second turn, Black had closed the gap and handed off to Derek Redmond just in front, having set a very fast time of 44.6 seconds. Redmond ran well, but the precocious teenager Quincy Watts streaked past him early on and maintained a lead to hand over about three metres in front of the British change. Although he did try to go wide around Everett as they came out of the second bend, John Regis simply couldn't make up the ground to give Kriss Akabusi any form of start over his anchor leg opponent. Which he desperately needed, as Antonio Pettigrew had already won the individual event and was currently the fastest man in the world over four hundred metres.

Around the first bend and into the first straight the Briton was tucked in behind the American and while there was at least a couple of metres between them, Akabusi didn't appear troubled. He almost looked relaxed out there. As they came into the second turn the distance seemed to have closed slightly, and Akabusi was biding his time, knowing he'd only get one chance. He waited. And he waited. What seemed like quite a while after that last turn, he struck and from about twenty metres out unleashed a killer kick that pushed him in front. Although the American did his best to react, he'd simply run out of track. Akabusi had run a masterful tactical race and held on to take the tape at 2 minutes 57.53 seconds, 0.04 seconds in front of the American.

> "I get recognized in the streets from time to time, mostly by people who want to hear my laugh. I don't think my laugh would have become so renowned had I not won that medal."
>
> Kriss Akabusi on the less-obvious advantages of coming first.

USA VS USSR: THE MIRACLE ON ICE
Winter Olympics Ice Hockey, Lake Placid, New York, 1980

When the US ice hockey team lined up for this medals (final) round match of the 1980 Winter Olympics it was against a Soviet Union team that so dominated the sport they had taken gold in five of the last six Winter Olympics, had only lost once in their previous thirty outings and had recently pounded the Americans 10–3 in a Madison Square Garden exhibition game. The Americans just about scraped into the top ten of the world rankings, and in recent games against the USSR had been outscored by a ratio 4–1. The US team was made up of college students and part-time players, because although the National Hockey League was a strong league, at that point the vast majority of players in it were Canadian. By contrast, although the Soviet players were technically not professionals, like so many of that country's top athletes they enjoyed cushy government "jobs" or were in the army, each situation allowing ample time for training in state of the art government-owned facilities. Each team had a different style too. While the Soviets relied on sports science, intricate tactical plans and detailed studies of opponents, the Americans had little time for such subtleties and concentrated on playing strong, hard and fast – an attitude that had seen them through this Olympics' preliminary round with four wins and a draw, while, as expected, the USSR had gone unbeaten, winning one game 16–0.

The atmosphere among the eight thousand-strong home crowd was electric, as Cold War-induced anti-Soviet feelings were running high – a background to these Games was President Jimmy Carter debating as to whether the US should boycott the summer Olympics in Moscow – and spectators were noisily behind the Americans from the beginning. It seemed to pay off too, as thanks to some inspired goalkeeping by Jim Craig and a sloppy piece of work by his opposite number, the first period finished 2–2. At which point the Soviets took the bizarre option to change their goalie. Not that it mattered too much as their outfield overwhelmed the Americans, with Craig working hard to keep them down to one goal scored. So it was 3–2, then, as they went into the third and final period. It was then that the crowd really went to work and that familiar chant of "U-S-A! … U-S-A!" was born at this point. It lifted the team to scramble two goals to take the lead with ten minutes left on the clock. The Soviets threw everything at their opponents in increasingly desperate attacks that were repelled by all means necessary. As the crowd and the commentator counted down the seconds, the US held on for a dramatic victory.

The American team went on to win the Gold, an event almost overshadowed by what immediately became known as "The Miracle on Ice", and has since been celebrated in two feature films and one TV documentary.

ENGLAND VS AUSTRALIA: BOTHAM'S ASHES
Fourth Test, Edgbaston, Birmingham, 1981

This series was so dominated by Ian Botham, with both bat and ball, that when England won it to retain the little urn, it became known as Botham's Ashes. However, this particular match managed to stand out even among his clutch of stellar performances.

At the start of this match the series stood at one game all with one drawn, but that wasn't really the full story as England had only won the previous match thanks to Botham's heroic – and face-saving – 149 not out as England were forced to follow on. They weren't faring too much better in this game either. Each innings was low scoring, but England's seemed unnecessarily so with 189 in the first and 219 in the second, while Australia made 258 in between. It left Australia chasing 151 with two days in which to get there. Everybody, including one or two of the England team, it later transpired, thought Australia had it in the bag. As it was, it was merely theirs to lose and Ian Botham was on hand to make sure they did just that.

Nobody had been making big scores with the bat in this game – the highest total was Mike Brearley's first innings of 48 – and Australia's second innings was no exception. Midway through the fourth day they stood at 105-5. Not brilliant, but still only needing 46. Then the ball was passed to Ian Botham. First Marsh went, clean bowled for four, then Bright went lbw with nothing added to the board. Next, he had Dennis Lillee caught behind and suddenly Australia were 120-8 and things looked very different. Then Kent went for only one more run, and Alderman, the last wicket, went back to the pavilion without troubling the scorer. Australia were all out for 121, giving England victory by 29 runs. Ian Botham's devastating fourteen over spell left him with figures of five wickets for just eleven runs. It was a sequence that included nine maidens and a period of just one run from twenty-eight consecutive deliveries.

Quite rightly he was awarded Man of the Match.

AUSTRALIA II VS LIBERTY: 132 AND OUT

The America's Cup, Newport, Rhone Island, 1983

This really wasn't remarkable because it was some unfancied chancers winning the America's Cup: their Australian yacht was the result of a great deal of expense and design expertise and really *ought* to have won. What was so shocking about it was that any boat other than one representing the New York Yacht Club, the defending champions, won, something that hadn't happened since 1851. Indeed, there were widespread rumours the NYYC were so confident that could never happen, they had bolted the silver claret jug to the base of its display cabinet. But this time things looked different as the smaller, nippier *Australia II*, representing the Royal Perth Yacht Club, was reckoned to be the most serious challenger to date, and had been showing its credentials during the qualifying rounds.

Not without controversy, though, as the twelve-metre boat was sporting a revolutionary new winged keel design that featured small panels sticking out at right angles on either side of its lowest edge. These provided added balance, allowing the boat to displace less water without sacrificing the stability that was crucial when travelling at high speed or into the wind. It gave *Australia II* quite an edge when it came to manouverability and the NYYC tried to have it declared illegal before the finals got under way. After a brief and nervy period of adjudication, the organizers decided it was legal and the best-of-seven races tournament could go ahead.

Technical difficulties dogged the Australian boat right from the start, and *Liberty* cruised past them in the first two races to go 2–0 in the series. In the third race those problems had been fixed and they pulled one back, but any euphoria didn't last long as *Liberty* took the fourth race to stand 3–1 up going into the fifth. But *Australia II* and her experienced skipper John Bertrand were just getting into their stride and won the next two with growing margins. A score of 3–3 was uncharted territory for the Americans, as in all the competition's history nobody had ever run their yacht this close – the America's Cup had never come down to the final race. But in 1983 it did, the Australians won it and the longest winning streak in any sport came to an end.

Miscellany

The highest, the longest and
the just plain weird

One of the main points about sport – any sport – is the result. Never mind what people tell you about playing the game being all that counts, really, everybody wants to know who won. And once you've got results you've got freak results. Bizarre scores, marathon matches and superhuman feats of strength, skill or endurance to earn a lasting place in the record books and taproom conversations. Here we list a few of the more interesting records and call attention to some of sport's most unusual occurrences.

Longest baseball game

On May 8, 1984, it took the Chicago White Sox eight hours and six munites to beat the Milwaukee Brewers 7–6, with a home run in the 25th innings . The game took place over two eveings, because an MLB rule states that an innings cannot be started after one am, so the players and fans had to come back the next night. (The average game takes beween three and four hours.)

Shortest baseball game

On 28 September 1919, the New York Giants beat the Philadelphia Phillies 6–1 in a mere 51 minutes. It was over so quickly because none of the Phillies batters lasted more than a couple of minutes, indeed they only managed eight hits in all nine innings

Youngest ever pitcher in major league baseball

Joe Nuxhall made his debut for the Cincinnati Reds against the St Louis Cardinals in 1944 at the age of fifteen years ten months and eleven days. Older players were involved in World War II at the time.

Highest scoring NBA (National Basketball Association) game

Detroit Pistons beat the Denver Nuggets by 186 to 184, in December 1983, for a combined points total of 370. If the Pistons had made even 85 percent of their free throws (they hit 61 percent) they would have broken the 200 points barrier.

Great Britain: Baseball World Champions

When the inaugural Baseball World Cup was staged in England in 1938 – five matches played in Liverpool, Rochdale, Kingston-upon-Hull, Halifax and Leeds – only Great Britain and the US took part. Britain won 4–1, making them the world champions. This was the last time they ever won, indeed the last time they took part, and since then it has been dominated by Cuba, who have won the now biennial tournament 25 times, with an unbeaten spell between 1984 and 2007, taking them to nine straight titles. The US's major league does not allow its players to take part: thus the US has only lifted the cup twice.

◀◀ Previous page: the annual Father Christmas Race, Middelfart, Denmark, 2010.

Carl Lewis in the NBA

In 1984, for no other reason than his celebrity status, Olympic athletics champion Carl Lewis was signed up by the Chicago Bulls basketball team. Although at 1.91 metres he was almost the right height, he had never played competitive basketball in his life.

Lowest scoring NBA game
Fort Wayne Pistons beat the Minneapolis Lakers 19–18 in 1950. Four years later, to prevent such low-scoring games, the NBA introduced the shot clock, meaning the team with the ball has to attempt to score within 24 seconds of gaining possession. Since then, the lowest score has been a combined 119 points, when Boston Celtics beat the Milwaukee Bucks 62–57.

All-time boomerang throwing record
In 1999, Manuel Schuetz threw his boomerang 238 metres (and yes, it came back to him) at the Swiss championships. This has proven to be an unbeatable distance – no other thrower since then has even managed to reach two hundred metres in competition.

A ringside seat for the Rumble in the Jungle between Muhammad Ali and George Foreman in 1974 (see p.196) cost $2490, which would be the equivalent of over $25,000 at today's prices.

Longest boxing match
On 6 April 1893, Andy Bowen and Jack Burke fought in New Orleans for the vacant lightweight championship, and they fought, and they fought. The bout lasted over 7 hours and 110 3-minute rounds, but when both fighters were too exhausted to get off their stools for the 111th round the referee wisely opted to declare it "No contest".

Biggest Test cricket wins
By runs: England beat Australia by 675 runs in Brisbane in 1928.
By an innings and runs: England beat Australia by an innings and 579 runs at the Oval in 1938.

Greatest number of Test wickets to fall in a single day
On day two of England vs Australia at Lords in 1888, 27 batsmen were dismissed for a total of 157 runs.

Lowest number of Test wickets lost in a single day
When England beat South Africa by an innings and 18 runs at Lords in 1924, they only lost two wickets, the lowest number for a winning Test match side.

The perfect bowling score

Six bowlers have dismissed all eleven opposing batsmen in the same Test match.

Bowler	Country	Against	Year	Venue	Figures
J.C. Laker	England	Australia	1956	Old Trafford	19 for 90
Srinivas Venkataraghavan	India	New Zealand	1965	Delhi	12 for 152
Geoff Dymock	Australia	India	1979	Kanpur	12 for 166
Abdul Qadir	Pakistan	England	1987	Lahore	13 for 101
Waqar Younis	Pakistan	New Zealand	1990	Faisalabad	12 for 130
Muttiah Muralitharan	Sri Lanka	South Africa	2000	Galle	13 for 171

Longest FA Cup tie

It took place in the fourth qualifying round of the 1971–72 Cup, when, in the days before penalty shoot-outs, Oxford City played Alvechurch FC for eleven hours until Alvechurch finally won the fifth replay 1–0. The scores in the previous games were 2–2, 1–1, 1–1, 0–0, 0–0.

The Premier League's safest keeper

David "Calamity" James would not be everybody's first thought, but he has kept 173 clean sheets, which is more than any other keeper. He also holds the Premier League appearance record having played 573 times for five different clubs.

Most expensive football shirt

This is the number 10 worn by Pelé on the famous day his Brazilian side beat Italy 4–1 in the 1970 World Cup final. It fetched £157,750 at an auction at Christie's, London, in 2002.

Riding the Ryder

The figure of the golfer on top of the Ryder Cup is Abe Mitchell, a British golf pro from the early twentieth century, who was a close friend and golf instructor of Samuel Ryder, the man who sponsored the first UK vs US tournament and donated the trophy.

Longest continuous keepy-uppies
Dan Magness from the UK juggled a football without it touching the ground for 24 hours in London in 2009.

Worst English international football disciplinary record
David Beckham: while gaining his record-breaking 115 caps, the midfielder was sent off twice and booked sixteen times.

Worst NFL (National Football League) teams
Since the NFL merged with the American Football League in 1970, two teams have gone the entire season losing every game: in 2008 the Detroit Lions lost sixteen and won none, while in 1976 the Tampa Bay Buccaneers only lost fourteen, but that was all they played.

> To make all the footballs used in an average NFL season 3000 cows are skinned.

Most uneven college football game
In 1916 Georgia Tech beat Cumberland College 222–0, in the biggest win ever. The reason being was that Cumberland, a Tennessee college, had scrapped its football programme and therefore had no proper team, but as details of this game had already been posted they faced a large fine if they didn't turn up. Some might argue they still didn't.

Highest score in an American football match
In almost a century, no team has beaten the record of Atlanta's Georgia Tech, who, as we've seen, slammed Cumberland University of Tennessee 222–0 in 1916. On the day, they achieved another unmatched record: 32 touchdowns.

The US's greatest jockey
Eddie Arcaro is the only jockey to have won the Triple Crown twice – the Kentucky Derby, Preakness Stakes and Belmont Stakes in the same year. He won

Breaking sixty

Five golfers have achieved a joint record lowest score of 59 on an official PGA Tour eighteen hole round, and surprisingly none of them are household names.

Golfer	Date	Venue	Course Par
Al Geiberger	1977	Colonial Country Club, Memphis	72
Chip Beck	1991	Sunrise Golf Club, Las Vegas	72
David Duval	1999	PGA West, La Quinta, California	72
Paul Goydos	2010	TPC Deere Run, Silvis, Illinois	71
Stuart Appleby	2010	The Old White Course, White Sulphur Springs, West Virginia	70

Table tennis tantrums

When, in 2009, six out of eight quarter-finalists in the US table tennis championships left in protest, demanding a prize-money raise, Michael Landers found himself with a straight passage into the final. He won, at the age of just fifteen. Aside from his age, he is also unusual in the sport in having a coach that works with him solely on fitness.

the Kentucky Derby five times in a career that lasted from 1931 to 1962, and the Preakness and the Belmont Stakes six times each (both of which are unbeaten totals). He rode 4779 winners in 24,092 races, was United States Champion Jockey six times in the 1940s and 50s, and amassed record-breaking career earnings of $30,039,543.

Highest ever ice hockey attendance

As an indoor sport, ice hockey attendances are a bit restricted, but on 11 December 2010, the University of Michigan and Michigan State University played in front of a record-shattering 104,173 fans at the Michigan American Football Stadium, where the rink had been placed on top of the artificial turf.

> The original ice hockey pucks were made from frozen cow pats.

Coldest marathons

With an average temperature of −20°C, to which wind chill will be factored in (winds can blow up to 40 kilometres per hour or 25 knots) and an altitude of over 2000 metres, (6500 feet), the Antarctic Ice Marathon is a real test of nerve for endurance runners. Not to be outdone, its sister event, the North Pole Marathon, recorded record-breaking temperatures of −37°C for its 2010 race, in which four siblings from France, the Michel brothers, finished in the top eight places.

Worst team in Australian Rugby League history

Sydney University, who competed in the professional New South Wales Rugby League Premiership for eighteen seasons between 1920 and 1937, finished bottom ten times and second from bottom on three occasions. Before they finally called it a day they had played 242 matches, winning 47, drawing 5 and losing 190 – between April 1934 and August 1936, they lost every one of the 42 games they played. The reason for this is that although they were in a professional league, the university's players were genuinely students, who could stay in the team for no longer than three years and who had to fit rugby in around their studies and other student activities.

Shortest Wimbledon championships tennis matches

For women, Marion Bandy lasted just twenty minutes against Susan Tutt at Wimbledon in 1969, before losing 6–0, 6–0. For men, in 1936, also at Wimbledon, Fred Perry beat Baron Gottfried von Cramm 6–1, 6–1, 6–0 in just forty minutes.

Six rainy day Options

Coin rugby

Facing each other across an empty table, players flick coins across the surface to score tries and conversions. Goalposts are created with angled thumbs and forefingers.

Formula D

French motor racing game originally called Formula Dé. Courtesy of seven dice – one for each gear, and one for hazards – players hurtle around famous Grand Prix circuits.

Owzthat

An approximation of cricket in which a "batting" player scores runs based on the throw of a dice, which has "Owzthat?" in place of the number five. When that comes up, the other player rolls their dice, which reads Not Out, LBW, No Ball, stumped, caught or bowled. You get the idea.

Subbuteo

The best known table-top sports game in the world, flicking round-bottomed "footballers" across green baize after a proportionately enormous ball has been with us since 1947. At one point the company branched out into table cricket, hockey and rugby with somewhat less successful results.

Totopoly

A bewilderingly complicated horse racing-based board game, that involved preparing your nags for the race before you got anywhere near the off. Then there was the betting and varying amounts of prize money to be taken into consideration.

Who's on first?

Referencing Abbott & Costello's inspired comedy sketch of the same name, contestants have to guess where on the baseball diamond-depicting board their opponents' players have been placed. Of course each participant has a player called Nobody, cue much hilarity: "Who's on first base?" … "Nobody."

Picture credits

The publishers have made every effort to identify correctly the rights of the rights holders in respect of all images used for this book. If, despite these efforts, any attribution is absent or incorrect, the publishers will correct this error once it has been brought to their attention in a subsequent reprint.

Cover images: Front cover: Chess Boxing, AP Photo/Miguel Villagran. Back cover: John Daly, © Ben Radford/Corbis; Robot Camel Racing, © Stephanie McGehee/ Reuters/Corbis. Inside front cover: Ostrich racing, © Sergey Dolzhenko/epa/Corbis. Inside back cover: Curling, © Reuters/Corbis.

Internal images: Page 7: © STR/Sri Lanka/X01315/Reuters/Corbis; 38: © Ashley Cooper/Corbis; 47: © Tami Chappell/Reuters/Corbis; 52: © Leo Mason/ Corbis; 73: Wolfgang Kaehler/Corbis; 140: © Pace Gregory/Corbis Sygma. Page 18: Koes Karnadi, © Dorling Kindersley; 24: Cecile Treal and Jean-Michel Ruiz, © Dorling Kindersley; 25: Alex Robinson, © Dorling Kindersley; 28: Laurie Noble, © Dorling Kindersley; 45: Nigel Hicks, © Dorling Kindersley; 49: Andy Crawford, © Dorling Kindersley; 60: Shaen Adey, © Dorling Kindersley. Pages 139, 189, 192, 203, 219, 225, 251, 255, 265, 261 265, 269, 273,273: Getty Images; 11: Getty Images/Hulton Archive; 125, 248: Popperfoto/Getty Images; 166: MCT via Getty Images; 175, 209, 241: AFP/ Getty Images; 179: Getty Images for Laureus; 199, 215: Bob Thomas/Getty Images. Pages 19, 23, 58: James McConnachie, © Rough Guides; 70: Tim Draper, © Rough Guides. Pages 1, 31: © windmoon/Shutterstock; 2: © Dennis Donohue/Shutterstock; 3: © fstockfoto/shuttterstock; 4, 116, 172: © Jose Gil/Shutterstock; 6: © Jeremy Richards/ Shutterstock; 15: © Amy Tseng/Shutterstock; 53: © Brandon_Perry/Shutterstock; 66: © Sean Nel/Shutterstock; 77: © Ben Haslam/Haslam Photography/Shutterstock; 82, 237: © J. Henning Buchholz/Shutterstock; 86: © J Helgason/Shutterstock; 88: © Neale Cousland/Shutterstock; 94: © Peter Guess/Shutterstock; 97: © Jamie Roach/ Shutterstock; 105: © Steve Broer/Shutterstock; 111: © Chudakov/Shutterstock; 112: © Pete Saloutos/Shutterstock; 114: © mountainpix/Shutterstock; 120: © Dariush M./ Shutterstock; 129: © Martin Lehman/Shutterstock; 135: © Pres Panayatov/ Shutterstock; 147: © Marc Pagan/Shutterstock; 152: © pix2go/Shutterstock; 160: © Gustavo Miguel Fernandes/Shutterstock; 186: © Mana Photo/Shutterstock; 283: © Carsten Medom Madsen/Shutterstock. Page 35: © Phil "Steam" Shaw; 80: courtesy of the Finnish Tourist Board; 91: Duncan Tunbridge, GB Boccia; 145: New York World Telegram & Sun Collection; 150: Press Association; 165: © Frances Holland & Nina Sharman; 278: NFL.

Index

Index entries referring to the Legends and 20 Cult Sports chapters are listed in bold.